P9-APA-022

STUDIES IN HISTORY, ECONOMICS AND PUBLIC LAW

Edited by the
FACULTY OF POLITICAL SCIENCE
OF COLUMBIA UNIVERSITY

NUMBER 498

THE PROPERTY QUALIFICATIONS OF MEMBERS OF PARLIAMENT

BY

HELEN E WITMER

THE PROPERTY
QUALIFICATIONS OF
MEMBERS OF PARLIAMENT

BY

HELEN E. WITMER

AMS PRESS
NEW YORK

98132

COLUMBIA UNIVERSITY
STUDIES IN THE
SOCIAL SCIENCES

498

The Series was formerly known as *Studies in History,
Economics and Public Law.*

Reprinted with the permission of Columbia University Press
From the edition of 1943, New York
First AMS EDITION published 1968
Manufactured in the United States of America

Library of Congress Catalogue Card Number: 68-58644

AMS PRESS, INC.
New York, N.Y. 10003

To

MY MOTHER

PREFACE

It is commonly agreed that the second World War of the twentieth century grimly portrays a struggle between the forces of totalitarianism and democracy. While the opening years of this war brought striking success to the Fascist countries, nevertheless, it was the British people who won praise and admiration, for their democratic government was able to withstand the mighty war machine of the enemy. The British government valiantly attacked the problems of war, and yet in the midst of the most devastating war of all ages, it found time to formulate post-war plans for the betterment of the people. Democracy was broadening its base; henceforth a true democracy would include far-reaching economic and social reforms.

Contemporary events focused attention on the British system, which had developed through evolution rather than revolution. The story of the growth of British democracy is a familiar one to the average reader of history. Strangely enough, this well-known story includes little material on the subject of property qualifications of members of parliament. The importance of the Qualification Act of 1710 in the history of the kingdom will always remain debatable. Writers and historians are divided on the subject. Some maintain that the Act was never enforced, while others vehemently assert that the Act preserved the political structure of the nation. Such alternate condemnation and praise of the Qualification Act aroused the interest of the writer and resulted in this book. The sole purpose of the work is to trace the colorful history of the Act, which truly depicts the perennial struggle between the forces of liberalism and conservatism.

The early history of the Qualification Act goes back to the period when the Julian Calendar was used by the people of the British Isles. To avoid confusion in the matter of chronology, the Old Style Calendar has been used throughout this book. Double dates, such as the Qualification Act of 1710/1711, are sometimes given, and should indicate to the reader that the main debate on the Qualificaton Act occurred in January and February of the new year. In this book the Qualification Act will be called the Qualification Act of 1710, the title usually used by writers and historians of British history.

At this time the writer would like to express her sincere appreciation to the members of the library staff of Columbia University for their interest, kindness, and assistance. She gratefully acknowledges Professor John Bartlet Brebner's critical analysis of the work. The author will always remain indebted to Professor Robert Livingston Schuyler, under whose discerning supervision and guidance this study was made.

HELEN E. WITMER.

NEW YORK,
JANUARY, 1943.

CONTENTS

9

98132

98183

CHAPTER I

MONEYED MEN AND LANDED MEN

No aspect of British history illustrates more clearly the unremitting conflict essential to the development of a people than the long and colorful history of the "Act for securing the Freedom of Parliaments, by the further qualifying the Members to sit in the House of Commons." With its passage in 1710, the prolonged and bitter struggle between the landed and moneyed classes in England reached its climax. The background of this act was a vivid one, and the events leading up to its actual passage were the index of a political conflict which began in the late Elizabethan period,[1] and continued unabated throughout the seventeenth century. In the reign of William III, efforts had been made to introduce such a measure; and early in the reign of Queen Anne another abortive attempt was made. Any study of the motives underlying this act, which provided for landed qualifications for members of parliament, reveals the determined efforts of the landed gentry to bar their rivals, the moneyed men, from the arena of political power.

While events of the times had militated against the men of landed property, they had assisted the rapidly growing moneyed classes to even greater power. Throughout the seventeenth century, the English government had pursued a policy of encouraging commerce, apparently with a view towards the security of the nation and as a means of bringing wealth into the country.[2] Considerably more important as a motive, however, was England's determination to weaken the commercial power of the enterprising Dutch. When James I ascended the English throne in 1603, little Holland was far ahead of England in the field of commerce. Her fleet, trade, and fisheries were far superior to those

1 Cunningham, W., *The Growth of English Industry and Commerce in Modern Times* (Cambridge, 1892), II, 5-6.

2 *Ibid.*, II, 110.

of England. But in the course of eighty years, England and Holland were to reverse places, this change being effected by the commercial policies of the government, and by the activities of the Levant, Eastland, Muscovy, and East India trading companies. At the time of the Glorious Revolution, England was rapidly approaching a position of commercial leadership, while the star of Holland's commercial supremacy was fast declining.[3]

Simultaneously, this growing commercial power of England was reflected in the growing political importance of the moneyed men, and in the rising hatred between the landed gentry and the *nouveaux riches*. Under existing conditions, moneyed men found ample opportunity for the creation of huge fortunes. Expansion of productive enterprises and the secular price movement, brought about by the currency debasement and an additional supply of precious metal, favored the owners of liquid wealth. Consequently other groups, particularly the landed men of England, suffered from the rising prices, being forced in many instances to live on fixed incomes while the cost of living steadily mounted.[4] This growing antagonism received added impetus in 1694 by the establishment of the Bank of England,[5] a Whig institution. Credit facilities of that bank encouraged the formation of new joint-stock companies and the expansion of old ones. Loose credit stimulated speculation, and stock-jobbing ran high.

Hand-in-hand with this speculation and the increase in liquid wealth, however, went an increase in corrupt practices. The rising tide of corruption aroused political leaders, who were determined to check the evil which tainted the reputations of some of the oldest political families of the kingdom. Neither

---

3 *Ibid.*, II, 102.

4 Heaton, H., *Economic History of Europe* (New York, 1936), pp. 248-52. For an explanation of the price revolution, see Hamilton, E. J., *American Treasure and the Price Revolution in Spain, 1501-1650* (Cambridge, 1934) ; also Rogers, J. E. T., *A History of Agriculture and Prices in England* (Oxford, 1882-87), V, 129-136.

5 Cunningham, W., *op. cit.*, II, 394-96.

major party was immune to the disease of corruption. Whigs and Tories, the English political parties struggling for power in the last decade of the seventeenth century, had first appeared at the time of the Exclusion Bill discussions. Both parties had been responsible for the downfall of James II and the accession of William and Mary;[6] but later their desire for political supremacy made them bitter enemies. The Tories, zealous defenders of the Crown and the Anglican Church, were mostly men of the land, landed gentry; the Whigs were the merchants, financiers, and stock-jobbers of the kingdom. The Whigs used their newly acquired fortunes to gain seats in the House of Commons. They found no difficulty in controlling the large commercial centers of England,[7] but aroused hostility when they invaded those boroughs formerly considered Tory strongholds. The Tories were incensed at the electoral activities of Wharton, the political manager of the Whigs, who was reputed to have controlled thirty parliamentary seats in the reign of James II. It was rumored that he had spent £12,000 in a later election.[8] These corrupt Whig activities were denounced by the Tories, who had been English overlords for generations. Not only did the landed men consider themselves the rightful guardians of the nation's welfare; but they feared that their political power would be usurped by the Whigs, and their interests neglected.

Some of the foremost political writers and statesmen of the day considered this problem in their writings. As classical students they were familiar with the story of Rome, and the causes of her downfall. All historians, ancient and modern, attributed the fall of Rome to the increase in wealth and the ensuing corruption. Like Cato of old, the contemporary writers lamented the rising tide of political evils. Among these Catonians was Algernon Sydney, best known for his political writings. Sydney

6 Lecky, W. E. H., *A History of England in the Eighteenth Century* (London, 1878), I, 10.

7 Morgan, W. T., *English Political Parties and Leaders in the Reign of Queen Anne* (New Haven, 1920), pp. 24-27.

8 *Ibid.*, p. 53.

had been associated with the most outstanding events of the seventeenth century. Born in 1622, the son of a wealthy family, Sydney had received the customary education of a wealthy boy, and spent some time on the continent. Throughout his life, he supported the rights of man, the laws of the land, and the Protestant religion, against the evils of arbitrary power and popery. He welcomed the Commonwealth régime, but later opposed Cromwell, whom he came to regard as a tyrant. When the Stuarts were restored to the throne of England, Sydney was in Denmark; and it was not until 1677 that he returned to England for the purpose of settling his private affairs. At home once again, he found it impossible to remain aloof from the politics of the day; and he soon found himself involved in the exclusion question and in French politics. Sydney was never regarded as a true supporter of the Stuarts; and in 1683, he was arrested for treason, levying war against the king. His protests of innocence proved fruitless, and he was executed in that year.[9] In his famous work, *Discourses on Government,* Sydney emphatically asserted that corruption would change the life of the nation. He was firmly convinced that any person who bought a position and entered upon a political life by corrupt means would tend to continue in his evil practices, expecting to make a profit large enough to cover the cost of the position. With profit as his goal, the mercenary official would sell favors and justice; and in time, even honors would no longer be a reward for merit, but would go to the highest bidder. Corruption, placing as it does a premium on money alone, would destroy the true sense of value of the populace.[10] Should this happen, the English people could be quite certain that the true interests of the nation would be disregarded, and the policies of the country would be determined by a dishonest few, who represented the moneyed interests only.

9 *The Dictionary of National Biography.*

10 Sidney (Sydney), A., *Discourses on Government,* ed. R. Lee (New York, 1805), II, 295.

The idea that landed men, by virtue of their stake in the country, were the true guardians of its welfare, was accepted not only by the Tories, but also by some of the Whigs. Many of the latter had invested part of their newly acquired wealth in the land, and others had married the daughters of Tory gentlemen; [11] as landlords and Tory sons-in-law, they had gradually adopted the Tory viewpoint on the matter. Perhaps here again, as classically educated students, they were influenced by the story of Rome. Had not Rome reached the zenith of her power when the Roman Senate was in the hands of the landed men? Had not a period of political dissension arisen when the Roman Senate was thrown open to landless men? Rome, however, had realized her mistake; and under Trajan, the earlier law was once more enforced, and the composition of the Senate again restricted to landed men. When competition arose between the landed and moneyed classes of the nation, England had need of just such a law.

Whether representation should be based on persons or on property had long been a perplexing problem to the English people. The question had been debated by the Army in 1647, when the Agreement of the People was under discussion. At that time Mr. Petty and Colonel Rainborough had recommended representation of persons, but such was not the opinion of Commissary Ireton and Colonel Rich. In voicing his ideas, Mr. Ireton said:

. . . I think that no person hath a right to an interest or share in the disposing of the affairs of the kingdom, and in determining or choosing those that shall determine what laws we shall be ruled by here—no person hath a right to this, that hath not a permanent fixed interest in this kingdom . . . [12]

Colonel Rich strenuously supported this opinion when he added:

. . . those that have no interest in the kingdom will make it their interest to choose those that have no interest. It may happen, that

11 Morgan, W. T., *op. cit.*, p. 26.

12 Woodhouse, A. S. P., *Puritanism and Liberty* (London, 1938), pp. 53-4; Firth, C. H. (Ed.), *The Clarke Papers* (Westminster, 1891), pp. 301-2.

the majority may by law, not in a confusion, destroy property; there may be a law enacted, that there shall be an equality of goods and estate . . . men that have no interest as to estate should have no interest as to election.[13]

The question of property qualifications for members of parliament, however, was not of paramount importance in this early period; it was not until after the restoration of the Stuarts that the intense hostility between the moneyed and landed classes brought the question to the foreground once more.

Another outstanding political leader of the last quarter of the seventeenth century who believed in the " stake in the country " theory was Anthony Ashley Cooper, Earl of Shaftesbury. This Earl of Shaftesbury (1621-1683) had taken an active part in the political struggles between Charles I and parliament, first supporting the king, and later the legislature. Years later, he assumed an important role in the political life of the Restoration. In return for his services, Charles II made him one of the Carolina proprietors. Locke, who was then in his employ, drew up a constitution for the colony, in which he proposed property qualifications for electors and representatives. Although Shaftesbury was distrusted by both the Whigs and the Tories of his day, he seems to have supported theories and doctrines which were to receive the approval of later generations.[14] In a pamphlet denouncing current political abuses Shaftesbury asserted that only men of landed property should be electors and representatives of the voters. He added:

It is not safe to make over the estates of the people in trust to men who have none of their own, lest their domestic indigencies, in conjunction with a foreign temptation, should warp them to a contrary interest, which, in former parliaments, we have sometimes felt to our sorrow. Wealth and substance will also give a lustre and reputation to our great council, and a security to the

13 Woodhouse, A. S. P., *op. cit.*, p. 63; Firth, C. H. (ed.), *op. cit.*, p. 315.

14 Brown, L. F., *The First Earl of Shaftesbury* (New York, 1933); Christie, W., *A Life of Anthony Ashley Cooper, First Earl of Shaftesbury* (London, 1871), 2 vols.

people; for their estates are then pawned, and so many pledges for their good behaviour, becoming thereby equal sharers themselves in the benefit or disadvantage which shall result from their own acts and councils.[15]

Shaftesbury did not believe, however, that landed property should be the sole qualification for representation. He deplored a situation that might place the government in the hands of untried young men, possessed of neither prudence nor experience, who through inheritance had acquired landed property. He made the recommendation that future members of parliament should be required to take an oath that they were the owners or possessors of £10,000, free and clear of all debts.[16]

Shaftesbury's ideas were unanimously supported by Henry Booth, Earl of Warrington. Born in 1652, the son of wealthy parents, he was very active throughout his political career in denouncing the existing political abuses. During the reign of William III, Sir Henry reached his pinnacle of success in the tenure of high positions in the government.[17] It was in this period that he wrote a pamphlet in which he described the characteristics and qualifications of an able and capable member of parliament. He urged the voters of the country to return men of good estates to the legislature. Such men, he argued, would consider the interests of the country, and be sparing in taxes, because they themselves would have to pay them.[18]

George Savile, the Marquis of Halifax, one of the most interesting men of the seventeenth century, held the same opinion as the Earl of Warrington. Halifax represented one of the oldest families in England, and was related by marriage to many of

15 Somers, J., *A Collection of Scarce and Valuable Tracts*, ed. W. Scott (London, 1809-1815). Shaftesbury's Pamphlet, " Some Observations concerning the Regulating of Elections for Parliament." Printed after Shaftesbury's death, VIII, 400-401.

16 *Ibid.*, VIII, 402.

17 *The Dictionary of National Biography.*

18 Lawrence, J. and Dunton, J. (ed.), *The Works of the Right Honourable Henry, late L. Delamer, and Earl of Warrington* (London, 1694). Pamphlet, " Monarchy the Best Government, and the English beyond all Others, with some Rules for the Choice of Members to serve in Parliament," p. 653.

the other outstanding families of the realm. Always a leader in parliament, he had served Charles II and James II, and had taken an active part in the English Revolution of 1688, continuing in active political life in the reign of William III. Of him Dryden wrote:

> Jotham of piercing Wit and Thought
> Endow'd by Nature and learning taught
> To move assemblies, who but tri'd.[19]

This friend of literary and political men belonged neither to the Whig nor the Tory party. He decried the Whig-Tory division, and denounced parties in general. In many instances, however, he seemed to lean toward the Whig side. Like Warrington, he too appealed to the voters to be careful to elect the right men to office. Like Warrington, he asserted that the landed property qualifications for membership in the legislative body would place the government in the hands of men most concerned with the welfare of the country. To insure the nation's well-being, he earnestly recommended that a future law provide a landed property requirement, because the interest of the country would then be in the hands of " such as have some share in it." [20]

The " stake in the country " theory as expounded by these prominent political leaders was accepted by many of the members of the 1694-1695 House of Commons. That body, composed mainly of " men of estates ",[21] was determined to eradicate bribery and corruption, and to use legislative means to weaken the growing political power of the moneyed men. Corrupt practices were widespread, and parliamentary investigations proved that several men in high government positions, as well as parliamentary members, had been involved in unsavory deals. Even King William became implicated when he accepted

19 Dryden, J., *Absalom and Achitophel.*

20 Raleigh, W. (ed.), *The Complete Works of George Savile, First Marquess of Halifax* (Oxford, 1912), Pamphlet, " Cautions for Choice of Members in Parliament," 1695, p. 155.

21 Burnet, G., *History of His Own Time* (London, 1734), II, 160.

the customary gift of money from the East India Company. That company's money had found its way into the pockets of those members of parliament who could advance the company's interests. Sir Thomas Cook, a member of the House of Commons and a director of the company, admitted to an astonished House that he had used £170,000 to influence some representatives to vote for the renewal of the company's charter. Another inquiry proved that several men, including Danby, Duke of Leeds, that veteran of corrupt practices of Charles II's reign, had been implicated in the scheme. Another House committee found that two army agents, together with a clothing contractor, had been involved in dishonest dealings. No sympathy was shown, and the three men were found guilty.[22]

An investigation into the circumstances of the passage of the Orphans Act revealed that bribes had been accepted by Mr. Hungerford and Sir John Trevor, Tory Speaker of the House of Commons. Both were expelled from the parliamentary chamber. Complaints against Ashurst and Overbury, Commissioners of Licenses for Hackney coaches, resulted in another investigation. Upon examination, both were acquitted; but others, Killegrew, Villers, and Gee, were found guilty of malfeasance in office, and removed.[23] These exposures played into the hands of the landed members of the Commons, who now began to agitate for a landed property qualification measure. Such a law, they held, would bar moneyed men, with their corrupting influence, from membership in the House of Commons.

To carry out such a purpose, in January 1695/1696, a landed property qualification measure was introduced into the House of Commons by Sir William Williams. Sir William (1634-1700), the sponsor of the measure, was recognized as an authority in the legal field, and had gained some prominence for prosecuting clergymen in the time of James II.[24] His Bill to

22 Rider, W., *A New History of England* (London, 1762-69), XXIX, 101-104.

23 Jenks, E., *Parliamentary England* (New York, 1903), p. 84.

24 Manning, J., *The Lives of the Speakers of the House of Commons* (London, 1851), pp. 378-382.

regulate Elections of Members to serve in Parliament provided
that a knight of a shire must be a natural born subject, and the
owner of landed property that would yield an annual income of
£500; a burgess member, likewise, must be a natural born subject of England, and the owner of landed property that would
yield an annual income of £200.[25] The proposed law would exclude landless men and naturalized subjects from membership
in the House of Commons. Many of the landless men and naturalized citizens were Dutch supporters of William III. Their
political activities were viewed suspiciously by the English
landed men, who considered themselves the rightful guardians
of the welfare of the nation. The bill was read twice and then
referred to committee.[26]

Before the measure was reported out of committee, protests
were heard from the Universities of Oxford and Cambridge,
and from the Cities of London and Bristol. The universities
complained that the measure would disqualify their parliamentary candidates; while the cities stated that their eminent merchants, who measured their wealth in personal property only,
would not be able to meet the provisions of the bill. An attempt
was made to exclude the universities and the City of London
from the operation of the proposed law, but it proved unsuccessful. The measure, without any amendments, passed the
Commons by a vote of one hundred and seventy-three to one
hundred and fifty.[27] Without any amendments, it was accepted
by the Lords, and was sent to William III for his approval. The
king found his position embarrassing. He knew that the commercial men and the important cities, centers of finance and
credit, opposed the measure. They, however, had been the chief

25 Historical Manuscripts Commission, *House of Lords, 1693-1697*, Provisions of Parliamentary Elections Bill, 1695/1696, pp. 199-201.

26 *Journals of the House of Commons*, XI, 410, 427, 451.

27 J. H. C., XI, 460. It is impossible to determine whether the vote followed
party lines. In the election of 1695, the Whigs, supporters of the foreign
policy of William III, gained a considerable majority. Lodge, R., *The History
of England from the Restoration to the Death of William III* (London,
1910), p. 393.

source of support for his wars. He therefore refused to give his assent to the measure, commenting that it would be " mischievous to his people ". [28] The supporters of the measure in the House denounced the king's advisers; and on April 14, 1696, they attempted to carry a motion to the effect that whoever advised the king to deny his assent to the measure was an " enemy to the King and Kingdom ".[29] Moderate Tories, fearing that the motion would lead to a political quarrel between the king and parliament, refused to support it; and the motion was lost.

The Tories attributed their defeat to the influence of the group which found its strongholds in the large commercial cities and in the Bank of England. It therefore seemed expedient to weaken that powerful institution. Robert Harley, Briscoe, and others revived the project of the Land Bank, which was to cater to the needs of the landed gentry by lending them money on property at low rates of interest. Thus the country gentlemen were to be granted independence from the Bank of England. It was very likely that some of the requests of landowners for financial assistance had been rejected by that institution, which found it more profitable to lend money for projects not involving land mortgages. Many Tories feared that unless the Land Bank was established, the Bank of England would control all the " cash " of the nation.

Briscoe, a member of parliament and a pamphleteer who used his pen to denounce the Whig financial institution, gave voice to this anxiety. He pointed out that the landed men were worth about £300,000,000, while the moneyed men were worth about £5,000,000. Yet the moneyed men held a position of power and influence in the nation which made them the masters, and the landed men, their servants.[30] Their wealth, accumulated in the

28 Macaulay, T. B., *The History of England* (New York, 1899), V, 144-146.

29 J. H. C., XI, 556; Chandler, R., *The History and Proceedings of the House of Commons from the Restoration to the Present Time* (London, 1742-1744), III, 24.

30 Briscoe, J., *A Discourse on the Late Funds, of the Million Act, Lottery Act, and Bank of England* (London, 1696), p. 161.

hands of the directors of the Bank of England, would enable them to buy the estates of the landed gentry; and in a few years, the directors would control not only the money, but also the land of England.[31] The concentration of wealth in the hands of a few men would, moreover, concentrate the control of policies of peace or war in the hands of the same few.[32] The availability to all purchasers of the stock of the institution was, in the eyes of Briscoe, most deplorable; for foreigners might be, as many of them were, stockholders of the Bank of England. As a result, it was possible that at some future time their money would leave England.[33] To this attack, the Whigs responded by denying the charges, by ridiculing the need for a Land Bank, and by predicting the failure of such an institution. The Whigs, however, forgot that the new institution would lend money to the government at a time when the government was sorely in need. William III had no objection to the creation of a Land Bank; therefore the Tories, having lost their bill for landed qualifications for parliamentary members, were appeased by the passage of the act which created the Land Bank.

During this period, the country was confronted with a depression which gradually spread over England in the spring and summer of 1696. In considering the causes for the poor economic conditions, the public began to suspect the reasons for the establishment of the new Land Bank, and questioned the stability of the older Bank of England. In consequence, the price of its stock fluctuated violently, and fell from 107 to 83.[34] Money was scarce and there were " runs " on banks. Meanwhile, Harley and Foley attempted to raise the necessary funds for the new bank. The moneyed people, being Whigs, refused to support what they considered a rival of their favorite, the Bank of Eng-

31 *Ibid.*, p. 35.

32 *Ibid.*, p. 135.

33 *Ibid.*, pp. 57-58.

34 Rogers, J. T., *The First Nine Years of the Bank of England* (New York, 1887), p. 50.

land. The landed people wanted the bank, but could not express their desire in terms of money, because most of their money was invested in land. Harley found himself unable to raise the required amount; and the Land Bank project collapsed.

Defeated in their aim, the country gentlemen turned their attention once again to their other " pet project ", landed property qualifications for membership in parliament. In the fall of 1696, a bill similar to the one that had been rejected by the king was introduced in the Lower House.[35] Immediately, petitions asserting that the proposed law would deprive many of their eminent citizens from serving in parliament, were sent in by the Lord Mayor, Aldermen, and Commons of the City of London, from the Borough of Southwark,[36] and from the people of the Borough of Honiton.[37] Defenders of the personal property-holders then suggested amendments. One such proposal, providing that a merchant, a natural born subject of England, worth £5,000 in real and personal property, would be eligible for membership in the House of Commons, was carried. It was specifically stated, however, that the owner of stock in the Bank of England or in any other company, was not a merchant of the country.[38] Mr. Vernon, a government official of William III, charged in a letter to a friend that the bill was a political measure, aimed to secure the next parliament for the Tories. He pointed out that the heated discussions in the House of Commons demonstrated the existence of two opposing groups, the landed or country group, and the moneyed group. He recounted one attack made in the Commons, which criticized the hunting and hawking pleasures of the heavily indebted country gentlemen, and raised the question whether the country gentleman or the active industrial leader was the better representative of the nation. Other members of the House, according

35 Hist. MSS. Comm., *House of Lords, 1693-1697*, Provisions of Parliamentary Elections Regulation Bill, 1696, pp. 375-378. *J. H. C.*, XI, 569.

36 *J. H. C.*, XI, 599.

37 *Ibid.*, XI, 631.

38 *Ibid.*, XI, 631-632.

to Mr. Vernon, praised the bill, saying it would result in good parliaments; and one member was quick to add that if the measure failed to pass this session of the House, it would be considered by future ones.[39]

The measure passed the House of Commons by a majority of forty votes,[40] and was sent to the Upper House. Surely it would meet no opposition there in the House of Lords, the home of the aristocrats! Contrary to expectation, and to the previous action of the Lords, who had approved the measure of the last session, the bill was rejected. The members of the Upper House had concluded that the measure was more favorable to the small landowner than to the large one! Although the Lords were the owners of large tracts of land, they lacked personal contact with their boroughs; and they feared that the bill would prevent them from naming their sons, relatives, and friends to represent those boroughs in parliament. Should they lose the power of nominating candidates, the Lords would lose much of their political power. With this in mind, to the dismay and annoyance of the Commons, on January 23, 1696/1697, the Lords rejected the measure by a vote of sixty-two to thirty-seven. A few days later, the resentful Commons proposed to tack the bill, which had been so unexpectedly rejected by the Upper House, to another measure. Paul Foley, the Speaker of the House, opposed the tacking clause, and stated that such action on the part of the House was unprecedented in parliamentary history. His arguments convinced his colleagues; and when the motion was put to a vote, it was lost by twenty-eight votes.[41]

John Toland, a Tory pamphleteer, severely condemned the House of Lords for its failure to pass the measure. In a pamphlet which he published a few years later, he reiterated the im-

39 Vernon, J., *Letters Illustrative of the Reign of William III, from 1696 to 1708*, ed. G. James (London, 1841). Vernon's Letter to Shrewsbury, November 28, 1696, I, 86-87.

40 *J. H. C.*, XI, 632.

41 Macaulay, T. B., *op. cit.*, V, 218.

portance of having men of landed property serve as representatives of the kingdom, and questioned whether men who were strangers to a community could serve its people, advance their interests, and redress their grievances. Moneyed men without land, he repeated, had no interest in the nation; and in proof, he cited the case of William Brown, who had moved his personal possessions to another country within twenty-four hours, and later followed them himself. Toland thought the act was an absolute necessity, and considered its adoption by the members of the next parliament, the highest duty they owed their country.[42]

While the Whigs controlled parliament, there was no attempt to reintroduce the measure. The election of 1702, however, returned the Tories to power; and in February, 1702/1703, a bill which differed little in wording from the previous ones, passed the House of Commons.[43] Its life in the Upper House was short. A motion to send it to committee failed to pass the House of Lords, whereupon twenty of the members protested, saying:

. . . the Design of that Bill was for hindering of Foreigners and Men of little or no Estate, from being capable of taxing and disposing the Rights and Estates of all England . . . [44]

Two years later, in January 1704/1705, a similar measure failed in the Upper House. Perhaps the attitude of the Queen persuaded some of the Tory members to reject their favorite measure. Her attitude was recorded by Archbishop Sharp, who wrote in his diary:

I was with the Queen again . . . She again fell atalking about the bill for qualifying people to be elected; and earnestly begged

42 Toland, J., *The Art of Governing by Partys* (London, 1701), pp. 164-166.

43 *J. H. C.*, XIV, 184.

44 Timberland, E., *The History and the Proceedings of the House of Lords, from the Restoration in 1660 to the Present Time* (London, 1742), II, 48.

of me that I would do what I could against it in our House. She said she depended upon me . . . [45]

Again the bill had failed to pass; and the Tories had to wait until the pendulum of political events swept them into power once more, before their measure became an actuality.

During the reign of Queen Anne, marked by the War of the Spanish Succession and the exploits of Marlborough, the struggle between Whigs and Tories continued unabated. While the English were victorious under Marlborough, the war was acclaimed by the people; but the defeat of the English in the Battle of Almanza, the failure of the expedition against Toulon, and the loss of ships and men, aroused opposition. The Tories questioned the management of the war, which had not brought about the defeat of France. They were suspicious of the growing power and of the demands of Marlborough, and complained bitterly about the burden of increased taxes. The approximate estimate of the war expenditures was as follows:

1702	£3,706,494
1703	£3,898,066
1704	£4,444,947
1705	£5,087,783
1706	£5,693,529
1707	£6,180,413
1708	£6,381,926
1709	£6,713,645
1710	£6,734,043 [46]

The burden of the war fell upon the landed men, who had opposed it, and not upon its supporters, the owners of stocks and bonds. St. John, later Viscount Bolingbroke, emphasized this fact when he wrote:

. . . But that which touched sensibly, even those who were but little affected by other considerations, was the prodigious inequality

45 Sharp, T. (ed.), *The Life of John Sharp, Lord Archbishop of York* (London, 1825), Recorded in diary, Saturday, January 27, 1704/1705, I, 299-300.

46 *A Short State of the War and Peace.* Printed for John Morphew (London, 1715), pp. 7-8.

between the condition of the moneyed men and of the rest of the nation. The proprietor of the land, and the merchant who brought riches home by the returns of foreign trade, had during two wars bore the whole immense load of the national expenses; whilst the lender of money, who added nothing to the common stock, throve by the public calamity, and contributed not a mite to the public charge . . . [47]

These money lenders and stock-jobbers were also denounced by Defoe, who called them the " plagues of commerce ", the men who encouraged neither trade nor manufacturing, but who became wealthy through the fluctuations in the price of stocks and bonds.[48] Such were the men who were buying up the estates of the gentlemen impoverished by the wars; [49] and such were the men who were buying their entrance into the House of Commons.

Other contemporary writers came to the support of Defoe, who continued his condemnation of these moneyed men.[50] One pamphleteer immortalized Sir Thomas Double, a fictitious Whig, who enumerated his wealth at £250,000, including the estates of two earls, and £80,000 invested in the stocks of the East India Company and the Bank of England.[51] Sir Thomas described an election which, at the cost of £8000, had returned him as a knight of a shire in a county where " none but of the First Quality, durst ever presume to offer themselves before." [52] Corrupt practices were also prevalent in the House of Commons, where money gifts and positions were used by the min-

47 Mallet, D. (ed.), *The Works of the Late Right Honorable Henry St. John, Lord Viscount Bolingbroke* (London, 1777), St. John's Letter to Windham, 1717, I, 11.

48 Defoe, D., *A Review of the State of the British Nation*, December 2, 1708.

49 *Ibid.*, January 22, 1706.

50 *Ibid.*, June 5, 1708.

51 Davenant, C., *Sir Thomas Double at Court and in High Preferments* (London, 1710), p. 12.

52 *Ibid.*, p. 14.

istry to induce members to support their measures. Although the Tories themselves were guilty of corruption and bribery, they were ever ready to place those evils at the doorstep of the moneyed men. In the election of 1710, the Tories admonished the freeholders of England to remedy the situation by returning Tory members to the House of Commons. The Tory candidates were described as landowners of England, men of untainted honor, and the proper guardians of the constitution. They would free the people from a burdensome war, abolish corrupt practices, and relieve the present and future generations of heavy taxes. It is doubtful, however, whether these campaign appeals would have brought the Tories into power, had not the country been aroused by the Sacheverell Affair.

Dr. Sacheverell, a minister of the Anglican Church, had preached in different parts of England; his ideas on religious intolerance and non-resistance were well known to the people. On November 5, 1709, in St. Paul's Cathedral, he aroused the enmity of the Whigs by describing the Lord Treasurer, Godolphin, the " able, cool, dispassionate minister " [53] who had served Charles II, James II, William III, and Anne, as Volpone, and by again expounding his theory of non-resistance and passive obedience.[54] Dr. Sacheverell's ideas not only jeopardized the government of England, which was based on the Revolution of 1688, but likewise endangered the Protestant Succession. The Whigs feared that a restoration of the Stuarts to the throne of Great Britain would not only deprive them of their power, but also destroy their investments.[55] Contrary to the advice of some of the ministers, the Whigs faced the issue, impeached the clergyman, and spent £60,000 to punish him. The trial gave the Tories, led by Harley and St. John, the opportunity to organize and consolidate their forces, and to employ pamphleteers to

53 Holland, F. (ed.), Walpole, S., *Essays, Political and Biographical* (New York, 1908), p. 68.

54 See Scudi, A. T., *The Sacheverell Affair* (New York, 1939).

55 Morgan, W. T., " The Ministerial Revolution of 1710 in England," *Political Science Quarterly*, June 1921, pp. 189-190.

spread their views. These writers reasserted their ideas on bribery and corruption, and their political theory regarding landed property qualifications for members in the House of Commons, as well as on Sacheverell's theory of non-resistance. The Tories denounced the principle of resistance as anti-monarchical and a republican idea.

The trial of Dr. Sacheverell, which was carefully followed by the Queen, aroused in her mind doubts and questions concerning her Whig ministers. During the trial, the noted preacher had asserted that there were false brethren in the state and church.[56] Marlborough had already been described by the Tories as the man who controlled the army, the fleet, and the revenue of the kingdom, while the people staggered under a load of debts.[57] Were he and Godolphin the false brethren? Harley believed that the trial forced the Whigs to declare publicly ideas which opposed royal authority.[58] The Queen, moreover, was happy at the outcome of the affair. The Lords found the clergyman guilty by a vote of sixty-nine to fifty-two; but his sentence was a light one. His writings were burned, his sermons condemned, and he was not permitted to preach for three years.[59] Following his struggle with the government, Dr. Sacheverell toured England, and was received everywhere by demonstrations of rejoicing and thanksgiving.

In the spring of 1710, addresses from different parts of England reached the Queen. All of them professed loyalty to her majesty, and promised to elect such representatives as were

affectionately Dutiful to Your Majesty, Religiously Zealous for

56 Vaillant, P. (Ed.), *Memoirs of the Marquis of Torcy* (London, 1757), II, 103-104.

57 Scott, T. (Ed.), *The Prose Works of Jonathan Swift* (London, 1901), V, "Memoirs relating to that Change in the Queen's Ministry in 1710" (London, 1714), 375-376.

58 Vaillant, P. (Ed.), *op. cit.*, II, 109.

59 Scudi, A. T., *op. cit.*, pp. 121-122; *Journals of the House of Lords*, XIX, 118.

our Holy Church, and have the tenderest Regard for the Lives, Liberties, and Estates of their Fellow-Subjects.[60]

These addresses, probably inspired by the clergy, heightened the Queen's dislike for the Whigs, and induced her to part with her Whig ministers. In May, 1710, she dismissed the Duke of Kent, the Lord Chamberlain; and on June 15, 1710, the unpopular Lord Sunderland, the Secretary of State, followed. The frightened Whigs considered these dismissals the first steps in their downfall. Stocks of the East India Company and the Bank of England were thrown on the market, and prices fell. The Tories criticized the Whigs for this depression, which frightened the Queen and the nation. A few days after the dismissal of Sunderland, the Duke of Leeds, accompanied by some of the officers and directors of the Bank of England, appealed to the Queen not to make any more changes. They stated that any future change in the Whig ministry would endanger the credit and finances of the nation. The Imperial Minister, Count Gallas, and the Dutch envoy added their protests against any contemplated dismissals.[61] Queen Anne promised not to relieve the Duke of Marlborough of his command; but she made no promises regarding her other ministers. In the summer and fall of 1710, other changes were made. Harley became the Chancellor of the Exchequer and was really the Chief Minister; and St. John became a Secretary of State. On September 26, 1710, the old parliament was dissolved and a new election called. Following the dissolution of parliament, the ministry became wholly Tory. St. John minimized the causes for the change in ministry which has been described, and said that:

the true original cause was the personal ill usage which she received in her private life, and in some trifling instances of the exercise of her power; for indulgence in which she would certainly

60 Boyer, A., The History of the Reign of Queen Anne, digested into Annals (London, 1703-1713), IX, 159.

61 Ibid., IX, 232; De Cize, E., Histoire du Whigisme et du Torisme (Amsterdam, 1717), p. 315.

have left the reins of government in those hands, which had held them ever since her accession to the throne.[62]

Swift, too, supported this opinion; but it is very unlikely that this was the " true cause " for the change in ministry in 1710. Like many events in history, not one but many causes contributed to the political upheaval, and the important roles of Harley and St. John must be considered also.

Robert Harley and Henry St. John, the statesmen brought into power as a result of the ministerial revolution of 1710, had much in common. Both held high positions in the reign of Queen Anne; both were patrons of literature; both worked for the Treaty of Utrecht; both received titles for their service to the state; and both ended their political careers in impeachment when the Whigs were returned to power on the accession of George I. Robert Harley, the son of Sir Edward Harley, was born in 1661; the younger statesman, Henry St. John, was born in 1678. The sons of illustrious families, both were Dissenters by parentage and education. Yet in 1710, they were the acknowledged leaders of the Tory Party, and the supporters of the interests of the Anglican Church and the landed gentry.

In the reign of William III, Harley had entered the House of Commons, where his parliamentary skill had won him the support of the Whigs and the Tories; and in 1701 he became the Speaker of the House. One year before, St. John, wealthy in his own right, and the possessor of a fortune of £40,000 through a fortunate marriage, had entered parliament as a member for Wootton Bassett in Wiltshire, where he and his wife had large landed interests. Dame Fortune had smiled upon the young St. John; this dignified and handsome man entered public life with a strong constitution, and the power and ability to express himself clearly and forcibly in speech and in writing.[63] His political ideas and his style of writing influenced many men in the eigh-

62 Mallet, D. (Ed.), *op. cit.*, St. John's Letter to Sir William Windham in 1717, I, 8.

63 Hassall, A., *Life of Viscount Bolingbroke* (London, 1889), pp. 11, 46.

teenth century. Swift said he possessed the " choicest gifts " of God, and spoke of his wit, beauty, quickness of apprehension, and excellent taste.[64] Others, however, saw in him the modern Alcibiades, because his fine characteristics were counter-balanced by his insolent manner, vanity, deceit, and dissipation. As Chesterfield said, " It is impossible to find lights and shades strong enough to paint the character of Lord Bolingbroke." [65] From the time of his entrance into the House of Commons, St. John attached himself to the virtuous and amiable Harley, and they became staunch friends. In 1704, St. John became Secretary of War. In that position, he supported the plans and policies of Godolphin and Marlborough in their conduct of the War of the Spanish Succession. In the same year through the influence of the Duke of Marlborough, Harley, the older and more experienced statesman, became a Secretary of State. Through Mrs. Masham, the new court favorite, Harley reached the ear of the Queen, and instilled in her the fear that the Anglican Church was in danger. His activities were discovered by the mistrustful Whigs; and in 1708, both he and St. John were dismissed from office. Harley wanted revenge, and in the next two years the two men did all in their power to consolidate and strengthen the forces of the Tories. Prince Eugene called St. John the " bull dog of the party ",[66] but it is more likely that Harley was the political boss who whipped the party into shape. The events of 1710 were in their favor, and with the support of the Anglican clergy and an able press, they were successful in obtaining their goal.

The fall of 1710 revealed a press campaign, as Tory and Whig pamphlets and newspapers appealed to the English freeholders for their votes in the coming election. *The Examiner,* the chief political organ of the Tories, displayed Swift's shrewd-

64 Scott, T. (Ed.), *op. cit.*, V, "An Enquiry into the Behaviour of the Queen's Last Ministry," 430.

65 Bradshaw, J. (Ed.), *The Letters of Philip Dormer Stanhope, Earl of Chesterfield* (London, 1892), III, 1413.

66 Turberville, A. S., *English Men and Manners in the 18th Century* (Oxford, 1929), p. 193.

ness, his knowledge of human nature, and his ability to express himself in the language of the people. Under his able leadership,[67] that paper denounced the acts and leaders of the Whig ministry.[68] Neither the War of the Spanish Succession nor the glorious military deeds of the Duke of Marlborough received any praise from Swift.[69] No thoughtful person could read *The Examiner* without coming to the conclusion that the Tories were the friends of the landed gentry, the friends of the Anglican Church, and the friends of the Queen.

The Whigs made feeble attempts to meet the charges of Swift. Their short-lived papers,[70] however, proved powerless against the scornful invectives of the Dean of St. Patrick's. Daniel Defoe, the friend of the mercantile class, claimed his paper, *A Review of the State of the British Nation,* was not a Tory organ,[71] but it could hardly be classified as a Whig one. The paper made no effort to vindicate the Whig ministry or deny many of the Tory charges. Defoe gave no active support to the opinion that the interests of the landed men conflicted with the interests of the moneyed men, although he acknowledged the great wealth of the Whigs in the following manner:

I have heard it suggested, that the Tallies, the Navy and Victualling Bills, the Exchequer Notes, the Annities, [*sic*], the Blanks and Prizes in the Lottery, the Stocks in the Bank and East India Company, the Sword-Blade Men, the Million Bank, etc. Amount to little less than sixty Millions Sterling; an Immense, Prodigious Summ, a Summ Foreign Nations are unacquainted with, and which would make a terrible Sound, put into French Livres, Dutch Guilders, or German Florins—Of this about seven Tenths they compute to be in the Hands of the Whigs . . . [72]

67 Swift managed the paper for about eight months. St. John, Atterbury, Prior, and others contributed to it.

68 Scott, T. (Ed.), *op. cit.,* IX; *The Examiner,* Number 15.

69 *Ibid., The Examiner,* Numbers 14, 17.

70 *The Whig Examiner* had five issues only. The Whig cause was taken up by *The Medley* and *The Observator.*

71 Defoe, D., *op. cit.,* Thursday, November 2, 1710.

72 *Ibid.,* Thursday, November 23, 1710.

The Whigs were more successful in their use of pamphlets to vindicate the Godolphin ministry, and to combat the attacks of the Tories. Most of the Whig pamphlets, including those written by Dr. Hare,[73] chaplain of the Duke of Marlborough, praised the military triumphs of Marlborough, and the glorious administration of Godolphin who had " the right Conception of Political Government both in Church and State." [74] Defoe's pamphlets, like his newspapers, were not very forceful in supporting the cause of the Whigs. In one pamphlet he attributed the downfall of the Whigs to

... a wicked Party of Men among us have, with too much Success, assisted the general Defection; have first spread a Cloud over the Eyes of the People, and then dug the Pit in their Way. By this Party some of the poor People have been brought to take Error for Truth, Falsehood for Sincerity, Hypocrisy for Friendship, Bondage for Liberty; and in short, Darkness for Light.[75]

This and similar statements would imply that Defoe was a supporter of the Whigs; and yet he remained friendly with Harley, and received money payments from him for work done in this period.[76]

While there were a few Tory pamphleteers who decried the methods used by the Tories in their climb to power, the majority of the Tory pamphlets held the Whig ministry responsible for corruption and bribery in recent elections, and for the heavy debt resulting from the war. To these charges, they added

73 Hare, F., *The Negotiations for a Treaty of Peace from the Breaking Off of the Conferences at the Hague to the End of Those at Gertruydenberg* (London, 1711), pp. 71-72; *The Management of the War* (London, 1711) ; *The Negotiations for a Treaty of Peace in 1709* (London, 1711).

74 Cockburn, W., *An Essay upon the Propitious and Glorious Reign of our Gracious Sovereign Anne* (London, 1710), p. 96. See also *A General View of our present Discontents*, Printed for A. Baldwin (London, 1710), p. 24.

75 Defoe, D., *A Word Against a New Election* (London, 1710), pp. 3-4.

76 Hist. MSS. Comm., *Portland MSS.*, IV, 584-585. Defoe's letter to Robert Harley, September 5, 1710.

a denunciation of those men who advanced their own interests at the expense of the landed men. One pamphleteer said:

Tho' the late Junto, and their Supporters, the Money'd Men, were, and still are able to Bribe many; yet was it not (and 'tis now less) in their Power to Corrupt All ... But then they met in their Career, a Set of Landed-men, Proof against Bribery; Stiff and Staunch in the Principles of Honour; Heartily Zealous for the support of our Happy Constitution in Church and State; and whom Profit could not allure, nor Power intimidate ... And, indeed, as there cannot be a Circumstance more dangerous to the Liberty of a Nation, than to have the real Right, Interest, and Property of Lands in one Hand, and the Power of being chosen into Parliament in another; so, to preserve the Rights of this Nation, we should be represented by such as have the greatest Share in Property.[77]

As would be expected, another pamphleteer attacked the moneyed men who used their wealth to enslave the people of England. He wrote:

. . . is not a Nation inslav'd, when two or three hundred Men shall get all the Money into their own Hands, so as to be able to govern the Cr—n, make the P————nt trample upon the Subjects, and over-turn the Constitution, contrary to the Wishes and Inclinations of five parts in six of the whole Kingdom? If this be not Slavery, what is? And how near that Project was to be effected, appears from the exceeding great Difficulty with which some late important Changes have been made ... [78]

The same opinion was expressed by Sir Richard Comover, a fictitious Tory, who condemned the Whigs for loading posterity with debts, and allowing:

the vilest Insects of the Land to get that Wealth, which should have provided for younger Children of the best Families: How

77 *An Essay towards the History of the Last Ministry and Parliament* (London, 1710), Printed for J. Baker in that year, also printed for J. Knapton in 1718, and A. Boyer, no date, pp. 47-49.

78 [Trapp, J.], *The Character and Principles of the Present Set of Whigs* (London, 1711), p. 10.

they have made the Country poor to inrich the City: How they have render'd the Landed Interest, in a manner vassal, and tributary to the mony'd Men ... [79]

He hoped that the spirit of the English people had not been broken, and that courage would be found

to defend the Landed, against the Mony'd Interest; for there I fancy the chief Trial of Skill will be. Tho' you are able to bribe our Burroughs, as yet, you have not quite bought us out of 'em; and hitherto, new Names and Families, out of the Scum and Lees of the People, sprung up in these corrupt Times, have not intirely over-run the Nation. God be thank'd, the Landed-Gentlemen of ancient Descent, are still powerful ... [80]

Swift took no active part in the war of pamphlets, giving his undivided attention to his newspaper, *The Examiner*. His pamphlets describing the political events of this period appeared in later years; but he never lost an opportunity to denounce the Whigs for mismanaging parliament, for crying down the landed interest and worrying the church.[81]

The election of 1710 proved that, despite the great wealth of the Whigs, their party lacked political organization and leadership. At first the Whigs had thought the dissolution of parliament an improbability. Even when it had become an actuality, they failed to organize their forces to counteract the growing power of the Tories. The Whigs forgot—or overlooked—the events of the day, and the great influence of the Tory newspapers and pamphlets. The Tories, meanwhile, found a powerful ally in the clergy, who influenced their parish voters to support the new administration by returning Tories to parliament. In a letter to Harley, Mr. Durden related that a clergyman invited a group of men to his home every Sunday evening, read

79 Davenant, C., *op. cit.*, p. 109.

80 *Ibid.*, p. 64.

81 Scott, T., *op. cit.*, V, " The Conduct of the Allies " (London, 1712), 100.

The Examiner to them, and then commented upon the paper. All the following week, he carried the paper with him, and read it to any voter " who was weak in the faith ".[82] On election days, the clergy went in a body to the polls, and this impressive ceremony had a lasting effect on the voters.[83]

The election of 1710 presented a picture of violence throughout the nation. One writer stated that the elections to parliament were carried on with such violence that the parliament might be called " the Parliament of Sacheverel and the mob." [84] In one district, a clergyman refused to attend a funeral, probably that of a Whig, or to preach the funeral sermon.[85] In the cities, mobs roamed the streets, " getting out the vote " for their candidates by threats. Voters were beaten, and the homes of men known to be supporting the Whig candidates were destroyed. In some cases, Whig voters were not permitted to approach the polls.[86] Whigs fortunate enough to be elected found themselves unseated by petitions later presented to the House. The author of *The Medley* attempted to find out why the voters supported the Tories in 1710. His interesting account was as follows:

I asked an honest Freeholder of Surry, why he was such a Blockhead as not to vote for Sir Richard? Lord! says he, they told me there shou'd be no more Taxes, but they wou'd carry on the War by Fines and Resumptions. A Livery Man of Wapping being check'd for giving his vote for the Colonel; In troth, quote he, I had not done it, but they said the Seamen shou'd be all paid off by Candlemas, and Navy-Bills be better than Par. I put such another Question to a West-Country Land-Jobber: Why truly, says he, I shou'd have voted right, but that I hate the Funds, and they swore they wou'd raise all the Money in the Year. A Jolly Parson

82 Hist. MSS. Comm., *Portland MSS.*, Letter of Mr. Durden to Mr. Harley, December 5, 1710, p. 641.

83 Roper, A., *The Post Boy*, October 26, 1710.

84 Rutt, J. (Ed.), Calamy, E., *An Historical Account of my Own Life* (London, 1829), II, 229.

85 Morgan, W. T., "An Eighteenth Century Election in England," *Political Science Quarterly*, Dec. 1922, p. 594.

86 Oldmixon, J., *The History of England during the reigns of King William and Queen Mary, Queen Anne, King George I* (London, 1735), pp. 451-452.

of Kent being ask'd why they us'd Mr. P——l so ill, reply'd roughly, Faith! we thought the Conventicles would have been shut up by this time, and the Barns put to their true Use.[87]

For various reasons, then, the election of 1710 went in favor of the Tories; and two hundred and seventy members of the old parliament lost their seats. In Cornwall, there was a Tory landslide. London, the stronghold of the Whigs, returned four Tory members to the Commons. Scotland followed the example of England. A list of Tory candidates, submitted by the government, received the approval of the dutiful Scots.[88] Yet in spite of all the efforts of the Tories, over one hundred Whigs were returned to the new legislative body.[89] The predominance of the Tories, however, cast a gloom over the Whigs, with the result that stocks fell by thirty per cent, and the Bank of England refused to discount foreign bills of exchange.[90] In commenting on the election of 1710, Swift said that the members of the new parliament were chosen without any " endeavors from the court to secure elections ";[91] but Defoe wondered how an election could be called a free one when violence, force, and bloodshed determined the votes of the freeholders.[92] The election of 1710 was not free in the modern sense of the word, and Ralph was probably correct in saying:

When the Ministry was in Alliance with the Whigs, the Majority of both Houses was Whig; when with the Tories, they became Tory.[93]

87 *The Medley*, Monday, February 26, 1711.

88 Mackinnon, J., *The Union of England and Scotland* (London, 1896), p. 408.

89 Morgan, W. T., *op. cit.*, December 1922, pp. 601-602.

90 Churchill, W., *Marlborough, His Life and Times* (London, 1933-1938), IV, 329.

91 Scott, T. (Ed.), *op. cit.*, V, " Memoirs relating to that Change in the Queen's Ministry in 1710," 386.

92 Defoe, D., *A Review of the State of the British Nation*, Tuesday, October 24, 1710.

93 Ralph, J., *Of the Use and Abuse of Parliaments* (London, 1744), I, 160. de Cize, E., *op. cit.*, pp. 316-317.

CHAPTER II

THE QUALIFICATION ACT OF 1710 [1]

THE Tory victory at the polls in the fall of 1710 brought great rejoicing to the landed men of the kingdom. They had eagerly followed the events of 1710 and the role played by their political rivals, the moneyed group. Many of the moneyed men had opposed Sacheverell, the martyr of the high church principle of non-resistance; and after the dismissal of Godolphin, efforts had been made by the same group to embarrass the government financially. The election of 1710, like previous ones, proved conclusively that the foreigners from Holland, drawn to England by her commercial triumph over the Dutch, and the importance of London as a money market, had swelled the ranks of the Whigs and not those of the Tories. The interests of this formidable foe were diametrically opposed to the interests of the landed men, and the victory at the polls must be used by the Tories to insure a legislative remedy for the situation.

The new House of Commons, which met on November 25, 1710, was composed of " men of estates ",[2] many of whom had been members of previous parliaments. As members of other legislative bodies, they were familiar with the fundamental issues

1 Following the Old Style Calendar, the Act for Securing the Freedom of Parliaments, by the farther qualifying the Members to sit in the House of Commons will be called the Qualification Act of 1710. Before 1793, it was not unusual for a measure to become a law on the first day of the parliamentary session, although royal assent might not have been given until many months later. Winfield, P. H., *The Chief Sources of English Legal History* (Cambridge, 1925), p. 78.

2 Owen, R., *An Antidote against Modern Slanders and Calumnies* (London, 1713), p. 10. " The Persons now in Power are Noted to be generally Men of good Estates... " *The Political State of Great Britain*, February, 1710/1711, pp. 195-196. " It may suffice to tell you, that as the Church-Party prevails in that House, so the Votes are in most Cases gone against the Whiggs: Which however is no more than the Whiggs have done before, when they had a Majority."

underlying the bitter struggle between the moneyed and landed classes of the nation. Many of the representatives, moreover, believed that the return of the Tories to power had indicated the voters' approval of all of the Tory principles, including landed property qualifications for membership in parliament. Shortly after the disposal of routine business, a landed property qualification measure was introduced into the House of Commons. In pleading for the adoption of the measure, St. John told the House members that unless they passed the Qualification Act, the time might come when the landed men would be excluded from the legislative body by the moneyed men.[3]

Little opposition developed in the Tory-controlled House, and even the Scottish representatives gave their approval to the bill. Scottish representatives were Tory sympathizers, and a bill which was not applicable to Scotland could hardly arouse their opposition. Tory leaders were fully aware of the true relationship between England and Scotland. The recent Act of Union had not served to strengthen the bonds of friendship between the two countries, and England hesitated to adopt any policy which might affect the representation of Scotland,[4] and further antagonize its population. Then too, Scottish landed estates were small, and any landed requirement for membership in the House of Commons would have been most difficult for the impoverished Scots to meet. Harley and St. John were well aware of these conditions, and also realized how zealously the Scottish representatives defended their constitutional rights. This attitude was shown by one of their representatives who assured a nobleman of Scotland that the Scottish members would be very cautious of any act which would

open the least door or give any opportunity for unhingeing our constitution, but will contribute as much as possible to strengthen it.[5]

3 Cartwright, J. (Ed.), *The Wentworth Papers, 1705-1739* (London, 1883), Letter of Lady Wentworth to her brother, December 21, 1710, p. 167.

4 Porritt, E. and A., *The Unreformed House of Commons* (Cambridge, 1909), I, 169.

5 Hist. MSS. Comm., *MSS. of the Earl of Mar and Kellie*, p. 486.

Scottish members supported St. John, Harley, and their followers, and the qualifying measure passed the House of Commons and was adopted by the House of Lords on February 22,
1710/1711.[6] The Queen was induced by her leading Tory ministers to approve the measure, which they claimed would place
the government in the hands of men who were the best friends
of the people.

The Qualification Act of 1710[7] provided that all future
members of the House of Commons must possess landed property. A knight of the shire must be in possession of an English
landed estate, freehold or copyhold, of the annual value of £600
after all debts had been paid; and every citizen, burgess, and
baron of the Cinque Ports had to meet the same requirements
for a landed estate of the annual value of £300. These provisions, however, applied to holders of bona-fide landed estates
only, and not to men who held mortgages unless they had been
the holders of such mortgages for a seven year period prior to
their elections. At future elections, a parliamentary candidate
could be called upon by the voters of the constituency to take an
oath that he could meet the landed property qualifications as required by law. Any successful parliamentary member refusing to
take the oath, was to lose his seat in the House of Commons.
These oaths were to be administered by local officials, and only
fees specified by law could be collected for them.

According to the provisions of the 1710 Qualification Act,
certain groups were excluded from the operation of the law.
The Act was neither applicable to the heirs or eldest sons of
peers and bishops, nor to the eldest sons of landed recusants,
who had declined in number since the days of William and
Mary. In refusing to take the oath of allegiance to those rulers,
Archbishop Sancroft, seven bishops, and about four hundred
clergymen had disqualified themselves as members of parliament.[8] Many of these recusants or non-jurors, however, were

6 *J. H. L.*, XIX, 233; *J. H. C.*, XVI, 432, 433, 440, 486, 502, 526.
7 9 Anne, c. 5.
8 Smith, G., *The United Kingdom* (London, 1901), II, 89.

very wealthy in land. Now, in accordance with the provisions of the Act, their eldest sons were permitted to serve as knights of the shires. This political concession was probably made to overcome the opposition to the bill of some of the members of parliament. Representatives of the Universities of Oxford and Cambridge were likewise excluded from the operation of the law. Both universities had opposed the earlier landed property measures, which, they maintained, would have disqualified their parliamentary candidates. The Act applied to England, the Dominion of Wales, and Berwick-upon-Tweed.

The passage of the Qualification Act produced no great storm of protest in the nation. For many years the question of landed property qualifications for members of parliament had been an issue, and the writers of that period had expressed their opinions on the subject. The adoption of the Act occasioned a recapitulation of its purposes. According to the historian Burnet, Bishop of Salisbury, the purposes of the Act were to place the government in the hands of the owners of landed property, and to weaken the power of the traders, courtiers, military and moneyed men.[9] This political purpose was stated by James Taylor in a letter to Horatio Walpole, in which he said:

I forgott to tell you in my last that the house of Lords had passed the Qualification Bill which I hear by a Computation will throw out above two hundred Members (at the next Election for a new Parliament) of the present house . . . [10]

Swift lost no time in expressing his whole-hearted approval in several numbers of *The Examiner*. For many months, he had vehemently asserted the importance of the landed interest, and he now praised the composition and the work of the House of Commons, which had recovered the honor of parliament by the adoption of the Qualification Act. Since the enactment of the measure would require future parliaments to be composed of

9 Burnet, G., *op. cit.*, II, 565.

10 Hist. MSS. Comm., *Townsend MSS.*, Letter from James Taylor to H. Walpole, February 27, 1711, pp. 79-80.

landed property men, the real property of the people no longer would be at the mercy

of those who have none themselves, or at least only what is transient or imaginary.[11]

A few months later, in June, 1711, he praised the Act as preserving the English constitution, which otherwise might lie

at the mercy of the moneyed interest: And since much the greatest part of the taxes is paid, either immediately from land, or from the productions of it, it is but common justice, that those who are the proprietors, should appoint what portion of it ought to go to the support of the public; otherwise, the engrossers of money, would be apt to lay heavy loads on others, which themselves never touch with one of their fingers.[12]

Swift never changed his high opinion of the Qualification Act, and many years later, in a letter to Pope, he said:

. . . there could not be a truer maxim in our government than this, That the Possessors of the soil are the best judges of what is for the advantage of the kingdom.[13]

The other contemporary newspaper, *The Medley,* disagreed with Swift's views, and denied that the landed men were the only true supporters of the government and that

a Man, who has a single Life in a Copyhold of £300 per ann. is fitter to be trusted than one worth £30,000 in Money.[14]

Swift's opinion was upheld, however, by Pittis, another writer, who praised the patriots in parliament for protecting the landed interest against the growing power of the Bank, East India Company, and other companies, arguing that originally the

11 Scott, T. (Ed.), *op. cit.,* IX, *The Examiner,* No. 35.

12 *Ibid.,* No. 45.

13 Bowles, W. (Ed.), *The Works of Alexander Pope* (London, 1806), Letter from Swift to Pope, January 10, 1721, IX, 32.

14 *The Medley,* April 23, 1711.

House of Commons had been composed of landowners, and this Act would restore the government to the hands that originally held it.[15] Another pamphleteer supported the Act because it placed the government in the hands of men of good estates, and therefore would prevent landless representatives from being bribed into adopting measures which might prove ruinous to the public welfare.[16]

To judge from contemporary accounts, the Qualification Act was not condemned on the score that the legal landed requirements were too difficult to meet. No complete study of the actual value of £600 and £300 estates in present day currency has ever been made, and any survey of prices for that period would be seriously handicapped by the lack of accurate index numbers. As early as 1696, however, Gregory King made an attempt to classify the English people according to their incomes. His interesting account was as follows:

Annual incomes of

160 families of the nobility with households of 40	£3,200
20 spiritual lords with households of 20	£1,300
800 families of baronets with households of 16	£ 880
600 Knights	£ 650
3,000 Esquires	£ 450
12,000 Gentlemen	£ 240
2,000 Merchants and Traders	£ 400
8,000 Lesser Merchants and Traders	£ 198
10,000 Lawyers	£ 154
2,000 Eminent Clergymen	£ 72
8,000 Lesser Clergymen	£ 50
40,000 Freeholders of the better class	£ 91
120,000 Freeholders of the lesser class	£ 55
150,000 Farmers	£ 42-10s.[17]

These estimates cannot be verified; and yet King's report would seem to indicate that many men in 1696 would have been able

15 Pittis, W., *The History of the Present Parliament and Convocation* (London, 1711), p. 98.

16 Wagstaffe, W., *The State and Condition of our Taxes Considered* (London, 1714), p. 35.

17 Robertson, J. M., *Bolingbroke and Walpole* (London, 1919), pp. 222-223.

to fulfill the provisions of the measure which failed to win the approval of William III. In the period after his reign, liquid wealth had increased, and some of it must have been invested in the land. Using the military law of England, a later writer concluded that many men could meet the landed provisions of the Qualification Act of 1710. The military law provided that owners of £500 per annum estates in lands, tenements, or hereditaments had to furnish the government with men and horses. He believed that there were approximately

3,000 men .... with £600 per Annum Estates
4,500 men .... with £500 per Annum Estates
10,000 men or more .... with £300 to £600 per Annum Estates

He concluded his account by saying:

So deducting, in a round Number, 200 for the Lords Spiritual and Temporal, out of 3000 computed to have £600 per Annum in Land of Inheritance, in Fee Simple, there rests 2,800, out of which to chuse about 120 Knights of the Shires, the Number qualified to be elected, is about 23 Times more than the Number to be elected.[18]

Despite the fact that there was no apparent objection to the practical requirements of the new law, the Act, originally designed to give additional security to the people, was severely criticized on the ground that it violated the English principle of freedom of elections. From time immemorial, the qualified voters of England had been free to elect any man to represent them in the House of Commons. The germ of political representation went back to the thirteenth century. First the clergy and the counties sent representatives, and later the cities and the boroughs. From that time to 1710, any man was eligible to be a representative of the nation. Until the rise of the moneyed group, it was customary for outstanding men of wealth, character, and integrity to be the representatives. The Qualification Act of 1710 limited the choice of the qualified voters of England to one group of men only—the landed men of the nation. Thus, freedom of choice, a basic principle of English liberty, had been

18 Boyer, A., *The Political State of Great Britain*, March 1740, Letter written by Mr. Daniel King, circa 1710, pp. 247-248.

destroyed, and henceforth there would be a sharp distinction between the landed men and the landless.[19] The landed gentry would control the legislative body of the government, and there was no assurance that they would not follow the precedent of the parliament of 1710/1711. Not only might the landed requirements be raised, but future parliaments might add other requirements for parliamentary candidates.[20] Should this happen, the House of Commons, originally composed of the representatives of the nation, would represent but a small aristocratic group. The House, acting in the interest of one small group, would control the destiny of all the people. Such a government, founded upon riches in land, might prove dangerous both to the people and to the crown.

Closely allied with the constitutional point of criticism was the complaint that landless men, qualified by ability, experience, and leadership, would be excluded from the House of Commons. A simple remedy would have been for these moneyed men to invest some of their wealth in urban property and thereby qualify as parliamentary candidates. Certain of the moneyed men followed this procedure, but many of their number refused to do so because their annual incomes would be decreased by landed investments, which were not as lucrative as commercial enterprises or stocks and bonds. An investment in land would yield no more than three per cent return, while an investment in other enterprises might yield a six per cent return.[21] Legally, these good business men, traders in many cases, and therefore trustees of that interest, could no longer be representatives in the Lower House. Before 1710, the landed interest had complained bitterly that their hated rivals, the moneyed group, jeopardized their interest; and now the traders returned the cry. Before the adoption of the Qualification Act of 1710, a gentleman of the House of Commons had assured the traders and manufacturers that they had nothing to fear, because

19 *Ibid.*, p. 248.

20 Somerville, T., *The History of Great Britain during the Reign of Queen Anne* (London, 1798), p. 423.

21 Oldmixon, J., *op. cit.*, p. 459.

he could think of none so proper to cultivate and improve them [home manufactures] as the Gentlemen from whose Lands they were produc'd, and who must of consequence, for their own sakes, as well as those of other Landed Persons whom they had the honour to represent, make use of the most hearty and effectual Measures for that End.[22]

This opinion was not accepted by many writers, who maintained that the exclusion of the commercial men from the House of Commons would prove detrimental to trade, and likewise strike at the very roots of the constitution, which intended to have all interests represented in the legislative body of the country. The exclusion of the landless men, the traders, would mean that the interests and welfare of corporations would no longer be safeguarded. They would be subservient to the landed interest, the sole ruler in the House of Commons.[23] Defoe, the friend of the merchants, came to their aid, and used his literary resources to admonish the landed men to protect trade, which had made the commons wealthy, had been a nurse to the land, and taken the products of the soil and distributed them to the world. He concluded:

Let your Landed Men that would crush our Trade, take the Hint —Whenever Trade dies, Land will, of course, feel the beginnings of Death—Land will pine, fade, Languish, and at last, die into its Original Poverty, and its mere native Condition.[24]

While Bishop Burnet did not support the opinion that trade, supervised by the landed representatives, would decline, he questioned the ability of many of the landed gentry to guide the future destiny of Great Britain. According to the worthy bishop, many of them were ignorant and corrupt.[25] True, they possessed landed estates; but if the charge of the bishop were valid, would

22 Pittis, W., *op. cit.*, p. 99.

23 Boyer, A., *The History of the Reign of Queen Anne digested into Annals*, IX, 322-323.

24 Defoe, D., *A Review of the State of the British Nation*, Tuesday, May 1, 1711.

25 Burnet, G., *op. cit.*, II, 565.

these landed representatives be invulnerable to corruption and bribery? Would the possession of land, which in some cases was heavily mortgaged, compensate for the absence of the characteristics of intelligence and political leadership? Time alone would tell.

In addition to excluding traders and moneyed men, whose chief assets were the stocks of the East India Company, the Bank of England, and other companies, the Tories had hoped that the Act would exclude military men.[26] The Tories, who had denounced the War of the Spanish Succession, claiming it had enriched the moneyed men and impoverished the landed gentry, accepted the opinion that the military men had but one interest, wars, on which they thrived. They claimed that it was the landed interest that had been called upon to support those wars in the reigns of William and Mary and of Queen Anne. When the military men were not actively engaged in a war, they were sponsoring a large standing army, which was contrary to English ideas of freedom and liberty.[27] Whether the provisions of the Qualification Act would exclude these military men was a debatable question. Certainly, the outstanding generals and admirals of the kingdom had large landed estates. One historian expressed the opinion that many of the military and naval officers in 1710 had greater landed interests than some of the members of the House of Commons.[28]

The fact that the Act subjected to the scrutiny of the House of Commons the titles and values of the estates of parliamentary representatives, caused some apprehension on the part of English writers.[29] To enforce the qualification provisions, it was necessary for the legislative body to have this right. True, the examination of titles and values of landed estates would only take place in contested elections; but the English voters, ever jealous of their liberty and freedom, feared that the additional power of the House of Commons might encroach upon their

26 Tindal, N., *The History of England* (London, 1745), XXIV, 65.
27 Wagstaffe, W., *op. cit.*, p. 37.
28 Oldmixon, J., *op. cit.*, p. 459.
29 Chandler, R., *op. cit.*, IV, 190.

individual rights. The power to return representatives to the House rested in the hands of the voters, but until the passage of the Grenville Act of 1770, all controverted elections were considered by the House as a whole, and determined by vote of all members present. These writers knew that contested elections aroused little interest in the House, and they feared that the political party in power would use the Qualification Act as a means for ridding the Commons of non-supporters of the government.

Writers of the period also advanced the idea that the law would bring about two undesirable economic results : a break-up of large landed estates, and an increase in the value of land.[30] It might prove profitable for an owner of a £600 per annum estate to divide his freehold into two estates of £300 per annum each, while the owner of a £15,000 per annum estate might divide his land into two estates of £600 per annum each, and one estate of £300 per annum. In this way, it would be possible for the younger sons of the owners to become eligible for parliamentary membership, and for landless men to buy the land so divided, in order to meet the requirements of the Act. It is utterly impossible, however, to predict the general results of such a practice had it been adopted throughout England. The wholesale break-up of large landed estates might have proved detrimental to the agricultural laborer, as fewer hands would have been needed on the smaller estates. Unemployment would have been the inevitable result, and wages of agricultural laborers would have fallen. On the other hand, smaller estates yield more readily to intensive cultivation, and the opposite results might have occurred. Despite the predictions of these " would-be economists ", it is most difficult to prove that the Qualification Act was one of the contributing factors in the great economic changes of the eighteenth century. A careful study of that period would undoubtedly show that the agricultural movement resulted from other causes, and was in no way connected with the operation of the Qualification Act.

30 *Ibid.*, IV, 190.

CHAPTER III
THE OPERATION OF THE QUALI-
FICATION ACT

IF the chief purpose of the Qualification Act had been to place the future control of the government in the hands of the Tories, the events of the next five years shattered the hopes of that party. Tory and Whig leaders, supported by their respective pamphlets and pamphleteers, struggled, in the first election after the enactment of the Act, that of 1713, for the political leadership of the country. The Whigs attacked the Tory administration, directing their most vehement denunciations against the Treaty of Utrecht, and appealing to the electorate to turn out the Tories, and return the friends of commerce and industry. The Tory ministers, however, controlled the country; and while the Opposition was successful in defeating some of the Tory candidates, it was unable to break the power of the Tory party in the House of Commons. It followed that, while the number of Tory members in the Commons was not as large as it had been in 1710, Tory control of both houses continued to be undisputed.[1]

The Tory success, however, was short-lived, for on August 1, 1714, Queen Anne died, and with her died the hopes and aspirations of the party which had so recently tasted success under the leadership of the brilliant Bolingbroke and Oxford. The new king, George I, was suspicious of the Tories, whom he regarded as Jacobites and supporters of the Stuart cause; his first official act was to appoint his ministers from the Whig party. The Dukes of Somerset, Shrewsbury, and Argyle, and Lords Cowper, Halifax, and Townshend were charged with the maintenance of the government pending the sovereign's arrival

1 Mahon, Lord, *History of England* (Phila., 1849), I, 32.

in England.[2] Bolingbroke viewed the appointments as the death-knell of his party, and wrote to a friend: " I see plainly that the Tory party is gone ".[3] In the election of 1714, which was necessitated by the death of Queen Anne, the king appealed to the electorate

to have a particular regard to such as showed a firmness to the Protestant succession when it was in danger; [4]

and his ministers did all in their power to influence the voters to support the Whig candidates. Again the Whigs attacked the Treaty of Utrecht, and emphasized the injury to the people of London and the other trading centers, arising from the decline in trade.[5] Boscowen, comptroller of the king's household, worked zealously for the Whig cause, and the results of the election were joyously received by the Whig leaders. Once more the Whig party controlled the House of Commons. In many of the towns and boroughs, the Whigs outnumbered the Tories two to one; and in the County of Cornwall, thirty-two of the forty-four representatives were Whigs.[6] The Scots returned Whig representatives, and all in all, there were only about one hundred and sixty Tories in the new House of Commons.[7] The Whigs had regained the political leadership of the country and were to hold it for about forty-five years, until the accession of the great grandson and namesake of George I, George III of .Great Britain.

The changes in political leadership during the eighteenth century, which were occasioned by the domestic and foreign problems of the day, had little effect on the fortune of the Qualifica-

2 *Ibid.*, I, 71.

3 *Macpherson Papers*, Original Papers; containing the Secret History of Great Britain, from the Restoration, to the Accession of the House of Hanover, Printed for Strahan, W., and Cadell, T. (London, 1775), II, 651.

4 Lecky, W. E. H., *op. cit.*, I, 169.

5 Boyer, A., *The Political State of Great Britain*, January 1715, p. 83.

6 *Ibid.*, February 1715, p. 161.

7 Feiling, K., *The Second Tory Party, 1714-1832* (London, 1938), p. 15.

tion Act. Theoretically and technically, the Act was enforced during this period. If one omits from consideration the eldest sons of peers and the Scottish representatives, to whom the provisions of the Act did not apply, it is very probable that the majority of the parliamentary representatives throughout the century were owners of bona-fide estates. On the whole, counties returned landed representatives, and were usually suspicious of non-resident candidates, whom they regarded as " foreigners " [8] Then too, ambitious moneyed men were buying estates from the old landed gentry, and thereby becoming landed proprietors. Some of the great wealth of the directors of the South Sea Company was invested in land in and around London. At the time of the collapse of the South Sea Company, an inventory of the wealth of the directors was made public by the government; and some of the directors were shown to have estimated their wealth as follows:

Sir John Fellows	£239,596
Sir John Blunt	£183,349
Robert Chester	£140,372
Edward Gibbon	£105,043
Sir Theodore Janssen	£226,278
Samuel Read	£117,297
Robert Surman	£112,321 [9]

The transfer of ownership in land from the old landed gentry to the moneyed men was noticed by the newspapers and writers of the day, and some commented upon the decay of the old landed gentry. In 1718, *The Freethinker* announced that Sir Robert Chaplin, a South Sea Company director, had purchased the estate of the late Lord Widdrington in Lincolnshire for the sum of £32,400; [10] and Defoe remarked that landed estates near London had been purchased by London merchants and traders. Defoe believed that in another age the families and fortunes of

8 Porritt, E. and A., *op. cit.*, I, 179.

9 Peele, J., *A Compleat History of the Late Septennial Parliament* (London, 1722), pp. 47-48.

10 *The Freethinker*, September 19, 1718.

these " newcomers " would equal the families and fortunes of the ancient gentry.[11] On another occasion, he stated that five hundred estates within one hundred miles of London, all former possessions of the old English gentry, had been purchased by Londoners who had acquired their wealth through trade, merchandizing, shopkeeping, and manufacturing.[12] The acquisition of land by the moneyed classes continued; and in 1740, an article in *The Political State of Great Britain* called attention to the magnificent palaces that had been erected within a few miles of London by Sir John Eyles, a merchant, Sir Gregory Page, the son of a brewer, and Sir Nathaniel Mead, the son of a linen draper.[13] In this way many of the moneyed men qualified for entrance to the House of Commons, thereby defeating one of the main purposes of the Act.

While it is true that in the century following the enactment of the Qualification Act many men became purchasers of landed estates with the express desire of fulfilling the provisions of the law, it is nevertheless probable that the law had its calculated effect, for some men, such as Tom Legh,[14] who failed to secure the necessary landed qualification, gave up the idea of being members of the House of Commons rather than face petitions likely to be presented to the House by their unsuccessful opponents. In some cases, great landed proprietors actually placed landed estates in the hands of their relatives in order that the latter might fulfill the letter of the law. Horace Walpole congratulated Henry Seymour Conway for making it possible for Conway's brother to become a parliamentary member; and, in another letter, the same author praised the Duke of Devonshire, not for his political work, but for his honesty, which manifested itself in the granting of estates of £600 per annum to two of his younger

11 Defoe, D., *A Tour through England and Wales* (New York [1928]), I, 15.

12 Defoe, D., *A Plan of the English Commerce* (London, 1749), pp. 83-84.

13 Boyer, A., *The Political State of Great Britain*, April 1740, p. 348.

14 Lady Newton (Ed.), *Lyme Letters, 1660-1760* (London, 1925), p. 232.

sons, in order to enable them to become knights of shires.[15] But these were unusual cases, and bankers, lawyers and landowners soon found a way to evade the provisions of the Qualification Act. Landed proprietors provided the necessary landed qualifications for a short time, only until the representative had taken his seat in the House of Commons. The fictitious landed qualification was used by the parliamentary candidate in various ways. It enabled him to swear to his landed qualification at election time, and the documentary landed estate could also be used if any political opponent petitioned the House regarding the election. For these reasons sham or fictitious titles to landed estates were eagerly sought by parliamentary candidates at every election.

The apparent weakness of the Qualification Act was recognized by the members of the House of Commons; and in 1713/1714, while the Tories were still in power, resolutions were adopted to strengthen the Act. The resolutions adopted in 1713/1714, and made Standing Orders of the House of Commons in 1717 read:

I. That, notwithstanding the Oath taken by any Candidate at, or after, any Election, his Qualification may afterwards be examined into.

II. That the Person whose Qualification is expressly objected to in any Petition relating to his Election shall, within fifteen days after the Petition read, give to the Clerk of the House of Commons a Paper, signed by himself containing a Rental, or Particular, of the Lands, Tenements, and Hereditaments, whereby he makes out his Qualification; of which any Person concerned may have a Copy.

III. That of such Lands, Tenements, and Hereditaments, whereof the Party hath not been in Possession for Three Years before the Election, he shall also insert in the same Paper from

15 Walpole, H., *Memoirs of the Last Ten Years of the Reign of George II* (London, 1822), I, 437. In the forties, Lord Egmont found time to record in his diary: " My son passed back to me the English estate I gave him for a qualification." Hist. MSS. Comm., *Egmont MSS.*, Diary of Viscount Percival, First Earl of Egmont, III, 264.

what Person, and by what Conveyance or Act in Law, he claims and derives the same; and also the Consideration, if any, paid; and the Names, and Places of Abode, of the Witnesses to such Conveyance and Payment.

IV. That if any Sitting Member shall think fit to question the Qualification of a Petitioner, he shall, within fifteen days after the Petition read, leave Notice thereof, in Writing, with the Clerk of the House of Commons; and the Petitioner shall, in such case, within fifteen days after such Notice, leave with the said Clerk of the House the like Account, in Writing, of his Qualification, as is required from a Sitting Member.[16]

To his friend George Kenyon, Peter Shakerley wrote that the resolutions sponsored by Mr. Ward were aimed at Kenyon, since the original period of time, ten days from the reading of the petition, would not have given Kenyon the opportunity of handing in his rent rolls. Shakerley described his active part in the debates that followed the reading of the resolutions, and the manner in which he finally won his point by having the time limit extended to fifteen days.[17] He urged his friend Kenyon to waste no time, but to return a statement

fairly written, signed by you, as the said resolutions require, and, least one should miscarry, send one to Sir Roger and another to me, both signed by you.[18]

Evidently, Kenyon followed the advice of his friend, for no action was taken on the petition which had been presented to the House by his political opponents.[19] Omitting the personal motive, the members of the House apparently intended that the first and second resolutions should compel the representatives of the House to be the true possessors of landed estates as required

16 Cobbett, W., *Parliamentary History of England*, 6: 1265. *J. H. C.*, XVIII, 629.

17 Hist. MSS. Comm., *Kenyon MSS.*, Letter of Peter Shakerley to George Kenyon, March 6, 1713/1714, pp. 454-455.

18 *Ibid.*, p. 455.

19 *Ibid.*, p. 455.

by the law. The fourth resolution aimed to make the task of the challenger or the petitioner more difficult; not only must the petitioner prove that the representative was not properly qualified, but the House would not proceed with the complaint unless the former's own landed qualification was submitted to the Commons within the specified time of fifteen days.

This procedure was carried out after the general election of 1714, which returned the Whigs to power. Petitions complaining of bribery and corruption at elections, and of failure to meet the requirements of the Qualification Act, were submitted to the House of Commons. In March, 1715, James Sheppard complained of an undue election for the Borough of Honiton, which had returned Sir William Courteney and William Yonge to the House of Commons. The returned representatives for Honiton requested the qualifications of the petitioner. James Sheppard failed to meet the demand, and the complaint against the sitting members was dropped.[20] A similar case, two years later, was that of George Caswall, whose election was questioned by Henry Gorges. Mr. Gorges failed to submit his landed qualifications to the House within fifteen days after he had petitioned that body, and his complaint against Mr. Caswall was not considered by that body.[21] In both cases, the failure to submit their landed qualifications according to the resolutions adopted by the House was solely responsible for the dismissal of the petitioners' complaints. This procedure on the part of the Commons was consistently followed, namely, in the elections which involved Harrison,[22] Grove,[23] Bertie,[24] and Cunliffe.[25]

The case of John Comyns differed considerably from the preceeding ones. The qualified voters of Malden had returned Comyns to the House of Commons, but the defeated parlia-

20 *J. H. C.*, XVIII, 71.
21 *Ibid.*, XVIII, 543.
22 *Ibid.*, XX, 368.
23 *Ibid.*, XXI, 66.
24 *Ibid.*, XXII, 395.
25 *Ibid.*, XXII, 426.

mentary candidates made the serious charge that the sitting member had not taken the oath of qualification.[26] Witnesses for both sides were heard, and the decision rendered was that, although Comyns had received the greatest number of votes, and therefore was acknowledged the elected representative, he had not taken the oath of qualification at the time of his election, nor at any time previous to the meeting of the Commons. Failure to take the oath as required by the Qualification Act rendered the election of Comyns void.[27] No reason was given for Comyns' strange behavior. Was it a case of ignorance of the existing Qualification Act, or was Comyns a landless representative, who found it an impossibility to swear falsely regarding his landed estate? Whatever the reason, Comyns lost his seat in the House of Commons.

Although the House of Commons had adopted the resolutions of 1713/1714, and had taken definite action in the cases described, many writers and members of parliament came to the realization that by the year 1722 the practice of using fictitious qualifications was very common.[28] As early as 1714, when the Whigs came into power, Abigail Harley had written to her brother that a young neighbor, Harton, took the oath of qualification in a trembling voice, and most of the voters present knew that he possessed no landed estate.[29] The same election saw the return of Mr. Lewis for Radnor, and his father's estate, had the former possessed it, would not have met the requirements of the law.[30] The same year found a writer complaining bitterly that the estates of many of the landed men were heavily mortgaged, and that the landed interest found it very difficult to obtain qualified candidates. He mentioned

Sir G. M. whose Land was in Twenty Counties, to patch up a Three hundred a Year; and C—ll.r, whose Land was in Drury

26 *Ibid.*, XVIII, 24.
27 *Ibid.*, XVIII, 129.
28 Porritt, E. and A., *op. cit.*, I, 171.
29 Hist. MSS. Comm., *Portland MSS.*, V, 506.
30 *Ibid.*, " Memoirs of the Harley Family," p. 663.

Lane, meaning a Pension from the Players; yet was he made a Member by the Recommendation of B——K, and One of the Twelve.[31]

Swift, the Tory pamphleteer, denounced the elections which followed the adoption of the Qualification Act, for many of the boroughs returned members to the House who did not possess one foot of land in the kingdom.[32]

Swift's opinion was supported by many of the members of the House of Commons. During the discussion of the Septennial Bill, a representative denounced the corruption and bribery existing in the country, and wondered how it was possible for so many representatives in the House to serve constituencies in which they had no

visible estates or interest, nay, some perhaps whose names were never heard of in the county a month before the election.[33]

Another member of the House of Commons held strangers responsible for the great increase in election expenses, and contended that many of these strangers had " no natural interest " to recommend them to their boroughs except bribery and corruption.[34] In the House of Lords, discussion on the Septennial Bill led the Earl of Ilay to compare the electors of England in 1716 with the electors of former times with this comment:

formerly the electors were either gentlemen or men of substance, whereas the majority of them are of the dregs of the people, and therefore more subject to corruption.[35]

The Septennial Bill became a law, and it was not until December, 1721, while Robert Walpole was in the midst of bringing order out of financial chaos, and the country was thinking about

31 *The False Steps of the Ministry after the Revolution*, Printed for J. Roberts (London, 1714), p. 19.

32 Scott, T. (Ed.), *op. cit.*, XI, 181.

33 Cobbett, W., *Parliamentary History of England*, 7: 328.

34 *Ibid.*, 7: 335.

35 *Ibid.*, 7: 302.

the spring elections, that Archibald Hutcheson proposed to amend the Qualification Act.

Born in Ireland in 1665, Archibald Hutcheson made a wealthy match, and in 1713 became a Tory member of the House of Commons. The change in political leadership in 1714 did not affect his position, and he continued to be a representative until 1727. He was a friend of the Duke of Ormonde and the Prince of Wales, and during the reign of George I, he received appointment as a Commissioner of Trade and Plantations.[36] Always the supporter of Tory principles and policies, he attacked the Bank of England, the East India Company, and the South Sea Company, which he considered beneficial only to certain private persons, including foreigners, and ruinous to the general public. He condemned the great wealth of these individuals, which surpassed the wealth of the old landed gentry and even the members of the nobility.[37] The Septennial Act and standing armies did not receive his support, and the financial policies of Walpole were severely condemned.[38] Bribery and corruption also bore the brunt of his disapproval, as did the interference of peers in the elections of Great Britain, for if the officers of the Crown, especially the Duke of Newcastle [39] and other peers, were to dictate to the voters of the kingdom regarding the election of their representatives, then

36 Nulle, S., *Thomas Pelham-Holles, Duke of Newcastle* (Phila., 1931), pp. 141-142.

37 Hutcheson, A., *Some Calculations and Remarks relating to the present State of the Public Debts and Funds*, Printed in *The Political State of Great Britain*, August, 1718, p. 92.

38 Feiling, K., *op. cit.*, p. 25.

39 The rapid rise of the Duke of Newcastle to important positions in the state was due in part to his possession of great landed estates, which made him a powerful factor in the Whig party; and in part to his connections with the outstanding families of the day—the Godolphins, Marlboroughs, Sunderlands, and Townshends. He possessed land in nine counties, and owned nearly all of Nottinghamshire. Winstanley, D., *Lord Chatham and the Whig Opposition* (Cambridge, 1912), p. 14. Feiling, K., *op. cit.*, p. 103.

the British Constitution is intirely at at End, and we are in the State of the most abject Slavery . . . [40]

Hutcheson proposed to remedy this situation by amending the Qualification Act in such a way that only bona-fide possessors of landed estates would be members of the House of Commons. Accordingly, on December 18, 1721, following a motion made by Hutcheson, the House designated Mr. Hutcheson and Mr. Robert Pitt to prepare a " Bill for the better securing the Freedom of Elections of Members to serve in Parliament." [41] On January 16, 1721/1722, the bill was read for the first time; [42] and one week later, on January 23, in the debate on the second reading of the bill, Mr. Hutcheson, who was responsible for the measure, defended it. His analysis of the Qualification Act was laudatory as to its purpose, but critical as to results, for by 1722, that Act, in his opinion, was of little use or service to the people of the country. Not only was the landed qualification too small, but all too often the parliamentary candidate swore to his landed qualification at the time of his election, and parted with it soon after. Hutcheson objected to the exemption of the eldest sons of peers and recusants from the operation of the law as this exemption left a " back door to many people ". His plea was for the adoption of his bill, which would establish free and independent parliaments for the people. He predicted dire consequences in the event that his measure was defeated. [43] Opposition, however, developed in the Commons, and some changes had to be made. To meet the objection of the Court Party, the provision prohibiting excise and customs officers from voting for members of the Commons, which would have decreased greatly the power of the current ministry, was dropped; and the pro-

40 Hutcheson, A., *A Collection of Advertisements, Letters and Papers, and some other Facts, relating to the last Elections at Westminster and Hastings* (London, 1722), p. 30.

41 *J. H. C.*, XIX, 697.

42 Cobbett, W., *op. cit.*, 7: 948. Chandler, R., *op. cit.*, VI, 271.

43 Cobbett, W., *op. cit.*, 7: 948-952. Boyer, A., *The Political State of Great Britain*, April, 1722, pp. 361-365.

vision that no person who did not pay scot and lot should be permitted to vote in a municipal corporation, was likewise stricken from the bill.[44] Provisions concerning bribery, writs, and duties of sheriffs remained intact, as well as the most important provision, which required that after March 22, 1722, every representative must give to the Clerk of the House of Commons a schedule of his lands, tenements, and hereditaments by which he claimed his qualification, and subscribe to the oath attached.[45]

The bill passed the Commons and went to the Lords, where it met with opposition. No doubt many of the peers believed that their control over the House of Commons would be weakened by its passage. Certainly, temporary landed qualifications would no longer be possible. According to the provision of the bill, the qualification handed in by the representative would be in the possession of the Clerk of the Commons for a probable seven years, the maximum life of the House of Commons under the Septennial Act. But this main objection could not be openly voiced by the members of the House of Lords. Hutcheson, realizing that opposition was developing in the Upper House, wrote to Lord Sunderland, emphasizing the importance to the king, the administration, and the nation's welfare, of a free and independent parliament, and urged the passage of the measure because:

The Bill now sent up to your Lordships from the Commons, relating to Elections, must be believed the sense of the majority of the House, as it certainly is of the nation, though not perhaps of the little boroughs of the kingdom.[46]

On the second reading of the bill in the House of Lords, objections were made to the oath provisions of the measure which

44 Chandler, R., *op. cit.*, VI, 276. In scot and lot boroughs, the right to vote depended on residence and contributions to the charges of municipal government.

45 Trenchard, J. and Gordon, T., *A Collection of Tracts* (London, 1751), Gordon, T., "A Compleat History of the Late Septennial Parliament" (London, 1722), II, 75-81.

46 *The Gentleman's Magazine*, June, 1839, Hutcheson's Letter to Lord Sunderland, February 9, 1721/1722, p. 582.

were thought to expose innocent persons to perjury charges.[47]
The Earl of Sunderland, Lord Townshend, and the Duke of
Argyle led the opposition, and when the motion was made to
refer the bill to committee, it was defeated by a vote of forty-
eight to thirty.[48] This action on the part of the House brought
forth a protest which was signed by twenty-six peers. The protest, read by Somerset, stated:

I. Because the Methods of Corruption made use of in Elections,
and now grown to an Heighth beyond the Example of
preceding Times, are, of all others, the greatest Blemish to
our Constitution, and must, if not remedied, prove fatal to
it; and did therefore chiefly deserve, as they can only admit
of, a Parliamentary Cure.

II. Because the Commons, who are the best qualified to judge
of the Growth of this Evil, and to point out proper Remedies
for it, having sent up a Bill complaining of the one, and
desiring our Assistance in the other, it was not, we apprehend, suitable to the Dignity and Wisdom of this House to
reject such a Bill, without entering into a free Discussion of
the Particulars of which it consisted, and thereby to give
an Handle for Reflections without Doors, as if we had
shewn a less Degree of Zeal against the Corruptions complained of than those from whose Elections it sprung; our
Opinion is, that we should rather have taken this favourable
Opportunity of joining our Endeavours with theirs, towards
the Cure of this Evil, than have made ourselves liable to
Objections for refusing to attempt it, even after such an
encouraging Step taken by the House of Commons.

III. Because a Law against Corruption, though always desirable,
is yet particularly seasonable and necessary at such a Junc-
ture as this, when new Elections of Members are coming
on, and the Parliament for which they shall (by what
Methods soever) be chosen, may continue for seven Years;
and, we think, the Lords are the more concerned to obviate

47 Timberland, E., *op. cit.*, III, 227.

48 Boyer, A., *The Political State of Great Britain*, February 1721/1722,
p. 218.

the ill Consequences of such a Choice, because the Septennial Act, which made so remarkable a Change in our Constitution, had its Rise in this House.

IV. Because we are persuaded, that by the Terror of the Penalties contained in this Bill, which were to have operated soon after it had passed into a Law, a mighty Check would have been given to the Growth of Corruption, though it should not have been absolutely cured; and we are confirmed in this Opinion by what we heard and believe, that while the Bill was depending in Parliament, and the Fate of it unknown, the impious Practices at which it was levelled were in some measure suspended; and should a further Stop have been put to Corruption and Bribery at the approaching Elections, by passing this Bill, such a Degree of Success might have given the Legislature Hopes of an entire Suppression of it.

V. Because supposing this Bill to have been defective in some respects, and not well adjusted in others to the End designed (a Supposition made, but not admitted by us) yet the true Way of supplying all these Defects, and making all proper Alterations, would have been by committing the Bill, and not by rejecting it: In other Cases, where a Bill of Publick Concern is laid aside by the House, they can easily make Amends for that Loss by bringing in a new one, which may more effectually answer the Good Ends proposed; whereas in this Case there is neither Time sufficient for repeating the Attempt, nor can any Bill of this Kind be ever begun in this House with any reasonable Prospect of Success.

VI. Because the Intention of many chief Clauses in the Bill is to provide for the more effectual Execution of Laws already made to secure the Freeedom of Elections, but hitherto evaded for want of such Provisions; and we know not that any Argument hath been or can be used against passing such Parts of this Bill into a Law, but what may with equal or greater Strength be urged for repealing those Laws, which yet are held sacred and inviolable.

VII. Because several Oaths are, by Laws now in Being, required to qualify Electors, and the Oaths enjoined by this Bill are intended only to strengthen the Obligations under which such Electors do, by the known Rules of our Constitution already lie; nor are these Oaths attended with any new Hardship or Difficulty, since they relate only to plain Matters of Fact, which are certainly known to the Electors themselves, and which they will be ready to attest with all Solemnity, if they are conscious of their own Innocence; and if they are not, the legal Punishment of Perjury to which they are subjected is light, in comparison of the heinous Nature of their Offence, and the mischievous Consequences of it.

VIII. Because that part of the Bill, which forbids the issuing of publick Money towards influencing Elections, relates to a Method of Corruption, which, of all others, ought the most carefully to be guarded against, and yet was admitted in the Debate to have been frequently practised; and therefore we cannot but wish, that this Bill had been passed into a Law for the sake of that Clause, which would have hinder'd what was given for the Security of the Subjects Rights, and the Safety of the Kingdom, from being ever employed to the Destruction of both: An Example, if thus set by Men in high Offices and Stations, cannot fail of spreading its Influence through all Ranks and Orders of Men, and Procuring Impunity and Applause for such Practices, as all true Lovers of their Country must wish might be universally detested and punished.

IX. Because we cannot understand how the Objection made to this Bill (That it removes Foundations) can, with any Colour of Reason be supported; on the contrary, we think, that the whole Design of it is to recover our old Constitution, and resettle it on those firm Foundations from which it has been removed, ever since Bribery has been made an usual Inlet to Parliament, and that Dangerous Traffick has been carried on between the Electors and the Elected, which has undermined the virtuous Principles, and may prove fatal to the Liberties of the free People of this Realm.

X. Because another Argument insisted on in Prejudice of the Bill (That it would give the House of Commons greater Latitude in deciding disputed Elections) seems to us to be equally groundless; for the Penalties intended to be enacted by this Bill are to take place only upon Prosecutions in the ordinary Courts of Justice, and cannot come under the Cognizance, or be inflicted by the Authority of the House of Commons; nor can the Courts below be checked in their Proceedings on this Head by the Determinations of that House, with which the Methods of punishing Corruption, prescribed by this Bill, do not in the least interfere: What therefore was alledged in the Debate can by no Means be allowed (That while the Commons are the sole Judges of Elections, 'tis in vain to think of restraining the Corruption of Electors) since the Methods here prescribed are such, as either operate upon the Conscience, or will, in the common Course of Law, execute themselves; and tho' they may be forwarded, yet cannot be frustrated by the Intervention of an House of Commons.

XI. Because as the passing this Bill would have been attended with no Inconveniences to the Publick, so great Mischiefs may, we apprehend ensue upon the rejecting it: The Honour of this House may suffer on that Account, and Corruption of all sorts will, we fear, receive new Life and Encouragement; it being a Matter of daily and certain Observation, that whenever a Bill is brought into Parliament to redress any great Disorders in the State, any Discountenance given to such a Bill will always countenance and increase such Disorders, and make them less capable of a Remedy in succeeding Times, especially when it shall be affirmed in the Debate, that all Bills of this kind do more Mischief than Good; which way of Reasoning, should it prevail, will effectually prevent all future Attempts towards curing this great Evil, and preserving the Constitution of Parliaments.[49]

Several members of the House of Lords condemned the protest, and urged the signers to reconsider their action and expunge the protest from the journal of the House. After some hesitation this suggestion was followed, and the protest expunged from the records of the House of Lords.[50] Hutcheson's bill, however, was lost; and it was not until a decade later that the House of

49 Timberland, E., *op. cit.*, III, 227-230.

50 *Ibid.*, III, 231.

Commons turned its attention once again to the Qualification Act.

Following the defeat of the measure, the political abuses rampant in England were attacked by the pamphleteers of the day. In 1727, on the eve of a general election, *The Craftsman* urged the electors of the nation to beware of brokers and stock-jobbers who made their money in Exchange Alley, and advised the election of men of abilities and estates. These men were the best representatives, the argument ran, for men of abilities would not follow crafty and designing leaders; and men of estates were above temptation.[51] In a letter to *The Political State of Great Britain* written that same year, a man described his encounter with a Jewish borough-broker who assured him that, regardless of his qualifications, he could be elected as a representative to the House of Commons. The borough-broker explained that victory at the polls could be guaranteed by his many agents, who kept the electors of various communities in a drunken state to accomplish their purpose. The letter writer lamented such corrupt practices as detrimental to the interests of the honest people, and in all probability productive of terrible consequences for the nation.[52] As in previous elections, advertisements appeared in the local papers announcing to the world that men were in the market to buy or sell seats in the House of Commons. The following notice appeared in *The Craftsman* in July, 1727:

SOME PERSONS WANT TO BUY

A Gentleman wants to buy a good Seat, for seven Years, in any Part of England. Another is willing to treat for only a Return. Another is willing to lodge £2000 in proper Hands, to be paid on Security of being a sitting Member.

SOME PERSONS WANT TO SELL

The perpetual Advowson of a Seat in the County of Bucks to be disposed of. The next Presentation to several Seats in Cornwall to

51 *The Craftsman*, August 5, 1727. Men of abilities would imply men of material power.

52 Boyer, A., *The Political State of Great Britain*, August, 1727, Letter to paper, July 31, 1727, pp. 153-154.

be had on easy Terms . . . A Gentleman, under some Misfortunes, is willing to dispose of a considerable Interest in the County of Wilts.

The Particulars will be given by Mr. Robert Goldsmith, Broker and Agent for Persons, who want any such Business to be done. He is daily to be spoke with from 12 to 3 at Garraways, in Exchange Alley . . . [53]

It seems paradoxical that this notice should appear in *The Craftsman,* whose sponsors, Bolingbroke and Pulteney, were always admonishing the electorate to return men of abilities and estates [54] to the House of Commons. The 1727 election was as notorious for drunkenness, bribery, and corruption as other eighteenth century elections had been and were to be. Although the House of Commons, which met in January, 1728, was controlled by the Whigs, some of whom had been returned by dishonest practices, the House was ready to remedy the existing evils. In May, 1729, a bill providing penalties for bribery at elections became a law.[55]

This act was praised by *The Craftsman* because the old country interest, which had been supplanted by the moneyed interest, would now return to its position of leadership in the nation, and would be able to return representatives to the House of Commons.[56] In another issue of the same paper, the traits of character of landed men were emphasized, and the importance of their positions in their respective communities stressed. The landed man, it was claimed, knew the needs of his community, and if elected to the House of Commons would redress the grievances of his constituency and advance its interests.[57] The country gentleman, unlike the moneyed man who purchased his seat, was above temptation. Once more, *The Craftsman* urged

53 *The Craftsman*, July 29, 1727.

54 *Ibid.*, August 19, 1727.

55 Cobbett, W., *op. cit.*, 8: 753-755.

56 *The Craftsman*, May 24, 1729.

57 *Ibid.*, January 10, 1729/1730.

the electors of England to remember the Qualification Act, because it was " often eluded, or but little regarded in other Places." [58]

A year after the passage of the Bribery Act, the House of Commons was ready to attack the question of pensions. A Pension Bill, introduced by Mr. Sandys, and supported by his followers, passed the Commons. The bill provided that all men holding pensions or any offices held in trust for them, were to be disqualified from membership in the Commons.[59] In this way, the members of the Opposition hoped to decrease the power of Walpole and his followers, for if Walpole were no longer able to tempt men with pensions and positions, it would naturally follow that the number of willing henchmen in the House of Commons would rapidly decrease. Walpole objected to the measure, but took no active part against it in the House, as he well knew that it would be defeated by the Lords. Sir Charles Wager, speaking against the Pension Bill, announced his opposition to all disqualifying bills, adding that the

Act which obliged every member to have an estate at least of three hundred pounds a year in land had disqualified ninety-nine persons of a hundred in the kingdom.[60]

The Pension Bill failed to pass the House of Lords, and members of the minority party continued to introduce similar bills in later parliaments.

The reforming spirit of the House of Commons manifested itself in various other ways, including another attempt to strengthen the Qualification Act. On February 23, 1731, the Commons ordered Mr. Windham, Mr. Pulteney, and Mr. Rolle to bring in a bill " to explain, amend, and render more effectual " the Qualification Act passed in the time of Queen Anne.[61] All three men were the possessors of landed estates, and all

58 *Ibid.*, January 10, 1729/1730.

59 Mahon, Lord, *op. cit.*, I, 372.

60 Hist. MSS. Comm., *Egmont MSS.*, Diary of Viscount Percival, I, 140.

61 *J. H. C.*, XXI, 811.

three believed that the Qualification Act should be so amended that evasion of the law would be an impossibility. William Windham, who owed his political success to Bolingbroke,[62] was a man of family and fortune; William Pulteney, later Earl of Bath, was a country gentleman of old family and large estates.[63] Pulteney had inherited considerable property from his father, and had received from Henry Guy, his guardian and benefactor, a legacy of £40,000, and an estate of £500 a year.[64] Both men were friends of Bolingbroke, and for a time, Pulteney, a leader of the discontented Whigs, wrote articles for The Craftsman. The bill drawn up by these men was defeated in the House of Commons by a vote of fifty-six to fifty.[65]

Pulteney and his friends were not discouraged by this defeat and a year later, on March 7, 1732, a similar measure was introduced into the House of Commons. During the debate, a member proposed that a qualification in public funds be recognized as well as a landed one. Robert Walpole and Sir William Young supported this view, but Sir William Windham, Sir John Barnard, and others raised strenuous objections, and the proposal was dropped.[66] It is difficult to understand Sir John Barnard's objection to the proposal, since Sir John's background, associates, and business activities would lead to the expectation that such a proposal would be welcomed by him. Sir John was a London merchant, and an expert in financial and commercial matters. He rose, unassisted by friends, learning, or wealth, to a position of honor and esteem in London, which city he represented in the House of Commons for many years.[67] He had opposed the Septennial Act for he believed in annual parliaments, and unlike other commercial and moneyed men, was of

62 Hervey, J., Memoirs of the Reign of George II (London, 1855), I, 26.
63 Lecky, W. E. H., op. cit., I., 374.
64 Coxe, W., Memoirs of the Life and Administration of Sir Robert Walpole (London, 1800), II, 150-151.
65 J. H. C., XXI, 859.
66 Hist. MSS. Comm., Egmont MSS., Percival's Diary, I, 240.
67 Hist. MSS. Comm., Onslow MSS., p. 469.

the opinion that electors, uninfluenced in any way, would always choose men of large property because they " would take the best care of the properties of their fellow-subjects." [68] A fellow member of the House of Commons, Henry Pelham, was of the same opinion, although he did not state his ideas in the 1732 session of the House of Commons. Henry Pelham, the brother of the Duke of Newcastle, has been severely criticized for indulging in the corrupt practices of his time. Although he manipulated elections in favor of the Whigs, he upheld the theory that not only should the representatives of the House of Commons be possessed of landed property, but also all officers of the kingdom should be required to qualify similarly, because the estate of an officer was

a pledge to the public, of fidelity as well as of honesty; as such a man is not surely so liable to be bribed by foreign courts, as one of no fortune.[69]

On the third reading of the 1732 bill, Mr. Pelham said that he had no objection to the measure, nor to the provision that required parliamentary candidates to swear to their qualifications at the Speaker's table, rather than at the time and place of their election; he did however, question the desirability of another oath. He complained that there were too many oaths, and recommended that this proposed oath be omitted.[70] Mr. Pulteney defended the provision, and pointed out that there was no multiplication of oaths, but that the bill merely changed the place of taking them. Pulteney firmly believed that since there were so many members who had no qualifications, this provision would make them known to the House of Commons.[71] Mr. Oglethorpe

68 Torbuck, J., *A Collection of the Parliamentary Debates in England from the Year 1668 to the present Time* (London, 1739-1742), XII, 116.

69 Coxe, W., *Memoirs of the Administration of the R. H. Henry Pelham* (London, 1829), I, 195. See Toynbee, Mrs. P. (Ed.), *The Letters of Horace Walpole* (Oxford, 1903-1905), III, 216. Walpole's Opinion of Henry Pelham.

70 Hist. MSS. Comm., *Egmont MSS.*, Percival's Diary, I, 244.

71 *Ibid.*, p. 244.

opposed the bill, and expressed the wish that there be no qualifications to limit the choice of the electors in electing their representatives. If representatives had disregarded the oath under the old law, he held, there was no reason why they would not do the same under the new law. Oglethorpe believed that all members of the Commons were qualified according to the intent of the Qualification Act, and if there were members who were not qualified, they should be made known to the House.[72]

When put to a vote, the bill went down to defeat, and immediately Mr. Pulteney moved that a committee be appointed to inquire into the qualifications of the members of parliament.[73] This motion aroused great opposition; and Mr. Camell, a member who had supported the bill, objected to the motion, which had been properly seconded, because it would subject the estates of five hundred men to a " narrow and critical examination " by a few men. Such an examination, he thought, might prove an inquisition, and might result in disastrous consequences. Mr. Walpole supported Mr. Camell, and when Mr. Pulteney's motion was put to a vote, it was lost.[74] The opponents of Pulteney's motion were members of the House of Commons who were not properly qualified, and members like Viscount Percival, who agreed with Mr. Camell that the small committee designated to examine the estates of members would really " spy out defects in their titles." [75] Percival also recorded in his diary that he opposed the measure because he believed that the former act did function, and that if members swore falsely under the old act, they were very likely to do the same before the House of Commons. He objected, moreover, to the general idea behind the bill, which seemed to imply that many of the members of the Commons were not properly qualified, and were not, therefore, the rightful holders of their seats.[76]

72 *Ibid.*, p. 245.
73 *Ibid.*, p. 245.
74 *Ibid.*, p. 245. The vote was 83 to 37.
75 *Ibid.*, p. 246.
76 *Ibid.*, p. 246.

The friends of the Qualification Act were not disheartened; and a little less than a year later, in January, 1733, a similar measure to amend and render more effectual the earlier act was introduced into the House of Commons by Mr. Rolle and Mr. Pulteney. Sir William Young opposed the measure, not only because it included the previously-rejected provision regarding the oaths, but also and more particularly because the handing over of the schedule of the landed qualification to the Clerk of the House would prevent the sale or disposition of the land for a seven-year period. One of the representatives of Liverpool, and an opponent of Pulteney, thought it was unreasonable to expect merchants to have landed estates. He was reminded by Mr. Pulteney that he was arguing against the old act, and not against the new measure, but Robert Walpole and his supporters cried out " Hear Sir Thomas ",[77] the Liverpool representative. Horace Walpole, Mr. Pelham, and others opposed the measure, using all the arguments previously given; but the strongest argument against the bill was never voiced during the discussion: no one suggested that the measure would decrease the power of the ministry which was responsible for and supported by many of the landless members of the Commons. It was a common practice for the Court Party to secure the election of the representatives of the Cornish boroughs. These men, recommended to the boroughs by the ministers in power, never appeared on election days, and were never questioned about their landed qualifications. The members of the Opposition hoped that the new measure, by forcing the parliamentary members to submit their landed qualifications to the Clerk of the House, would remedy this evil. Supporters of the measure were successful in winning Percival and a few others to their side; but when the vote was taken, Walpole and his followers scored the victory: the measure was defeated by a vote of 159 to 120.[78] While he voted in favor of the bill, Viscount Percival, in his diary, criticized some of its provisions. He wondered why a

77 *Ibid.*, pp. 332-333.

78 *J. H. C.*, XXII, 212, 245. Hist. MSS. Comm., *Egmont MSS.*, Percival's Diary, I, 346.

mortgagee holding property for a seven-year period should be eligible to represent a constituency, while that same mortgagee did not have the right to vote. He remarked that a similar situation existed in the case of men who held leases on property for a number of years. Percival also feared that it was possible for a representative to swear to his landed qualification and discover later that he had been mistaken, and thus find himself, although innocent, adjudged guilty of perjury under the law.[79]

Undaunted by defeat, the supporters of the Qualification Act made another unsuccessful effort to strengthen it in February, 1734,[80] with the intention of diminishing the political power of Walpole and the Whigs in the national election of 1734. Within the House of Commons, Walpole's manipulations of elections were attacked by Sir John Barnard. In a speech advocating annual elections, Sir John implied that treasury money was used to oppose the country gentlemen who had natural interests in the community, and were the logical and rightful representatives of their constituencies.[81] The House of Commons was divided on the question, some supporting Sir John in his condemnation of corrupt practices in the nation, and others actually denying that the conditions he deplored existed. Robert Walpole belonged in the latter group; his comments were:

There may, Sir, be some bribery and corruption in the nation; I am afraid there will always be some; but it is no proof of it, that strangers are sometimes chosen; for a gentleman may have so much natural influence over a borough in his neighborhood, as to be able to prevail with them to choose any person he pleases to recommend; and if upon such recommendation, they choose one or two of his friends, who are perhaps strangers to them, it is not from thence to be inferred, that the two strangers were chosen their representatives by the means of bribery and corruption.[82]

79 *Ibid.*, p. 347.

80 Boyer, A., *The Political State of Great Britain*, September, 1734, p. 262.

81 Torbuck, J., *op. cit.*, XII, 116-117.

82 Coxe, W., *Walpole Memoirs*, II, 277. Walpole was considered a political boss by Chesterfield. See Maty, M. (Ed.), *Miscellaneous Works of the late Philip Dormer Stanhope, Earl of Chesterfield* (Dublin, 1777), I, 347. Torbuck, J., *op. cit.*, XII, 151.

The indignant Walpole then attacked Sir John's speech, and denied that government money was used in elections. He added:

To insinuate, Sir, that money may be issued from the public treasury for bribing elections, is really something very extraordinary, especially in those gentlemen who know how many checks are upon every shilling that can be issued from thence . . . [83]

But bribery and corruption, the results of which Sir Robert attempted to deny or minimize, were rampant in the election of 1734. Walpole and the Duke of Newcastle used large sums of money to retain their political positions. Walpole was reputed to have used £60,000 of his own money for election expenses; [84] and Hervey wrote that, in violation of the Bribery Act of 1729, money " was never more plentifully issued ",[85] to buy the votes of the electorate, and to buy food and drink for the community. By corresponding with many men, by reprieving the sentences of prisoners, by bestowing revenue officers' places on hesitant voters, by placing business in the hands of non-friendly Whigs, Newcastle and his agents were responsible for the sixty or seventy members who were returned in the interest of the government from places dominated by the Duke.[86] Although the discontented Whigs and the Tories attacked the excise scheme, the standing army, and the Septennial Act, as well as the whole administration of Walpole, they were not able to defeat the old leaders.

The new parliament met in January, 1735, and although the Whig majority was smaller, the Duke of Newcastle characterized the new assembly as " a good one ".[87] A month later, in February, 1735, the parliament rejected a bill to amend the Quali-

83 Torbuck, J., op. cit., XII, 151.

84 Mahon, Lord, op. cit., I, 405.

85 Taylor, G. R. S., Robert Walpole and his Age (London, 1931), p. 266.

86 Williams, B., " The Duke of Newcastle and the Election of 1734," The English Historical Review, July, 1897, pp. 448-488.

87 Mahon, Lord, op. cit., I, 405.

fication Act.[88] Shortly thereafter, in April, James, Lord Lime-
rick, petitioned the House complaining that John Boteler, the
returned representative from the Borough of Wendover, was
not the possessor of a landed estate as required by law. It was
true that Boteler was the owner of land which he had inherited
in 1708, but by 1735 the accumulation of debts had decreased
the value of the estate. Accordingly, the election of Boteler was
declared null and void.[89] Other petitioners were not successful in
unseating their political opponents. Although in 1739 a petitioner claimed that Mr. Clarke was not properly qualified according to law, the Commons declared that Clarke was
duly elected.[90] The Commons on the whole seemed to favor
their parliamentary colleagues, especially if they were members
of the party in power. In many cases, however, petitions complaining of the evasion of the Qualification Act were not considered because the petitioners had failed to submit their own
schedules of landed qualifications within the specified time.
Therefore, either because the critics of the Qualification Act
could not prove definitely that the existing act had been violated
or evaded in a wholesale manner, or because other questions—
the Gin Act, the repeal of the Test Act, the poor conditions of
the weavers, the quarrels of the royal family, or the increasing
tension between Spain and Great Britain—seemed more important, no further attempt to amend the Qualification Act was
made until February, 1739. In that month, a bill prepared by
Mr. Bottle and Mr. Rushout met the same fate as had the previous bills.[91]

The repeated failure of Pulteney and his followers to amend
the Qualification Act induced them to abandon their efforts; for
the next twenty years, there was no movement in the House of
Commons for any amendment of that act. In the forties, Pul-

88 *J. H. C.*, XXII, 550.

89 *Ibid.*, XXII, 466-468.

90 Oldfield, T., *An Entire and Complete History of the Boroughs of Great
Britain* (London, 1794), I, 317-319.

91 *J. H. C.*, XXIII, 449.

teney and the opponents of Walpole endeavored to weaken the existing Whig ministry by a Place Bill. In 1740, while the Place Bill was being debated on the floor of the Commons, John Selwyn, an opponent of the bill, referred to the Qualification Act, which he lauded as preserving the constitution; [92] and Pulteney, who naturally supported the Place Bill, raised the question of whether gentlemen of family, fortune, character, and interest in their country were the only ones chosen by the voters to represent them in the House of Commons. The fact that such men were not the only ones chosen was due, he said, to the ministers, who were able to have their supporters, men of no character, fortune, or interest in the country, returned to the House.[93] Another supporter of the Place Bill made no comment on the composition of the House of Commons in 1740, but said that former parliaments were composed of

mercenary wretches, who, Esau-like, sold their birth-rights, and from being born free, became slaves to their purchasers . . . [94]

With the Court Party against the Place Bill, it is needless to say that it met the same fate as had the bills to amend the Qualification Act.

Temporarily dropped by Pulteney and others, the question of the Qualification Act and its operation was kept alive by the contemporary writers. In 1740, *The London Magazine* remarked that though the purpose of the Qualification Act was a good one, it did not accomplish its purpose, for evasion was possible by the temporary possesion of fictitious qualifications.[95] In the same year, the author of an article in another magazine stated that, while he could not point out by name any representative as not being properly qualified according to law, yet he did know of three or four sons or brothers of great families who represented boroughs, and he wondered if they would have

92 Cobbett, W., *Parliamentary History*, 11 : 333.
93 *Ibid.*, 11 : 354.
94 *Ibid.*, 11 : 377.
95 *The London Magazine*, February, 1740, p. 91.

proper landed qualifications if all their debts were paid. He added that the landed qualification was a pledge of independence, and proof of the representative's interest in the country and in the welfare of the people. The Qualification Act should be retained on the statute book, he felt, and should be enforced; false swearing should be severely punished, and cases involving evasion of the law should be tried by jury. The writer recommended further that the landed qualification of any representative, once elected, should be questioned within a year after his election, and that the qualification should be raised.[96]

In 1747, when the attention of the nation was directed to a national election, the Qualification Act again assumed some importance for the political pamphleteers. In June, 1747, the electorate was urged to examine the character, the experience, and the fortune of the parliamentary candidate. The fortune of the prospective House member was cited as most important, for a large fortune would place him beyond the reach of corruption and influence, while a small one might induce him to seek a seat in the House in order to improve his material wealth.[97] A few months later, another magazine article restated the provisions of the Qualification Act, and recommended several amendments: (1) that the value of the landed estate necessary for qualification be increased: double for the knights of the shires, and increased to £600 per annum for the citizens and burgesses, and (2) that no estate should qualify any candidate except one of free inheritance.[98] In a letter to a friend, Bishop Thomas described the electoral activities of a peer and criticized the nobleman for supporting a relative who had " not a foot of Land in the County nor any Relations to it." [99] A year later,

96 *The Gentleman's Magazine*, September, 1740, p. 450.

97 *Ibid.*, June, 1747, p. 275. Quoting an article from the *Westminster Journal* entitled, " Topics of Self-Enquiry for Electors, and Candidates before Voting."

98 *Ibid.*, August, 1747, p. 366. Quoting an article from the *Westminster Journal*, entitled, "Amendments suggested to Laws of Election."

99 Hist. MSS. Comm., *Weston MSS.*, Letter from Bishop Thomas to Edward Weston, January 1, 1747, p. 296.

when the works of Bolingbroke were offered to the public, it was noted that they contained a considerable statement of the author's views on the Qualification Act. Although Bolingbroke had taken no active part in the political life of the kingdom since the days of Queen Anne, his ideas had greatly influenced a good many men, among whom were William Windham and William Pulteney. These two men, as leaders of the two groups in the House of Commons—Pulteney the leader of the discontented Whigs, and Windham the leader of the Tories—had worked zealously for the enforcement and amendment of the Qualification Act. While Bolingbroke in his works did not attack the existing political abuses, he did restate the main purpose of the Act, which had been to place the government in the hands of men of independent fortunes, and thus render the representatives beyond the reach of temptation and bribery.[100] The opinions of the writers of the forties were restated by the writers of the fifties, but their blasts of attack on political abuses of the day had little effect on a House of Commons composed of men returned by Bubb Dodington, James Lowther, and the Duke of Newcastle.

The national election of 1754 was described by *The Connoisseur* as a noisy one which kept many a town in an "uproar". London bankers offered themselves as parliamentary candidates, and too often they depended upon the strength of their liquor rather than that of their arguments, to convince the electorate of their worth. The important role played by liquor in elections was emphasized by the writer of a letter to *The Connoisseur* thus:

. . . The merits of a treat has often recommended a member, who has had no merits of his own. For it is certain, that people, however they may differ in other points, are unanimous in promoting the grand business of eating and drinking.[101]

100 Bolingbroke, Viscount, *A Collection of Political Tracts* (London, 1748), " Of the Constitution of Great Britain," p. 259.

101 Chalmers, A. (Ed.), *The British Essayists* (London, 1802), Letter written to *The Connoisseur*, April 25, 1754, XXX, 66.

Buying votes, and supplying food, drink and entertainment, made victory at the polls an expensive undertaking for any candidate. Then again, there was always the possibility that the battle won at the polls might have to be fought again in the House of Commons. Horace Walpole, the contemporary commentator on events in the reigns of the Georges, wrote to a friend that a lawyer had estimated that the contest between the Lowther and Thanet interests in 1754 was likely to cost more than " five and fifty thousand pounds ".[102] Another writer believed that the Oxfordshire election in 1755 cost the successful candidate, Sir Edward Turner, £240,000.[103] The landed men realized that it was impossible to cope with the situation. They found it difficult to compete with the borough candidates who were supplied with sums of money from the Duke of Newcastle's pocket. During a six-year period while the Duke controlled the purse strings, £243,000 was spent in " secret service ", and about £51,000 was spent for election purposes.[104] The representatives returned in this manner, according to the landed men, were not the true representatives of the voters, for these parliamentary members held fictitious landed qualifications, swore falsely, and degraded the dignity of the House of Commons by their dependence upon a ministry which they followed in return for money. Once again, in 1760, the supporters of the Qualification Act sponsored a movement to amend the existing law. They hoped that such an amendment would prove valuable in the coming election by insuring the return of landed men to the Commons, thus weakening the power of the Duke of Newcastle and his followers.

On January 31, 1760, the House of Commons appointed a committee to bring in a bill " to enforce and render more effec-

102 Toynbee, Mrs. P. (Ed.), op. cit., III, 242-243.

103 Dickins, L. and Stanton, M. (Ed.), An Eighteenth-Century Correspondence (London, 1910), p. 253.

104 Namier, L. B., The Structure of Politics at the Accession of George III (New York, 1929), I, 258.

tual " the Qualification Act of 1710/1711.[105] The bill, similar to the earlier ones sponsored by Hutcheson and Pulteney, was introduced into the House by Sir John Philipps. James Grenville, Pitt, and others, believing that something should be done for the Tories, supported it.[106] Pitt's attitude induced other House members to follow suit. Lord Egmont objected to the measure, which he feared would subject the estates of the members of the House of Commons to an examination of a committee, and queried whether estates, mortgaged in many cases, if carefully investigated, would be able to meet the requirements of the proposed law. Although opposed by the Duke of Newcastle, Lord Strange, and others, the bill was passed by the Commons; [107] and on May 21, 1760, it was accepted by the Lords.

The amended Qualification Act did not apply to Scotland, to the universities, to the eldest sons of peers, temporal or spiritual, or to the eldest sons of landed recusants. With the exceptions noted, it compelled a newly elected House member to hand to the Clerk of that body, while the House was in session and the Speaker presiding, a signed statement describing fully his landed qualification and its exact location. He must further take an oath that he was the true owner of the landed estate, and that such land had not been granted or made over fraudulently for the purpose of qualifying him to be a member of the House of Commons. This signed statement would remain in the hands of the Clerk, could be examined at any time, and was to be kept up to date, since any change in the schedule must be reported to the Clerk of the House. Any person attempting to sit in the House, or vote on any measure, before handing in his schedule of landed qualification, would have his election declared void.[108] The landed men were satisfied with their act, and felt that their victory would have met with the approval of Hutcheson and Pulte-

105 *J. H. C.*, XXVIII, 741.
106 Walpole, H., *Memoirs of George II*, II, 435.
107 *Ibid.*, II, 436.
108 33 George II, c. 20.

ney. They believed that the 1760 act would plug the loopholes of the Qualification Act by abolishing fictitious qualifications, and that future parliaments would be composed of men who were bona-fide possessors of landed estates. Such a parliament would not be venal, nor dependent upon the Crown.[109] Apparently neither purpose was completely accomplished, however, for in the years from 1760 to 1800, seats in the House of Commons continued to be bought, and men willing to pay the price for them did not hesitate to obtain fictitious landed qualifications in order to take their seats in the House. It is true, however, that these prospective candidates found it more difficult to obtain the necessary landed qualifications, since these were now required, not for a day, or at the most three days, but for a period of time covering the duration of parliament, which might legally be seven years.[110]

The first test of the amended Qualification Act came in the general election of 1761. Contemporary pamphlets were an active factor in the election. *The Gentleman's Magazine* printed the provisions of the 1760 act, and inquired how it was possible for so many landless candidates to canvass counties, towns, and boroughs. It called upon them to consider the oath to God that must be taken by them if they were successful in obtaining parliamentary seats.[111] *The London Magazine* likewise appealed to the voting population to return men of " real estates ".[112] Horace Walpole commented on the venality which was grosser than ever " because West Indians, conquerors, nabobs, and admirals, attack every borough." Competition existed everywhere, and there were nine parliamentary candidates for Andover.[113] The new king, George III, took an interest in his first general election by personally naming the candidates for

109 *The London Magazine*, January, 1761, pp. 9-13.

110 *Ibid.*, January, 1761, p. 9.

111 *The Gentleman's Magazine*, February, 1761, p. 56.

112 *The London Magazine*, March, 1761, p. 117.

113 Toynbee, Mrs. P. (Ed.), *op. cit.*, Walpole's Letter to Thomas Mann, March 3, 1761, V, 29.

those boroughs which belonged to the Crown.[114] Of the English representatives returned to the House there were fifty-nine army officers, twenty-one naval officers, seven regular civil servants, five diplomats, forty lawyers, fifty merchants;[115] and it was not improbable that some of these representatives, especially many of the merchants and friends of the king, held fictitious landed qualifications from patrons and bankers. It must not be forgotten, however, that many of the moneyed men, like all good business men, had some landed investments. This was especially true of Richard Glover, the merchant, returned by Bubb Dodington for Weymouth, who was reputed on his death to be the owner of property valued at £40,000 or £50,000 and including

mortgage and bond, in land, and houses, freehold and copyhold, in the city of London, in Buckinghamshire, and in Kent, where he possessed the Manor of Downe. He had also lands in South Carolina . . . [116]

On the whole, the membership of the 1761 House of Commons differed little from previous ones. About forty per cent of the representatives were returned by constituencies which had been previously served by their ancestors; about thirty-five per cent were members of old parliamentary families; and about twenty-five per cent of the membership was without parliamentary ancestry.[117]

Like members of previous parliaments, however, the landed members of the House realized that a new foe in the form of the East and West Indian adventurers was now competing for membership. In 1761, only two of their number, Robert Clive

114 Hunt, W., *The History of England from the Accession of George III to the close of Pitt's First Administration, 1760-1801* (New York, 1905), p. 19.

115 Namier, L. B., *England in the Age of the American Revolution* (London, 1930), pp. 254-255.

116 *An Inquiry Concerning the Author of the Letters of Junius* (London, 1814), p. 53.

117 Namier, L. B., *The Structure of Politics* . . . I, 208.

and John Walsh, were successful in obtaining seats in the House of Commons, but the landed men feared that this moneyed interest would grow stronger in future years. The election of 1768 proved this opinion correct. These *nouveaux riches* attacked the strongholds of the old landed gentry, and their activities, together with the Wilkes case, agitated the country. The Bentincks and the Lowthers spent £40,000 each in the election of 1768,[118] and Chesterfield wrote to his son:

Elections have been carried to a degree of frenzy hitherto unheard of: that for the town of Northampton has cost the contending parties at least £30,000 a side, and George Selwyn has sold the borough of Luggershall, to two members, for £9000.[119]

Following the election of 1768, innumerable petitions complaining of undue elections were presented to the House of Commons, and delayed the regular business of the House. To remove this obstacle and to regulate the trials of controverted elections, were the purposes of the Grenville Act. Its sponsor believed that the measure would remove delay, inconvenience, and expense which usually accompanied the hearing of election petitions. The Grenville Act of 1770 abolished the practice of hearing petitions by counsel at the Bar of the House of Commons, and established a definite procedure for all cases involving controverted elections. Thereafter, contested elections were to be delegated to House committees. A Select Committee was to have broad powers in hearing witnesses and examining papers for both sides, and in rendering a final decision.[120] This act, however, concerned elections only, and the landed men continued their agitation for other measures which would make it more difficult for the new moneyed interest to obtain seats in the Commons. This sentiment on the part of the landed men increased after the election of 1774. According to Horace Wal-

118 Marriott, J. A., *English Political Institutions* (Oxford, 1915), p. 220.

119 Bradshaw, J. (Ed.), *op. cit.*, Chesterfield's Letter to his son, April 12, 1768, III, 1376.

120 10 George III, c. 16.

pole, the newly elected House of that year was an " assemblage of patricians and plebeians and knights," among whom was a waiter, Robert Macreth, who had been returned to the House of Commons by Lord Orford, his debtor.[121] Lord Folkestone, a member of the Commons, was fully resolved to weaken this unaristocratic group. In February, 1775, he moved that all schedules of landed qualifications be printed. The opponents of the motion, fearing the dire consequences of such a step, argued that there was no need for such a motion, since any member of the House had access to the schedules. When put to a vote, Folkestone's motion was lost.[122]

This election of 1774 did not escape the criticism of the polit-ical pamphleteers of the day. They attacked the existing corrup-tion, which had already resulted in the seating of tavern waiters and common gamblers in payment of debts. Major Cartwright added the story of the Cheshire gentleman who ordered the voters of his borough to elect his colored footman. The corpora-tion begged forgiveness for offending him, and requested that he send a white candidate.[123] The same writer earnestly urged that all election laws be enforced, and that every parliamentary candi-date should submit to the sheriff, or to the chief magistrate of his locality, a statement of his qualification. In the county the qualification should be in land, and he recommended

£400 per annum might be sufficient: for London it might be the same; or a property in the kingdom of £12,000; for other cities and towns £300 per annum in land, or £9000 in other property; clear of all debts and demands.[124]

This idea that property, other than landed property, should be used as a qualification for membership in the House of Com-mons was not accepted, however, by the members of that body.

In April, 1780, the House of Commons considered once more

121 Toynbee, Mrs. P. (Ed.), *op. cit.*, IX, 66, 75.

122 Almon, J., *The Parliamentary Register* (London, 1775), I, 254.

123 Cartwright, J., *Take Your Choice* (London, 1776), p. 38.

124 *Ibid.*, p. 69.

the question of the qualifications for membership in its halls. In that month, a committee was appointed to draw up a measure to amend the 1710 Qualification Act.[125] The committee reported to the House that, while the purposes of the Act passed in the reign of Queen Anne, and the amendment adopted in the reign of George II, were of good intent, the Acts had been evaded and were of little actual value. In order to secure the independence of parliament, they recommended that the landed qualifications be raised, and that all members of the House be fully qualified throughout their term of membership in that body. To punish evaders, the bill provided that any member attempting to vote or sit in the House without handing in a schedule of his landed qualification, would be called upon to forfeit a sum of money to any person who might sue the sitting member, and a like sum to Christ Hospital in London.[126]

This measure was attacked by James Luttrell, who, in a speech on May 23, 1780, charged that it was detrimental to the freedom of parliament. He added that the amendment adopted in the reign of George II was " to court the landed interest ", but that any measure to raise the landed qualifications for members of the House was unconstitutional, and might lead to such high requirements that only a few men would be able to meet them. He disapproved of all qualification acts, and stated that if members thought the existing acts were being evaded, they should prove their accusations. Could it be safely said that evaders of the acts were responsible for the American Revolution, or that the eldest sons of peers, and Scottish representatives, were strong opponents of ruinous measures? He thought not, and believed that the Court Party was more powerful among men of first rank in the country. He disagreed with the theory that landed men were the only true representatives of the nation. He doubted whether men of £300 per annum estates

125 *J. H. C.*, XXXVII, 780.

126 Bill to Explain and Amend the several Acts for securing the Freedom of Parliament, by farther extending the Qualification for Members to sit in the House of Commons, and for rendering the same more effectual, 1780.

were not corruptible, and pleaded that future parliaments be chosen for ability, integrity, and knowledge.[127] He objected to the provision of the proposed law that landed estates, smaller than those for the English representatives, should be required for the Scottish representatives. He pointed out that some of the peers in the House of Lords were landless, and yet their eldest sons were eligible for membership in the House of Commons. Whether it was because of the presence of the new moneyed but landless interest, or because of the belief that the new measure would result in an aristocratic House similar to the Lords, the motion that the bill be committed was defeated by a vote of eighty-nine to twenty-eight.[128]

While no attempt was made in the period from 1780 to 1800 to strengthen the Qualification Act, that act nevertheless continued to hold an important place in the political life of the country. In 1781, the charge of bribery and nonpossession of landed estate resulted in the voiding of the election of the representative from Honiton;[129] and in 1784, Sir Robert Smith petitioned the House of Commons alleging that Christopher Potter, the returned representative from Colchester, did not have the necessary landed qualification. Sir Robert asserted that Mr. Potter had been declared a bankrupt in 1783, and could not have acquired the necessary land for his election. A careful investigation proved the truth of these assertions, and revealed that at the time of his election, Mr. Potter had submitted a signed statement asserting that he was the possessor of the necessary land. The schedule of his landed qualification, however, had not been handed to the Clerk of the House of Commons. Counsel for Mr. Potter declared that he was the owner of a landed estate of the legal requirement, and that he had not handed in his schedule because he had not taken his seat in the House of Commons. The House Committee decided that since Potter had not complied with the standing rule of the House,

127 Cobbett, W., *op. cit.*, 21 : 624-625.

128 *Ibid.*, 21 : 626.

129 *J. H. C.*, XXXVIII, 18, 49, 320.

which required that the landed qualification of any member objected to in a petition must be filed with the Clerk within fifteen days after the reading of the petition; his election was void, and a writ for a new election was issued.[130] In another instance, the Qualification Act operated indirectly in the election of representatives for the City of Canterbury. At the time of the election, two freemen called upon the four candidates to swear to their landed qualifications. Two complied with the request, and two refused to state their qualifications. The latter lost the election, for the returning officer refused to register any votes cast for them.[131]

The renewal of interest in and enforcement of the Qualification Act in the eighties brought great concern to many parliamentary candidates, who found it a difficult task to secure the necessary landed qualifications. Among such men were Anthony Storer and Daniel Pulteney. In 1781, Anthony Storer wrote to Lord Carlisle:

I arrived in town this morning, time enough to do all in my power to send to Gregg, to try if I can get a qualification to take my seat tomorrow. My qualifications have been always embarrassing to me . . . [132]

A year later, the penniless Daniel Pulteney, in a letter to the Duke of Rutland, bitterly referred to his defeated hopes of obtaining a seat in the Commons. He called upon the Duke to use £1500 or £2000, the usual sums lost in gambling, or the price paid for some famous picture, to buy him a seat in the House; and he mentioned two owners of seats that had been offered for sale.[133] In another letter, he begged the Duke to pro-

130 Luders, A., *Reports of the Proceedings in Committees of the House of Commons, upon Controverted Elections* (London, 1785), I, 415-459.

131 *The Gentleman's Magazine*, May, 1784, p. 373.

132 Hist. MSS. Comm., *Carlisle MSS.*, Letter of Anthony Storer to Lord Carlisle, November 26, 1781, p. 535.

133 Hist. MSS. Comm., *Rutland MSS.*, Letter of Daniel Pulteney to the Duke of Rutland, December, 1782, pp. 65-66.

vide him with a landed qualification. Evidently his creditors had been molesting him, and his thoughts on evading the creditors, along with the provisions of the Qualification Act, are interesting. He wrote:

. . . In point of law, Mr. Hill will see how absurd any scruple can be on the subject, but what is a sufficient answer as to creditors is this. If I had a known grant of £300 a year in any register county known precisely to a creditor, and he had sufficient time to sue out a proper process against it, it would be certainly subject to an execution, but for this purpose it is requisite the creditor should know the terms of the grant, the situation of the land it issues from, and have time to form this process, etc., whereas all that would pass in this case would be to receive the grant from your Grace in the morning, the contents of which nobody could know but Mr. Hill, deliver it in and swear to it, before George Sutton perhaps, and sign a reconveyance to your Grace at night . . .

He assured the nobleman that any landed qualification that might be assigned to him would never be the subject of any attack by any creditor, pointing out that creditors had not taken any action against some of the members of the House. He added:

Lord E. Bentinck's horses have been sold by advertisement; Will Hanger, Stanhope, and 50 others have at this time all sorts of demands upon them and judgements against them, but nobody ever thought or heard of any claim on a qualification, which with one third at least of the House is known to be fictitious . . . [134]

It is interesting to note that Daniel Pulteney became a member of the House, increasing the number of members who held fictitious landed qualifications. His membership in that body did not improve his material wealth, however, and in a letter to the

---

[134] *Ibid.*, Letter of Daniel Pulteney to the Duke of Rutland, May 14, 1783, p. 95. Another pamphleteer of that period estimated that one half or 279 members of the House of Commons were "the near relatives or connections of peers, without property or pretence except such relationship or connection to be chosen by a county." Laprade, W., *Parliamentary Papers of John Robinson, 1774-1784* (London, 1922), p. 10—Introduction.

Duke of Rutland, he pleaded with him to speak to Mr. Pitt for an Indian appointment. This the Duke attempted to do by writing Mr. Pitt:

I very much wish to obtain an office of about £400 per annum, not preclusive of a seat in Parliament for Pulteney. He has nothing to live upon. I must either support him out of my own pocket, or he will be forced into the arms of the Opposition . . . [135]

The Duke of Rutland was not the only nobleman or great landed proprietor who provided the necessary landed qualifications for members of parliament.[136] Fortunately, all of the would-be members of the House were not as poor as Daniel Pulteney. The Duke of Bedford provided a landed qualification for John Sackville;[137] Philip Yorke, the future Chancellor of England, owed his landed qualification to a wealthy relative;[138] and Earl Temple furnished John Wilkes with the necessary land to enable him to stand for Middlesex.[139] Mr. Pitt, who represented Appleby, was indebted to Sir James Lowther, the future Lord Lonsdale, for his entrance into the House of Commons.[140] In fact, at the very time that Pitt was recommending the abolition of the rotten boroughs, Wraxall, whose political memoirs are famous, wrote that he believed the parliamentary leader to possess little or no landed property.[141] The same was

135 Hist. MSS. Comm., *Rutland MSS.*, Letter of the Duke of Rutland to Mr. Pitt, August 31, 1785, p. 238.

136 For the power of the boroughmongers see Oldfield, T., *An Entire and Complete History of the Boroughs of Great Britain* (London, 1794), 2 vols. Seymour, C., *How the World Votes* (Mass., 1918), I, 84-85.

137 Cavendish, Sir Henry, *Debates of the House of Commons, 1768-1771* (London, 1841), Private Journal of John, Fourth Duke of Bedford, p. 609.

138 Porritt, E. and A., *op. cit.*, I, 173.

139 Nicholls, J., *Recollections and Reflections, Personal and Political, as connected with Public Affairs during the Reign of George III* (London, 1822), I, 30.

140 Wraxall, N. W., *Historical Memoirs of My Own Time* (Philadelphia, 1837), p. 250.

141 *Ibid.*, p. 303.

true of Sheridan, Burke, and Fox. Fox had been returned for the Borough of Midhurst, the property of Viscount Montagu, who supervised the election of young Charles while that young man was busy enjoying himself on the continent of Europe.[142] Fox rose to high positions in the state, but his debts likewise mounted. It is very doubtful whether at any time he was the true owner of a landed estate. Fox considered, moreover, that the vigorous enforcement of the Qualification Act would " exclude talents from obtaining entrance into the house." [143] If these prominent representatives used sham qualifications in the face of friends and enemies, it is very probable that the practice was widespread.

In the latter part of the eighteenth century, political writers on the subject of the Qualification Act were gradually falling into three groups : those like William Paley, who were content with the existing law, but believed it should be strictly enforced ; those like Josiah Tucker, who advocated a somewhat different scheme, still based on the main idea of property ; and the third and last group, the reformers, who attacked the structure of the whole political system of Great Britain. William Paley believed that the system of representation which existed in 1785 was to be credited for the House of Commons of five hundred and fifty-eight members, among whom were landowners, merchants of the kingdom, heads of the army, the navy, and the law, and other prominent men.[144] He praised this excellent group of men as not being easily influenced by corrupt motives, and wondered what scheme of representation could promise " more wisdom " or produce greater integrity.[145] Unlike Paley, Josiah Tucker, famous for his opinions on trade and colonies, advocated some changes in the system of representation. He recommended that a parliamentary candidate for a county should deliver to the

142 Seymour, C., op. cit., I, 83-84.

143 Wraxall, N. W., op. cit., p. 303.

144 Paley, E. (Ed.), The Works of William Paley (London, 1830), III, 392-393.

145 Ibid., III, 393.

sheriff or returning offcer, at least ten days before the election, a schedule of his landed estate which should consist of at least one thousand acres of land, on which there were ten occupied houses; and this schedule should appear on the doors of public buildings and in the newspapers. For the cities and boroughs, the parliamentary candidate should possess five hundred acres of land on which there should be five occupied houses. Failure of the parliamentary candidates to meet these requirements would result in the imposing of a fine, and not only the loss of a seat in the House of Commons, but ineligibility as a parliamentary candidate for a period of three years thereafter.[146] But more important than the conservative group that was willing to keep the " status quo ", and the small group which desired to make some changes, was the group of reformers inspired by the changing ideas and ideals of the period. The question of representation raised by the American Revolution naturally led men to question their own political system. In the eighties, the Reform Movement began to take root. During the nineties and the early part of the following century, it grew slowly, and a decade later it burst into full bloom.

146 Tucker, J., *A Treatise Concerning Civil Government* (London, 1781), pp. 278-283.

CHAPTER IV

THE REFORM MOVEMENT AND THE QUALIFICATION ACT

THE Reform Movement in England in the latter part of the eighteenth century received its impetus from many sources. Faint whisperings had been heard in the time of the Earl of Chatham, who had declared himself in favor of reform, but no machinery of political agitation had been created by that famous statesman to carry on his work.[1] A more potent factor in arousing public opinion was the famous Wilkes Case. The election of John Wilkes, and his subsequent expulsion from the House of Commons in 1768 and 1769, focused the attention of the people on the struggle between the parliamentary candidate and the government. Wilkes' conflict with the government made him a popular hero; his writings emphasized the fact that he, the legal representative of the voters of Middlesex, had been unable to take his rightful seat in the House of Commons. Although it was short-lived, the Wilkes Case stimulated criticism, and called into existence those political organs—meetings, pamphlets, and organizations—which were to be used successfully by later radicals.[2]

The Middlesex Election received added attention because it occurred at a time when not a few Englishmen were being awakened by the dispute with the American colonies to a consideration of the whole question of representation.[3] This dispute, which culminated in the American Revolution, aroused the interest of many men in the political abuses of the day, especially in the unrepresentative character of the House of Commons. The silent Industrial Revolution, which had been in progress

1 Veitch, G. S., *The Genesis of Paliamentary Reform* (London, 1913), p. 24.
2 *Ibid.*, pp. 26-34. Kent. C. B., *The English Radicals* (London, 1899), p. 46.
3 Veitch, G. S., *op. cit.*, p. 26.

for some time, had brought about a great shift in population, and the large centers of industrial activity were now clamoring for representation in the House. In the eighties many Englishmen became active in movements which sought to bring about improved conditions in the social, economic, and political status of the people. In the political field societies were founded which worked indefatigably for the redistribution of seats in the House of Commons, for shorter parliaments, and for franchise reform. Petitions were sent to the House of Commons, and demonstrations for political reform were frequent.

Of the many political reformers of that day, none was more prominent than Major Cartwright, already mentioned in connection with the election of 1774. John Cartwright was the son of a country gentleman of Nottinghamshire. From his father he had inherited a small estate which supported him, and afforded him the leisure time to participate in the political questions of the day. In early life, Cartwright had been interested in naval affairs; but at the time of the American Revolution, he showed keen interest in the conflict between Great Britain and her colonies.[4] By 1780, Cartwright, called by many historians "the Father of Reform," had become the idol of the English people, who knew him through his political speeches and pamphlets, which advocated annual parliaments, universal suffrage, and the ballot. His advocacy of universal suffrage went back to 1776. In that year, he had written a pamphlet, *Take Your Choice,* in which he severely condemned the idea that men of property were the only ones who had "stakes in the country." He disagreed with the idea that men without land, gold, herd, or flock were not interested in the government. Such men, he wrote, possessed wives and children, and

by birthright a property in the English constitution: which, if not unworthy of such a blessing, will be more dear . . . than would be many acres of the soil without it.[5]

4 Cartwright, F. D., *The Life and Correspondence of Major Cartwright* (London, 1826), 2 vols.

5 Cartwright, J., *Take Your Choice* (London, 1776), p. 19.

For the rest of his life, Cartwright never wavered in this opinion, and through the societies which he had helped establish, and through numerous political writings, he supported the idea that all men should have the right to vote.

Deeply interested in the questions of suffrage, duration of parliament, and the ballot, Cartwright gave but little attention to the Qualification Act. That the act was evaded he could not deny, for he himself had allowed his own father to supply the necessary landed qualification when he stood as a parliamentary candidate for the County of Nottingham in 1778.[6] In his famous pamphlet already mentioned, Cartwright made no recommendation for the abolition of property qualifications for membership of the House, but stated that the qualifications for a county member of the House should be a landed estate and

£400 per annum might be sufficient: for London it might be the same; or a property in the kingdom of £12000; for other cities and towns £300 per annum in land, or £9000 in other property; clear of all debts and demands.[7]

These property qualifications for members of the House of Commons were restated the following year, 1777, when the second edition of the same pamphlet was published, but Cartwright followed these qualifications by the comments:

Were parliaments and elections once restored to what they ought to be, and the time should return when the members should demand their wages for doing a duty unprofitable to themselves, perhaps all monied qualifications might not only be unnecessary, but improper; as too much restraining the constituents in the free choice of their representatives; of whose fitness or unfitness, worthiness or unworthiness, they doubtless would be the properest judges.[8]

Three years later, in 1780, in a pamphlet entitled *The People's Barrier Against Undue Influence and Corruption,* Cartwright

6 Cartwright, F. D., *op. cit.,* I, 123.

7 Cartwright, J., *Take Your Choice,* p. 69.

8 Cartwright, J., *The Legislative Rights of the Commonalty Vindicated: or Take Your Choice* (London, 2nd Edition, 1777), pp. 164-165.

again discussed his general plans for restoring the government to the people. No mention was made of property qualifications of members of the House of Commons, and he explained the omission by stating:

I have purposely omitted to propose any landed or monied qualification of members; because I apprehend that this bill would render every such qualification totally useless. If so, their continuance would be an injurious abridgement of the people's freedom, and might exclude from parliament the fittest men in the kingdom for the duties of a laborious, unprofitable office, not ministering to the aristocratical pride of its possessor.[9]

The rapidly awakening interest in the Reform Movement was shown by monster meetings which were held throughout the country. As early as January, 1780, clergymen, nobles, and freeholders met at York and petitioned parliament for political reforms.[10] On February 2, 1780, under the chairmanship of Charles James Fox, the freeholders of Westminster likewise considered the question of parliamentary reform, and appointed a committee to correspond with other sections of the country. A few months later, one of its sub-committees rendered a report in which a definite plan of parliamentary reform was outlined. The committee recommended annual parliaments, ballot, universal suffrage, and salaries for members of the House of Commons. On the question of property qualifications for membership in parliament, the committee further recommended that all men eligible for voting should be eligible for parliamentary candidacy.[11] These political demands, which were to be the demands

9 Cartwright, J., *The People's Barrier Against Undue Inflence and Corruption* (London, 1780), p. 109. Because Cartwright made few comments on the Qualification Act and its operation, many writers agree with Veitch, who said, "Cartwright retained a belief in the property qualification for membership of the House of Commons." Veitch, G. S., *op. cit.*, p. 48. As late as 1808, in making constitutional recommendations for the Spanish people, Cartwright stated: "the representative to have a qualification in landed property." Cartwright, F. D., *op. cit.*, I, 364.

10 *The English Chartist Circular*, Number 29, p. 113.

11 *Ibid.*, p. 113. Harris, W., *The History of the Radical Party in Parliament* (London, 1885), pp. 28-32.

of the Chartists many decades later, caused no literary revival in the field of political pamphleteering.

Joseph Towers, however, a contemporary of Cartwright, in a pamphlet written in 1782, questioned whether the Qualification Act had been of any service to the people. He denied that the existing law had added to the corruption of the day, although he knew that the government official who held the purse strings could qualify " the meanest of his creatures to represent a Cornish borough." [12] He argued that the Qualification Act limited the power of the people.[13] Nor was he unmindful of the fact that property carried weight in any community, and that in an election, the person of property was often preferred to the candidate of no property. Yet the possession of wealth was no assurance against corruption, for history had proved that men of large fortunes could be bought by government officials. He thought the present law was useless and undesirable.[14] In 1783 this opinion was opposed by Lord Carysfort, who, while admitting that the existing Qualification Act was "absolutely nugatory," [15] recommended its enforcement, using the old argument that the landed requirement made for independence on the part of the representative. He thought it mattered little whether the property was real or personal; but he deemed it absolutely essential that every member of the House of Commons take an oath at the opening of each session that he was the possessor of a yearly income, clear of all debts, of the sum fixed by law.[16] Another pamphleteer, writing in 1784, did not think that the landed qualification fixed by law should be the sole qualification for parliamentary candidates, since, he thought, the younger sons

12 Towers, J. A., *A Vindication of the Political Principles of Mr. Locke* (London, 1782), p. 107.

13 *Ibid.*, p. 103.

14 *Ibid.*, pp. 103-107.

15 Carysfort, Lord, *Thoughts on the Constitution, with a View to the Proposed Reform in the Representation of the People, and Duration of Parliaments* (London, 1783), p. 49.

16 *Ibid.*, p. 49.

and brothers of noble or opulent families were excellent parliamentary material.[17] True, these men were not the owners of landed estates; but they were vitally interested in government matters, much more so than the " indigent Irishman or any other stroller," [18] who found entrance into the House of Commons. To insure a good House of Commons, he strongly recommended the enforcement of the Qualification Act. He would make one exception, however: that of allowing the sons and brothers of peers and of wealthy commoners possessing landed estates of a certain value, to be eligible for membership in the House of Commons.[19] He closed by reminding the reader that

As very bad consequences have resulted from the little attention that has been paid to the essential article of qualification, it is to be hoped that care will be taken to prevent a possibility of evasion, under any plan of reform that may be adopted.[20]

It was only logical that the political agitation of the people in the eighties should find an echo in the House of Commons. In that period many of the House sessions were devoted to the question of parliamentary reform. In 1780, when there had been an unsuccessful attempt to strengthen the Qualification Act, the Duke of Richmond introduced an equally unsuccessful measure to extend the suffrage and to restore annual parliaments.[21] In 1782, William Pitt, a newcomer to the House of Commons, showed his interest in the problem, by moving that a committee be appointed to inquire into the state of representation in the House of Commons.[22] The motion, unsupported by the members of the House, was lost by twenty votes. One year later, on May 7, 1783, Pitt made another attempt to reform the House

17 *A Letter to the Right Honourable William Pitt.* Printed for J. Stockdale (London, 1784), p. 11.

18 *Ibid.,* p. 11.

19 *Ibid.,* p. 65.

20 *Ibid.,* p. 71.

21 Cobbett's *Parliamentary History of England,* 21 : 686-688.

22 *Ibid.,* 22 : 1416-1422.

of Commons. This time he brought forward three resolutions for the prevention of bribery, for the disfranchisement of corrupt boroughs when a majority of their electors had been found guilty of corruption, and for the addition of one hundred new members for the counties.[23] These resolutions did not win the support of the House; but undaunted by repeated failure, Pitt made still another attempt, two years later, to amend the representation in the Commons. In April, 1785, Pitt, as Prime Minister of Great Britain, asked leave to introduce a Reform Bill which sought to increase the number and the importance of the county representatives. Pitt further proposed the compensation of the patrons of those boroughs which, in accordance with his measure, were to be deprived of their representatives.[24] The motion failed to win the approval of Pitt's conservative colleagues, for they were not ready to consider any plan of reform.

The failure of all these attempts to reform the House of Commons demonstrated the strength of the opposition to such measures. Any attempt to democratize the government of Great Britain in the eighties met with either indifference or open opposition from the majority of the members of the House. Many of the members were indebted to George III, the greatest boroughmonger of the eighteenth century, for their seats in the House. His great political power had been summarized by Dunning in his famous resolution of 1780, which read, " that the influence of the Crown had increased, was increasing and ought to be diminished ". But how could George III's power be checked? Any reform, no matter how slight, encountered his opposition, and his attitude was reflected in the House of Commons. To many of the House members, moreover, it seemed that the Reform Movement was supported by only a small group of radicals, and not by a majority of the people. This may have been true to a certain extent, because the financial reforms made in this period eased the burden of the taxpayer, and the return of prosperity dampened the spirit of reform. By 1785, even Pitt,

23 *Ibid.*, 23 : 827-846.
24 *Ibid.*, 25 : 432-450.

discouraged by repeated failure, turned his attention to other governmental problems. By the time of the French Revolution, the Reform Movement in England was slumbering quietly; but the repercussions from the revolution across the channel aroused it, and brought it once again to active life in English thought and politics.

It was not surprising that the rights of the individual as expressed by the French Declaration of the Rights of Man, and the political, social, and economic reforms of the French National Assembly, should attract the attention of the English people. In England, the renewed interest in the Reform Movement was expressed in the revival of societies such as the Society for Constitutional Information, which had been established in the eighties, and in the formation of new ones, such as the Society of the Friends of the People. The main purposes of the latter organization were " to restore the Freedom of Election, and a more equal Representation of the people in Parliament, and to secure to the People a more frequent Exercise of their Right of Electing their Representatives." [25] By the realization of these purposes the members of the society sought to reestablish the right of the people to participate in their own government. In 1792, another organization, the London Corresponding Society, composed mainly of English workers, was founded with the main purpose of establishing the representation of the common people in the House of Commons.[26] Such societies were supported by the English working people, who apparently found in them an expression for their ambitions.

The obvious discontent of the people caused some members of the House of Commons to introduce petitions which begged for more equal representation in that body. One petition, presented on May 6, 1793, stated:

. . . the present system of representation gives to it [property] a degree of weight which renders it independent of character; en-

25 *Proceedings of the Society of Friends of the People* (London, 1793), p. 4.
26 Brown, P., *The French Revolution in English History* (London, 1919), p. 55. Maccoby, S., *English Radicalism 1832-1852* (London, 1935), pp. 15-16.

ables it to excite fear as well as procure respect, and confines the choice of electors within the ranks of opulence; because, though it cannot make riches the sole object of their affection and confidence, it can and does throw obstacles, almost insurmountable, in the way of every man who is not rich, and thereby secures to a select few the capability of becoming candidates themselves, or supporting the pretensions of others.[27]

Although the petition did not attack the existing Qualification Act, it did attack the power held by the peers in the election of members of the House of Commons. The petition charged that one hundred-fifty members of the House of Commons owed their election to the interference of peers, and further that forty peers controlled the boroughs that returned eighty-one members to the House of Commons.[28] Mr. Grey, afterwards Earl Grey, followed up the presentation of this petition condemning the great power of the boroughmongers, with the motion that it be referred to a committee. This motion opened the way for discussion, but Mr. Pitt, once the supporter of the Reform Movement, now pointed to the horrible example of France, and questioned whether moderate reforms could possibly be accomplished in Great Britain without confusion. He added:

I would rather abandon what I conceive to be the best plan of Reform, than risk the consequences of any hazard to the Constitution, as it at present subsists.[29]

Mr. Pitt's plea for the maintenance of the " status quo " found a staunch supporter in the person of Mr. Jenkinson, a member of the House, who defended the existing political structure of the government by declaring that the landed interest should

27 *Authentic Copy of a Petition praying for a Reform in Parliament, presented to the House of Commons on Monday, May 6, 1793,* Printed for J. Debrett (London, 1793), p. 87.

28 *Ibid.,* p. 89.

29 *Speeches of the Rt. Hon. Wm. Pitt, and Rt. Hon. Charles J. Fox on Mr. Grey's Motion for a Reform in Parliament.* Printed for J. Debrett (London, 1793), p. 21.

have the predominant weight in a country since it was the
" stamina of the country," [30] and that the close boroughs had
been responsible for the introduction of outstanding men in the
House of Commons.[31] Duncombe, Francis, and others rallied to
the defense of Grey, but they were unable to move the conservative spirit that dominated the House of Commons. The vote,
two hundred eighty-two against forty-one,[32] showed that the
House was in no mood to consider any question of parliamentary reform at that time.

Was the mood of the House of Commons influenced in any
way by Burke and his writings? His important work, *Reflections on the French Revolution,* published in the winter of 1790,
had expressed his admiration for the existing British government; and he had warned against sudden and violent changes.
Whether or not this work was responsible for the wave of conservatism that swept over the kingdom is a debatable question.[33]
Very likely, Burke did nothing more than express the opinion
of the upper classes, who feared that reform might lead to revolution and chaos. Such was the opinion of Gibbon, who in a
letter to Lord Sheffield wrote:

If you trifle with this solemn business, if you do not resist the spirit
of innovation in the first attempt, if you admit the smallest and
most specious change in our parliamentary system, you are lost.[34]

Mr. Wyvill, a Yorkshire clergyman who was interested in
affairs political more than in those religious, was quite sure that
the slightest change would result in subsequent changes, and
that the principles of the French Revolution—Liberty and

30 *Authentic Report of the Debate in the House of Commons on the 6th
and 7th of May, 1793.* Printed for J. Debrett (London, 1793), p. 16.

31 *Ibid.,* p. 20.

32 *Ibid.,* p. 135.

33 Brown, P., *op. cit.,* p. 75.

34 Prothero, R. E. (Ed.), *Private Letters of Edward Gibbon* (London,
1897), Letter to Lord Sheffield, May 30, 1792, II, 298.

Equality—would result in Anarchy and Ruin.[35] Like Burke and Wyvill, Arthur Young condemned the Reform Movement, and expressed his belief that dire results would take place if property were placed at the disposal of landless representatives. He assured the people that if demagogues of the mob were admitted to the House of Commons, Great Britain would follow France's example,[36] and he added:

The principle of our constitution is the representation of property; imperfectly in theory, but efficiently in practice; by means of apparent defects, but which, perhaps, are disguised merits, the great mass of property, both landed, monied, and commercial, finds itself represented; and that the evils of such representation are trivial, will appear from the ease, happiness, and security of all the lower classes, hence possibly virtual representation takes place, even where the real seems most remote.[37]

Young's pamphlet caused Daniel Stuart to question the property of the members of the House of Commons, and he asked:

. . . where is the property (divested of their places and pensions, and other political emoluments) of Mess. Pitt, Dundas, Jenkinson, Long, Rose, Steele, Addington, and Burke? These are the leading men in Parliament, yet, according to Mr. Young's argument, they must lead to mischief, because they have little or no property . . . Go up to the House of Peers, and search for the property (places and pensions excepted) of Lords Grenville, Hawkebury, [sic], Chatham, Auckland, and Loughborough. Compare the leaders of administration and opposition throughout, and it will be found, that the former are poor, and the latter are wealthy.[38]

But more forceful than the battle of political pamphlets and the activities of reform societies in crystalizing the parliamen-

35 Wyvill, C., *A Letter to Rt. Hon. Wm. Pitt* (London, 1793), p. 19.

36 Young, A., *The Example of France—A Warning to Britain* (London, 1794), p. 53.

37 *Ibid.*, p. 106.

38 Stuart, D., *Peace and Reform, Against War and Corruption* (London, 1794), p. 59.

tary attitude toward reform, was the march of revolutionary events in France. The harsh treatment of the non-juring clergy, the execution of Louis XVI and Marie Antoinette, and finally the Reign of Terror, caused even the most progressive minds among the ruling class of Great Britain to shy away from all thought of reform. As early as 1793, the year in which Charles Grey had presented the petition describing the great control of the peers in elections, editors of radical pamphlets and leaders of demonstrations had been arrested and imprisoned. Membership in radical organizations had dropped, and many groups had ceased to exist. In 1795, the British government adopted a series of laws which all but extinguished the flame of reform. Temporarily, at least, the English Reform Movement was dead; and with the appearance of Bonaparte upon the scene, the nation directed all its energies toward one end: the defeat of the conqueror of Europe, Napoleon I.[39]

While the British government concerned itself with combating the economic plans of Napoleon, and maintaining the balance of power, the people, although hard pressed by the continental system and the heavy taxation occasioned by the war, nevertheless continued their interest in political affairs of the day. Outwardly, the political structure of the British government remained the same, although the union of Ireland with Great Britain in 1801 added to the number of representatives in the Commons and the Lords, and extended the landed qualifications of the English parlimentary candidates to those of Ireland.[40] As usual, the parliamentary elections held during the Napoleonic period received a great deal of attention from the English electorate. The elections in the opening years of the nineteenth century were very similar to those of the eighteenth. Election expenses were high; petitions questioning the qualifications of returned members flooded the House of Commons after each election; and the Qualification Act came in for its customary bombardment of praise and condemnation. In 1802 an un-

39 Brown, P., *op. cit.*, pp. 150-158.

40 *J. H. C.*, LVI, 664. 40 George III, c. 38.

successful Whig candidate spent £15,690 4s 2d in an effort to gain the parliamentary seat for Carmarthenshire. The sum included payment for

11,070 breakfasts, 36,901 dinners, 684 suppers, 25,275 gallons of ale, 11,068 bottles of spirits, 8,879 bottles of porter, 460 bottles of sherry, 509 bottles of cider, and eighteen guineas for milk punch. The charge for ribbons was £786 and the number of separate charges for horse hire was £4,521.[41]

In 1807, the expenses of the three parliamentary candidates for the County of Yorkshire amounted to the sum of £250,000.[42] Following the general election of 1802, the electors of Coventry petitioned the House of Commons to the effect that the newly elected members from Coventry, Francis William Barlow and Nathaniel Jefferys, were not properly qualified according to the laws of Great Britain.[43] The committee appointed by the House of Commons to consider the case, confirmed the charge against Nathaniel Jefferys, and declared that since he was not propertly qualified according to the law passed in the reign of Queen Anne, his election was null and void.[44]

Attention was again focused on the Qualification Act as the result of a by-election in Middlesex, when the provisions of the Act were put in force. On January 28, 1805, the electors of Middlesex petitioned the House of Commons complaining that the victorious member, George Mainwaring, was not the possessor of a landed estate. In describing the election, the petitioners charged that George Mainwaring had refused to state his qualifications because, he said, the law did not apply to him as the eldest son of a person qualified to serve as knight of a shire. The petition further charged that this response had not met with the approval of many of the electors present, and that Mainwaring had then proceeded to take the oath, and to describe his landed

41 Williams, D., *John Frost* (Cardiff, 1939), p. 7.

42 Ashton, J., *When William IV was King* (London, 1896), p. 52.

43 *J. H. C.*, LVIII, 52.

44 *Ibid.*, LVIII, 251.

estates. The petitioners questioned his election because they doubted the statement of his landed qualifications. The committee appointed by the House to consider the question declared the election of Mainwaring null and void because he failed to meet the landed qualifications as fixed by law.[45] Very likely the decision of the House committee was greatly influenced by the fact that Mainwaring was a severe critic of the government in power.

A year later, in a letter to the *Political Register,* one individual openly complained about the widespread use of fictitious qualifications which enabled landless men to enter the House of Commons. The writer estimated that about one hundred members of the 1806 House of Commons were not bona-fide possessors of landed estates. He added that many of the representatives acquired fictitious qualifications which enabled them to comply with the letter of the law, and that after taking their seats in the House of Commons, these representatives returned the landed estates to their rightful owners. The writer of the article was quite certain that the object of the Qualification Act was a good one: to place the government beyond the reach of corruption; in order to carry out this commendable purpose, he recommended the enforcement of the existing law and suggested that (1) the landed qualification be registered, (2) the landed qualification be examined at every meeting of parliament, (3) the creditors of a parliamentary representative be given the right to sue and to attach such landed estates.[46] This letter, unsigned, appeared in a paper which was owned by William Cobbett. Since his return from the United States in 1800, Cobbett had become the champion of the Reform Movement. A writer on all subjects, Cobbett found his greatest pleasure in the political topics of the day. He was not a party man, and no political leader of the time, whether Whig or Tory, was safe from attack in his publications. His chief aim in life was to aid

45 Cobbett's *Parliamentary Debates,* 3: 147-148. *J. H. C.,* LX, 22, 225.

46 Cobbett's *Political Register*—Letter to the *Political Register,* October 19, 1806. Found in November 1, 1806 issue.

the poor and oppressed; and his numerous publications were directed to gain parliamentary reforms for the common man. Because his cheap publications educated the English people as to the dire need for parliamentary reform, Cobbett holds an important position in the development of the English Reform Movement.[47] Like Major Cartwright, Cobbett labored primarily for a redistribution of the seats in the House of Commons, and for the abolition of corruption, which, he thought, would be partly accomplished by the abolition of sinecures.

It seems strange that the knowledge of the widespread evasion of the Qualification Act did not call forth a champion from the ranks of the reformers to lead a movement for its abolition. That the law was being shamefully evaded was an acknowledged fact. Henry Clifford in a letter to Samuel Whitbread said:

I need not observe how miserably this provision [landed qualification provision] has at all times been evaded and defeated.[48]

In the general election of 1807, Richard Brinsley Sheridan was one of the parliamentary candidates for the City of Westminster. His electioneering methods were severely condemned in a pamphlet which described the first day of the election in the following manner:

On the first day of Election, the outrageous, and perhaps justifiable, insults you met with from your creditors, and the exasperated independent Electors, furnished you with a modest hint of their estimation of your pretensions to confidence . . . in fine, the most disgraceful scenes of iniquity have been practised to procure your passport to the House of Commons, for an Election it cannot be called, unless you can get rid of the idea, that choice is a necessary ingredient in its legal interpretation.[49]

47 Melville, L., *The Life and Letters of William Cobbett in England and America* (London, 1912), 2 vols.

48 *Observations on some Doctrines advanced during the Late Elections, in a Letter to Samuel Whitbread from Henry Clifford* (London, 1807), p. 57.

49 *An Address to Richard Brinsley Sheridan, Esq. on the Public and Private Proceedings during the late Election for Westminster* (London, 1807), pp. 3-4.

If the above is a true picture of the election proceedings for the City of Westminster, it is very unlikely that Sheridan, pursued thus by his creditors, was the true possessor of a landed estate which would enable him to take his rightful place in the House of Commons.

The year 1807 turned the attention of the English people from the Qualification Act to another political problem which the pamphlets of the day were vigorously attacking. On July 7, of that year, Cochrane in the House of Commons proposed an inquiry into the sinecures and places held by the members of parliament. The inquiry was delegated to the Finance Committee, and while·that committee collected the necessary data, the political pamphleteers denounced with vehemence the entire system of sinecures and pensions. The report rendered by the committee, in June, 1808, was not a startling one, for it merely recommended the abolition of some of the sinecures and the retention of others. Naturally this did not meet with the approval of some of the members of the House of Commons. In 1809, the committee was reduced in number, and the smaller group produced a report which gave Cochrane and his supporters the desired information. From the report, it appeared that seventy-six members of parliament held offices of some kind to the value of over £150,000, and out of the seventy-six, twenty-eight held sinecures or received pensions amounting to £42,000.[50] For the next three years, 1809-1812, the topic of sinecures and pensions was frequently discussed in parliament; but all attempts to abolish these evils ended in complete failure.

Another question that held the attention of the English people in this period, was the selling of parliamentary seats. On May 4, 1809, Mr. Curwen, parliamentary representative for Carlisle, and an opponent of bribery and corruption, explained the importance of having the landed interest represented in the House of Commons. The country gentlemen were peacefully-minded, he said, and an increase in their number in the House would check the rage for an increase in foreign commerce and

50 Roberts, M., *The Whig Party, 1807-1812* (London, 1939), pp. 186-187.

the demand for additional colonies.[51] To decrease bribery and corruption, Curwen asked leave

to bring in a Bill for better securing the Independence and Purity of Parliament, by preventing the procuring or obtaining Seats in Parliament by corrupt Practices; and likewise more effectually to prevent Bribery.[52]

Curwen's Reform Bill was a very comprehensive measure which would impose penalties for the sale of parliamentary seats, extend the existing bribery laws, and apply the oaths against bribery and corruption to elected persons. His measure was in reality another attempt to decrease the power of those men who, having grown rich during the Napoleonic Wars, were using their newly gained wealth to buy their entrance into the House of Commons. Curwen, supporter of the landed interest, sought to check this influx by legislation. Subsequent meetings of parliament were devoted to the analysis of the various provisions of the bill. A parliamentary colleague, George Johnstone, vigorously opposed the measure because, he said, it tended

to exclude moneyed men from Parliament, who were of no party, and amongst the most independent.[53]

The oaths provision, as well as the provision for the trial of election cases by the courts, caused opposition; but the measure was finally carried by a vote of ninety-seven to eighty-five.[54] The Curwen Act was far from perfect, but it did have many admirable features, and provided some check on bribery and corruption. Parliamentary seats were no longer advertised in the daily publications, nor were they bought and sold in the open market like common commodities of merchandise.[55]

51 Cobbett's *Parliamentary Debates*, 14: 362.

52 *Ibid.*, 14: 367.

53 Colchester, Lord (Ed.), *The Diary and Correspondence of Charles Abbot, Lord Colchester* (London, 1861), II, 187.

54 Cobbett's *Parliamentary Debates*, 14: 1015. 49 George III, c. 118.

55 Halévy, E., *A History of the English People in 1815* (New York, 1924), p. 164.

Throughout this period from 1807 to 1812, when other important issues were before the English people, the Qualification Act naturally received very little attention. It returned briefly into the limelight in 1812, however, when, in an election address, Walter Honywood Yate admonished the English electors to be

particularly careful, that those whom you choose be duly qualified, according to law, and that no deceit be practised in obtaining temporary qualifications. You ought to inquire into their estates, and how they came by them: and if they have none, as many who stand candidates, I am told, have not, you may guess who assists them, and what hopeful services are to be expected from them. Such men, you may be sure, will never speak your sense in parliament—nor their own, if they have any; but that of their masters.[56]

The election of that year, contrary to the hopes of the Whigs, returned the conservative Tories to power, and they were able to hold this dominant position for over fifteen years.

After the defeat of a Reform Bill in 1812, the subject of parliamentary reform was not discussed in the House of Commons until after the downfall of Napoleon. There were several reasons for this. First, the interest of the people was devoted to one chief concern: the defeat of Napoleon; and there was little time in the Tory House for considering other problems such as reform. Then, too, there was no strong leader in the Commons to direct the Reform Movement. It does not seem likely that Brand, Burdett, or Whitbread could have assumed the position of leadership, because not one of them had the characteristics of a great leader, nor the personality that would appeal to the English people. Divided as they were among themselves, it was difficult for the reformers to gain the support of the Whig Party, which they considered necessary for the success of their movement. Yet the period 1812-1815 was not devoid of activity. Reform pamphlets continued to appear, and societies bent on spreading reform propaganda among the English people flour-

56 Yate, W. H., *A Candid and Admonitory Address to the Independent Electors of the United Kingdom* (London, 1812), pp. 31-32. Pamphlet later published in 1825.

ished. But the reformers were waiting—waiting until they had gained the support of the Whigs, and until the time should appear ripe for the launching of their movement.

The return of peace in 1815 brought domestic affairs to the foreground for the first time in many years. The leaders of the Reform Movement were convinced that the opportune time had arrived for the adoption of some of their demands. In 1816, through the efforts of Cartwright, Cobbett, and Hunt, Hampden Clubs were established throughout the kingdom for the expressed purpose of arousing a demand for parliamentary reform. The chief demands were for annual parliaments, universal suffrage, and secret ballot; and occasionally some speaker, such as Mr. Draper, a clergyman, would attack the existing Qualification Act. At one such meeting, he said:

If we look to those above us, we shall find they have confounded two things that nature had kept distinct, and that is man and property—the property belongs to the man, but the man never ought to be carried along with the property. It is a libel on mankind and common sense, that no man should sit in the House of Commons who has not £300 a year. I know several Gentlemen in the House of Commons whom I admire, but not for their property. I know of but two qualities necessary for a Representative in Parliament, integrity and intelligence.[57]

The work of the Hampden Clubs was fostered by the publications of William Cobbett, which gained daily in popularity and circulation. His cheap publications, "two penny trash", directed the reading public to the cause of their suffering—misgovernment; and recommended one cure—parliamentary reform. The lower classes embraced the demands wholeheartedly; but the upper classes were not favorably impressed. They were willing to surrender none of their power to the masses, whose leaders they despised, and whose cause and methods they denounced. The perturbed state of the nation in 1816, with its bread riots,

57 *A Full Report of the Proceedings of the Meeting Convened by the Hampden Club*—The Freemasons' Tavern, Lincoln's Inn Fields, June 15, 1816 (London, 1816), pp. 20-21.

demonstrations, and secret meetings, forced the officials of the conservative government to take action. In 1817, the suspension of the Habeas Corpus Act drove William Cobbett to America,[58] and other measures suppressed political demonstrations, silenced the reform leaders, and closed the reform clubs. Such repressive measures, however, could not destroy the Reform Movement, the roots of which went back to the latter part of the eighteenth century. Occasionally in the succeeding years, the voice of reform was heard: in 1818, when for the eighteenth time Sir Francis Burdett made his annual motion that the House consider the state of representation; and in 1819, when the people of Manchester in a great demonstration demanded parliamentary reforms. On that fatal day thousands of people assembled demanding " Vote by ballot," " No Corn Laws," and " Equal Representation." Unfortunately, there was a clash between the yeomanry and police, several people were killed, and many were wounded. The events in the kingdom during the summer and fall of 1819 [59] convinced many of the members of the House of Commons that action would have to be taken against the radicals. When the House met in November 1819, it speedily passed the celebrated " Six Acts " by which freedom of press, speech, and assembly were virtually destroyed, and radicalism, for a time, was silenced.

No sooner were the radicals silenced, however, than the landed interest discovered that another group, the moneyed men, again threatened them. The Napoleonic Wars, like other wars, had affected the fortunes of many Englishmen. Government contracts and inflation had benefited some persons at the expense of others. As in previous times, a new moneyed group, in defiance of the Curwen Act was invading the House of Commons to occupy purchased seats. The interest of this moneyed group was in direct conflict with the old landed interest. In 1812, the year of a general election, a writer of an article in *The Edinburgh Review* complained that

58 Melville, L., *op. cit.*, II, 81.

59 Bamford, S., *Passages in the Life of a Radical* (London, 1844), I, 176-225.

An unprincipled Jew may cause the best and most respectable man in England to ruin himself, or give up his seat; and even where no such case occurs, no sooner is a vacancy declared, than some man of mere money, and with no other earthly qualification, has a chance, next to a certainty, of getting into Parliament if he chuses to spend so much as the speculation requires . . . [60]

William Cobbett was quick to recognize that the purchase of parliamentary seats by this new moneyed class was rapidly changing the character of the membership of the House of Commons,[61] and in his pamphlets, he attacked the sale of parliamentary seats. Cobbett explained how many of the seats in the House of Commons were the property of the leading Whigs and Tories, and that these were sold in fee simple, or rented for one, two, three meetings of the Commons, or for the entire session of parliament.[62] To strengthen his argument, Cobbett named men who had bought or rented seats. Among those named were Brougham, a lawyer who held one of the seven seats owned by Lord Darlington; Horner, also a lawyer, who held a seat owned by the Marquis of Buckingham; and Wilberforce and Romilly, who rented their seats in the House of Commons.[63] One person described the political situation as follows:

The country belongs to the Duke of Rutland, Lord Lonsdale, the Duke of Newcastle, and about twenty other holders of boroughs. They are our masters! If any little opportunity presents itself, we will hang them, but most probably there will be no such opportunity; it always is twenty to one against the people . . . [64]

As usual the contemporaries of Cobbett found pleasure in discussing the pros and cons of the British representative sys-

60 *The Edinburgh Review*, July, 1812, p. 138.

61 Cobbett's *Weekly Political Register*, Published in New York, June 4, 1816, pp. 129-130.

62 *Ibid.*, p. 131.

63 *Ibid.*, Published in New York, April 27, 1816, p. 520.

64 Holland, Lady, *A Memoir of the Rev. Sydney Smith* (London, 1855). Letter to Mrs. Meynell, Feb. 12, 1821, II, 215.

tem, and the subject of the boroughmonger attracted attention until the passage of the Reform Bill of 1832. Since most men of large estates, whether Whig or Tory, were guilty of selling parliamentary seats, they showed little interest in Cobbett's accusations. They were vitally interested in only one problem, namely, that of keeping out of the House of Commons those men whose interests and political doctrines did not coincide with their own. This could be accomplished by the strict enforcement of the Qualification Act, and by the rejection, in contested elections, of all representatives of the moneyed class. Curiously enough, very few members of the House of Commons in the period from 1816 to 1830 were declared ineligible because of the Qualification Act. This is, however, easily explained. A moneyed man, anxious to obtain a parliamentary seat, could easily purchase the necessary land to enable him to be properly qualified. Moreover, a patron responsible for the entrance of a man into the House of Commons, would not hesitate to provide him with a fictitious landed qualification.

Yet in this period a few cases had to be decided by the Select Committees appointed by the Commons. One of these cases entailed the interpretation of the wording of the Qualification Act, which had been passed in the reign of Queen Anne. In the general election of 1818, Lord Binning, Robert Torrens, and Mr. Barnett were the parliamentary candidates for the City of Rochester. When requested to state their landed qualifications, Lord Binning said he was the eldest son of Earl Haddington of Scotland. Lord Binning and Mr. Barnett were successful in the election; but in the opening session of the House of Commons, a petition was presented questioning the eligibility of the former.[65] The question raised was whether or not the eldest son of a Scottish peer could represent an English county, city, or borough. This was the first time that such a question had arisen, and the Select Committee, appointed by the House of Commons, had to interpret the wording of the Qualification Act, which stated that nothing in the act should extend to the eldest

65 *J. H. C.*, LXXIV, 60.

son or heir apparent of any Peer or Lord of Parliament. Did
" Peer or Lord of Parliament " include Scottish peers? Contrary to opinions of eminent English lawyers and various members of the House,[66] the Select Committee decided that the
Scottish peers were included; and Lord Binning was declared
the duly elected representative. As for the petition, that was declared " frivolous and vexatious." [67]

The same session of the House of Commons had to decide
upon a petition from the qualified voters of the Borough of
Leominster, complaining about the election of Sir William
Cunningham Fairlie. The signers of the petition stated that Sir
William had tendered his own oath in writing at the time of the
election, but that the voters refused to accept it and called upon
Sir William to take the oath as prescribed by the Qualification
Act. It was also pointed out to Sir William that his landed
qualifications were not located in Great Britain. Sir William
assured the voters that he had forgotten his English estates,
which he then proceeded to describe. After some hesitation, Sir
William took the prescribed oath of qualification. The petitioners asserted that Sir William's landed qualification was a fictitious one, and was not worth £300 per annum. Moreover, the
deed of conveyance was said to be fraudulent, and was not
stamped according to the laws of the kingdom. On the whole
there was considerable doubt that Sir William was the true
possessor of such landed estates.[68] Accordingly, a Select Committee was appointed by the House of Commons; and after due
time, Sir Charles Morgan, the chairman, reported to the members of the House that Sir William was not duly qualified according to the Qualification Act, and that therefore, he was not
the rightful representative for the Borough of Leominster.[69]

66 Torrens, R., *A Letter to the Independent Freemen of the City of
Rochester* (London, 1819), pp. 8-10.

67 *J. H. C.*, LXXIV, 228. Corbett, U. and Daniell, E. R., *Reports of Cases
of Controverted Elections, in the Sixth Parliament of the United Kingdom*
(London, 1821), pp. 229-238.

68 *J. H. C.*, LXXIV, 20-21.

69 Corbett, U. and Daniell, E. R., *op. cit.*, pp. 1-25. *J. H. C.*, LXXIV, 127.

The election of Daniel Whittle Harvey was likewise declared null and void by an 1820 House committee,[70] which confirmed the claim of some of the qualified voters of Colchester that he was not the owner of a landed estate as required by the Qualification Act.[71]

In both these cases, the House of Commons took action after petitions had been received from the qualified voters. Quite different, however, was the case of Mr. Southey, a conscientious Englishman, who believed that he could not serve the electors of the kingdom because he was not properly qualified. In 1826, in a letter to the Commons, which was read by the Speaker of that body, Mr. Southey explained his case in the following manner:

Having, while I was on the Continent, been, without my knowledge, elected a Burgess to serve in the present Parliament, for the borough of Downton, it has become my duty to take the earliest opportunity of requesting you to inform the Honourable House, that I am not qualified to take a seat therein, inasmuch as I am not possessed of such an estate as is required by the Act passed in the ninth year of Queen Anne.[72]

In view of the widespread practice of the day, it may seem surprising that Mr. Southey did not acquire a fictitious landed qualification, and assume his seat in the Commons. Judging from his travel on the continent, he was a man of means; and his return to the House of Commons by the voters of the Borough of Downton indicates that he was known to some extent. That he refused to take his place in the Commons must, therefore, be assigned either to a sense of honesty, or to the fact that he did not believe that a contested election was worth the money it would entail. Then too, his political views as well as the political power of his defeated opponents must be taken into consideration. Whatever the reason, Mr. Southey took the easiest way out by refusing to take his seat in parliament.

70 *J. H. C.*, LXXV, 374.

71 *Ibid.*, LXXV, 189.

72 *Ibid.*, LXXXII, 28.

It could hardly be expected that in the period between the downfall of Napoleon and the opening years of the thirties, the conservative members of the House of Commons, opposed to radicalism and intent upon enforcing the Qualification Act, would consider any measure that might change it. Indeed, throughout this period no member of either house made any attempt either to strengthen or abolish the Act. Probably any attempt at its abolition would have met with failure; such was the fate of all proposals and plans for parliamentary reforms. Within the Commons the question of property qualifications for members did come up for discussion, however, in 1819. In that year, Sir George Warrender presented a bill, which later became law, making the possession of property in Scotland a satisfactory qualification for members to serve in the United Parliament of Great Britain and Ireland.[73] Some of the other topics that commanded the attention of the Tory legislature were the question of Queen Caroline, the Corn Laws, reforms in administration and finance, the Test and Corporation Acts, and Catholic Emancipation. The attention of the House was directed not only to the domestic affairs, but also to the trend of events in Europe. For the success or failure of the " concert of powers " would, in all probabilities, affect the commercial policies and the position of Great Britain.

Although the people of Great Britain were primarily interested in the course of domestic and foreign affairs, as is shown in the literature of the post-Napoleonic Period, Cobbett and the reformers did not permit these topics to overshadow completely the question of reform. They continued their attacks on the boroughmongers; and their demands for redistribution of the seats in the House of Commons, annual parliaments, and universal suffrage, kept alive the flame of reform. But that flame did not touch the question of property qualifications for the members of the House of Commons. That subject was overshadowed by other political demands; and it was not until the thirties that the issue of property qualifications for membership

73 *Ibid.*, LXXIV, 244, 529. 59 George III, c. 37.

in the House of Commons came to the foreground. For that reason, few pamphlets for or against the Qualification Act appeared during that period. In 1818, a pamphlet, *The Freedom of England,* contained a poem by an unknown writer who criticized the use of sham or fictitious qualifications in verse—such as it was!

> Well, well, said Senex, if the county must
> Elect a tool, ev'n let that tool be Cust;
> Whose legal conscience bids him roundly swear,
> His lands are worth six hundred pounds a year: [74]

The writer continued his condemnation of that system which would allow Mr. Cust, who possessed no landed estates, to be elected to the House of Commons as a representative. He asserted that Lord Brownlow had given the necessary land to Mr. Cust, and that a legal transaction enabled the parliamentary member to take his seat in the House.[75]

In the same year, another unknown writer, in *Two Addresses to the Freeholders of Westmorland,* stated that while the letter of the Qualification Act might have been affected by recent events, he was certain that the spirit of the law had been preserved and enforced.[76] One took it for granted that a county representative should be a man of substantial landed property, for not only would such a representative have the landed interests at heart, but also his own land would stand for the people as a pledge for his conduct. He thought the legislators of Queen Anne's day had been wise and just in passing a law which made landed property the qualification for membership in the House of Commons. Property showed that

a man had something that might be impaired or lost by mismanagement; something which tended to place him above dependence from need; and promised, though it did not insure, some degree of education to produce requisite intelligence.[77]

74 *The Freedom of England* (London, 1818), p. 1.
75 *Ibid.,* pp. 3-4.
76 *Two Addresses to the Freeholders of Westmorland* (London, 1818), p. 47.
77 *Ibid.,* pp. 47-48.

He added that men of large estates had many duties; and that in their relations with others, their honesty, justice, consideration, and other characteristics necessary for a good legislator would appear.[78] The pamphleteer closed his article by reminding the reader that freeholders of past times " knew that their rights were most likely to repose in safety, under the shade of rank and property." [79] This address was nothing, if not a campaign appeal to the electors of that community to return men of landed estates to the House of Commons. By way of contrast, there was a pamphlet written by Mr. Knox, a clergyman, which appeared in 1821. This writer, whose position brought him in contact with all kinds of men, disagreed with the theory that riches, independent of personal merit, could be a sufficient recommendation for members of parliament.[80] To him, membership in the House of Commons was a trust, and required a good education, strong natural abilities, a just, honest, and upright heart, manly firmness, and " enlarged philanthropy." [81] He did not understand why such men could not be found in any part of the nation, and he knew they would be found when

the corrupting idea shall be exploded, that Property is the best qualification for a national counsellor and lawgiver.[82]

But several decades were to pass before Knox's idea was to be fully realized. The members of the legislative body in the closing years of the twenties and the opening years of the following decade were occupied with other political reforms; and it was not until the middle thirties that agitation forced the House of Commons to consider the question of property qualifications for its members.

78 *Ibid.*, p. 49.

79 *Ibid.*, p. 50.

80 Knox, V., *The Spirit of Despotism* (London, 1821), p. 51.

81 *Ibid.*, p. 51.

82 *Ibid.*, p. 51.

CHAPTER V

THE REFORMING THIRTIES

ALTHOUGH the closing years of the twenties might have indicated to the people that at last the House of Commons was in a receptive mood for reformative measures, the leaders of the Reform Movement were not too hopeful when the parliament met in February, 1830. The Catholic Emancipation Act of 1829 had not been favorably received by all of the people, and the passage of the act had caused hard feeling among some of the members of the legislature. It soon became apparent that the lack of cooperation and unity in the spring session of 1830 would result in the failure of all proposals and plans for parliamentary reforms. As early as February 18, 1830, the Marquis of Blandford, a Tory member of the Lower House, condemned the existing political abuses, and moved to bring in a bill " to restore the Constitutional influence of the Commons in the Parliament of England." [1] His plan called for the appointment of a House committee of twenty-one for the purpose of investigating thoroughly the representation of the cities, boroughs, and every part of the country. Should this committee report that because of a shift in population, the number of inhabitants in a given place had declined sharply, that place would lose its representation in the House of Commons in proportion to its loss in population; and those places which had expanded would receive additional representation in the House. His comprehensive plan included salaries for the members of the House of Commons, and extension of the suffrage to copyholders and certain leaseholders.[2] Lastly, he recommended repeal of the Qualification Act which had been passed in the reign of Queen Anne.[3] Such a plan would certainly

1 Hansard, *Parliamentary Debates*, New Series, 22: 698.
2 *Ibid.*, 22: 688-691.
3 *Ibid.*, 22: 692.

have placed the government of the kingdom in the hands of the people; but this plan, as well as all others introduced in the spring session of 1830, met with defeat.

Meanwhile, the nation was laboring under a period of economic stress which manifested itself in riots, demonstrations, and the formation of various societies and organizations. As early as March, 1830, Mr. Huskisson called the attention of the House of Commons to the growth of an organization in Birmingham, the main purposes of which, in his words, were " to raise a universal cry for Parliamentary reform; and to carry the question by exaggerating the difficulties, abuses, and distresses of the country." [4] Another organization, the National Union of the Working Classes, was formed in June, 1830, and had for its main purposes the betterment of the conditions of the working people, and the adoption of parliamentary reforms.[5] Its suggested reforms for the House of Commons included annual parliaments, extension of the suffrage, secret ballot, and abolition of property qualifications for membership because

until intelligent men, from the productive and useful classes of society, possess the right of sitting in the Commons' House of parliament, to represent the interests of the working people, justice in legislation will never be rendered to them.[6]

The purpose and work of this organization, which was largely composed of working men, were made known to the English people through its newspaper, *The Voice of the People*. About this time, William Carpenter, a pamphleteer, became interested in the Reform Movement; joining Cobbett and the other reformers, he used his pen to record in cheap periodicals the purposes and work of the reform societies. Like Cobbett, Carpenter did much to further the Reform Movement.

It was during this state of political and economic unrest that King George IV died on June 26, 1830. The death of the sove-

4 Harris, W., *op. cit.*, p. 221.

5 *Ibid.*, p. 181.

6 Carpenter, W., *op. cit.*, p. 181.

reign necessitated the summoning of a new parliament; and the reformers were hopeful that the new election would return more of their number to the House of Commons. Events in France in 1830 also stimulated interest in liberal movements. The arbitrary government of Charles X caused the French liberals to revolt, and to set up a new government under Louis Philippe. This revolution occurred at the very time that parliamentary elections were being held in Great Britain, and when reformers were directing their efforts toward the return of " liberal " representatives to the House of Commons. Nor were their efforts in vain, for when the new House of Commons met in the fall of 1830, the reforming element was predominant.[7] Nevertheless, the hopes of the reformers were not to be realized, because it became apparent at the opening session of the new parliament, that the Duke of Wellington, the Prime Minister, would oppose all plans for parliamentary reform. Not until November, 1830, when the Duke of Wellington was replaced by Lord Grey, the friend of parliamentary reform, did the prospect of political reform begin to grow brighter.

The English people, meanwhile, continued their agitation for parliamentary reform by means of pamphlets, meetings, resolutions, and petitions. Redistribution of the seats in the House of Commons and universal suffrage were the chief political reforms demanded; but other desirable political reforms were not entirely forgotten. At a public meeting, called by the Birmingham Political Union on December 13, 1830, resolutions were adopted and a petition to parliament drawn up. Among the provisions of the petition was one which read:

The right of sitting and voting in the Commons' House of Parliament, when lawfully chosen, without the qualification of property which was fixed unconstitutionally by the Act of 9th of Queen Anne.[8]

7 Harris, W., *op. cit.*, p. 224.

8 Carpenter, W., *Political Letters and Pamphlets*, "A Political Compendium," Dec. 18, 1830, p. 15.

Carpenter, though his greatest energies were directed against the powerful boroughmongers, did not forget to urge the representative of the scot and lot borough of Preston, Henry Hunt, the advocate of universal suffrage, secret ballot, and annual parliaments, to work for the repeal of the Qualification Act. Writing in December, 1830, Carpenter pointed out that the Act operated most injuriously by excluding from the House of Commons men of practical knowledge. He explained that for membership in the House of Representatives of the United States, a body which " exhibits a large share of direct plain intelligence, which is most valuable in directing the affairs of any commercial people," [9] no such qualifications were required by law. But secret ballot, annual parliaments, and abolition of property qualifications for the members of the Commons were forgotten for the time being, when the reformers in and out of the House decided to work for the adoption of the great Reform Bill,[10] which finally became law in 1832.

While the Reform Bill for England was being debated in the House of Lords in 1832, the question of property qualifications for members of parliament was being discussed in the House of Commons. The question arose when, during the discussion of the Reform Bill for Scotland, a provision was inserted requiring the Scottish members of parliament to have landed property to the value of £600 a year if representing a Scottish county, and £300 a year if representing a Scottish borough.[11] During the discussion, Sir George Clerk recommended the adoption of the landed qualification provision, arguing that uniformity would then exist throughout the kingdom. The Chancellor of the Exchequer proposed an amendment requiring landed qualifications for representatives of Scottish counties only. He supported Sir George Clerk's contention that it might be wise to have a uniform law for the entire kingdom, but he questioned the feasibility of such a law by adding:

9 *Ibid.*, "A Political Digest," Dec. 23, 1830, p. 4.
10 Roebuck, J. A., *History of the Whig Ministry* (London, 1852), II, 111.
11 *Ibid.*, II, 394. Hansard, *op. cit.*, 3rd Series, 13: 390-397.

I think it would be very impolitic to enforce this very strictly. The House is aware that this has been the case in this country; for if it had been enforced very strictly, some of the brightest ornaments of this House would have been deprived of their seats; and without being guilty of invidious generalities, . . . I might mention the names of Mr. Pitt, Mr. Sheridan, Mr. Burke, Mr. Tierney, and others. I think there is no question that if in these instances the qualification had been enforced, great injury would have been the result. . . . The truth is, the necessity of such a qualification never yet excluded permanently any man, however obnoxious or unworthy, but only serves as a means of insult or annoyance. It promotes mischievous and expensive litigation, gives rise to unworthy subterfuge, and serves to break down the distinction which ought to exist between truth and falsehood.[12]

Robert Dundas, Mr. Pringle, and others supported the provision establishing landed qualifications for Scottish representatives; but Scotland and the Scottish representatives vigorously objected. Petitions were received from Edinburgh, Renfrew, and from the Glasgow Political Union;[13] and Mr. Dixon, a Scottish representative, asserted that the existing Qualification Act should be enforced in England, and that if it were not enforced, it should be repealed.[14] Mr. Hume suggested that the abolition of the Qualification Act was preferable to the continuous infraction of it by those men who entered the House of Commons improperly qualified,

any more than Mr. Fox, or Mr. Canning, and many others . . . For you who are the law-makers to be the law-breakers, is setting the worst of all examples.[15]

One member thought some changes should be made in the existing law, and another wondered why the Act should exist at all

12 Roebuck, J. A., *op. cit.*, II, 395-396. Hansard, *op. cit.*, 13 : 1057-1058, John Charles Spencer, Viscount Althorp.

13 *Ibid.*, 13 : 1057.

14 Roebuck, J. A., *op. cit.*, II, 396.

15 *Ibid.*, II, 396.

in any part of the kingdom.[16] Sir Robert Peel attacked the problem from a different angle. He protested that any concession to Scotland would be used by the discontented people of England as an argument for change in the Qualification Act. Sir George Warrender thought the existing law, if considered good, should be enforced; but if the law were evaded in England, it should not be imposed on the Scottish people.[17] Finally, the Reform Bill for Scotland, without any landed qualifications for the members of the Commons,[18] passed both houses. Sir George Murray, commenting on its passage, said:

the qualification will be done away with even in England, and that the omission of it in Scotland will in future be an argument for its abolition.[19]

The sections of the 1832 Reform Act, hailed in all areas of the civilized world, which provided for the redistribution of seats in the House of Commons and the extension of the suffrage, did not produce any startling changes in the composition of the new House of Commons. It was true, however, that the reformed House of Commons, which met after the general election of 1832, included many men who supported the ideas of the reformers. How many, it is difficult to determine;[20] but the increased number of reformers in the House could not dominate that body, still controlled by the representatives of the landed interest. Among the reformers returned to the House of Commons were John Hobhouse, man of culture and scholarship; Sir Francis Burdett, the supporter of parliamentary rights for the people; and Joseph Hume, who was returned from Middlesex. Hume, fellow-student of James Mill at Montrose Academy, and friend and supporter of Benthamism, was neither a brilliant nor a very original thinker. According to

16 Hansard, *op. cit.*, 13 : 1066.

17 *Ibid.*, 13 : 1069.

18 *Ibid.*, 13 : 1069.

19 Roebuck, J. A., *op. cit.*, II, 396.

20 Harris, W., *op. cit.*, pp. 233-234.

Hobhouse, he was considered a " shabby, shuffling fellow " who would, in the House of Commons, advance the interests of the reformers and the people.[21] Two of the newcomers in parliament were William Cobbett and George Grote. Cobbett, the crusader for parliamentary reforms, reached the pinnacle of his ambition when he was returned by the electors of Oldham. Unfortunately, however, he never played an important role in the House of Commons. His position there seemed to be overshadowed by younger men who had appeared upon the scene; and his sudden death in 1835 put an end to all potential parliamentary actions. George Grote, the future historian of the Greeks, was returned for the City of London. Grote's interest in parliamentary reform went back to 1821, in which year he published a work which described the political abuses of the day, and showed the need for reforms. In a later work, *Essentials of Parliamentary Reform,* published in 1831, Grote refused to support the opinion that property was the only suitable basis for representation.[22] Grote believed not only in the extension of the suffrage, but also in more frequent elections of parliament, and secret ballot.[23] In the years to follow, Grote never changed his opinions; and as a member of the Commons, he did all in his power to influence that body to adopt secret ballot.

John Roebuck, returned for Bath, was only starting his parliamentary career; but he soon showed himself the opponent of the upper classes and their interests, and the friend and supporter of the principles of the reformers. For a time, however, it seemed likely that Roebuck would lose his seat in the House of Commons because of the provisions of the Qualification Act. In the election of 1832, at the request of two electors, Roebuck took the oath of qualification, stating that he was properly

21 Dorchester, Lady (Ed.), *Broughton, Lord, Recollections of a Long Life* (New York, 1910), IV, 30. Wallas, G., *The Life of Francis Place, 1771-1854* (London, 1898), p. 183.

22 Bain, A. (Ed.), *The Minor Works of George Grote* (London, 1873), " Essentials of Parliamentary Reform," pp. 19-20.

23 *Ibid.*, pp. 37-50.

qualified, and that his landed estate was in the parish of Camberwell, Surrey.[24] Mr. Roebuck was known for his radical views; and after his return for Bath, an attempt was made to unseat him. The petitioners claimed that he was not properly qualified according to the law of the kingdom, that he could not be the owner of property in the parish of Camberwell because no such parish existed. According to the explanation given by his biographer, Roebuck had made all arrangements for the necessary landed qualification, for which he paid over £5000; but the legal formalities had been delayed, and had been completed only one or two hours before Roebuck had taken the oath of qualification.[25] The problem confronting the Select Committee of the House of Commons was a difficult one. Legally, Roebuck was qualified; but his fictitious qualification certainly violated the spirit of the Qualification Act, since he was not the " true possessor " of a landed estate. The committee was divided on the question, and Roebuck almost lost his seat. The petition was dismissed only after the decisive vote had been cast by the chairman of the committee. Commenting on the case, Roebuck's friend, Mr. Leader, explained that many parliamentary candidates used fictitious qualifications; and Roebuck himself asserted that not one man in ten possessed

before his candidature the sort of estate qualifying him to sit.[26]

Roebuck, however, did not forget his experience; and when he had to obtain another landed qualification in a later election, he was extremely careful about the legal formalities. A friend described the incident in the following manner:

As Roebuck had no landed qualification, I gave him one charged on my estate of Burston, in Buckinghamshire. He was particular

24 Perry, H. J. and Knapp, J. W., *Cases of Controverted Elections in the Eleventh Parliament of the United Kingdom* (London, 1833), pp. 21-30. *J. H. C.*, LXXXVIII, 16-17. Leader, R. E. (Ed.), *Life and Letters of J. A. Roebuck* (London, 1897), p. 49.

25 *Ibid.*, p. 49.

26 *Ibid.*, p. 49.

in affairs of that kind, that he insisted on having all legal forms observed, and he actually brought me bank-notes of the requisite value, which had been lent him by our friend, George Grote, and which I, of course, immediately returned to Grote.[27]

It is interesting to note that the electors of Bath in 1832 cared little about Roebuck's landed qualification. They showed their opposition to the 1710 Qualification Act, by petitioning the House of Commons to abolish " the Act of Queen Anne, which renders Qualifications necessary, for becoming Members of the Legislative Body." [28]

Besides Roebuck, the friend of the people, two other distinguished members of the reformed House of Commons should be named. These were Charles Buller and Sir William Molesworth. Buller was recognized by his contemporaries as a man of genius and superior intellect. Like many men of his day, he was keenly interested in colonial affairs, and under Lord Durham, he performed numerous important services in that field. Buller's friend and companion was Sir William Molesworth, who belonged to an old Northamptonshire family. Educated at Cambridge and Edinburgh, young Molesworth continued his education on the continent, and on the death of his father in 1823, succeeded him in the baronetcy. With his money and leisure time, Sir William moved in the society which included Mill and Grote; and he accepted the ideas and principles expounded by the liberals of the day.[29] Richard Cobden, however, was not greatly impressed by Sir William, whom he described as follows:

not a man of superior talents, and let him say what he pleases, there is nothing about him that is democratic in principle . . . [30]

27 *Ibid.*, Letter written by John Temple Leader to editor, February 19, 1896, p. 50.

28 *J. H. C.*, LXXXVII, 432.

29 Fawcett, Mrs., *Life of the Right Honourable Sir William Molesworth* (London, 1901). *The Dictionary of National Biography.*

30 Morley, J., *The Life of Richard Cobden* (Boston, 1881), p. 93.

Roebuck, on the other hand, saw in Molesworth a man of wealth and position who would lend distinction to the cause of the reformers.

Now, it is of great importance in this wealth-loving aristocratic country to have among those men a rich man, of good standing and rank. Molesworth filled up this gap for us. Moreover, he did so with great effect, as he is a person of no mean ability and very great industry. He is ever anxious to learn, is studious, and in the right away. Being young, he would soon acquire the art of speaking, which older men cannot.[31]

Roebuck's opinion was shared by Redding, who remembered Molesworth as a person of ability " and unimpeachable political integrity ",[32] who used his position in the House of Commons to work for free trade, colonial reforms, prison reforms, and for the abolition of property qualifications for membership in the House of Commons. Not only did Molesworth support the demand for reforms, political, social, and economic, in the House of Commons, but he also founded the *London Review,* which he later united with the *Westminster Review,* to spread more effectively the ideas of the reformers among the people. In and out of the House of Commons, Molesworth was an indefatigable worker for reform. Both his spirit and his labor were justly acknowledged in his epitaph, which reads as follows:

A laborious and thoughtful student from an early age, both of speculative truth and of the practical questions of political life. His opinions were his own. He lived to see some of them triumphant partly through his own efforts, and died as he had lived, faithful to them all.[33]

With such an impressive group of reformers in the House of Commons, it was to be expected that the legislation of the thirties would be noteworthy for its liberal character. As fol-

31 Leader, R. E. (Ed.), *op. cit.,* p. 81.

32 Redding, C., *Personal Reminiscences of Eminent Men* (London, 1867), II, 1.

33 Elliot, H. (Ed.), *The Letters of John S. Mill* (London, 1910), I, 188.

lowers of Bentham, James Mill, Ricardo and other philosophical radicals,[34] Molesworth and his friends were determined to attack the existing political, social, and economic conditions. Undoubtedly, their membership in the House gave assurance to the passage of the liberal measures of the thirties; but they found it an impossibility to force the House to accept their program of parliamentary reforms.

The early sessions of the reformed House of Commons were devoted to routine work, and after that, election petitions were considered. Some of the petitions claimed that the representatives returned to the House of Commons were not properly qualified according to the Qualification Act. For example, on February 7, 1833, a petition was received from the qualified voters of Tiverton, in the County of Dover, describing the recent election in which John Heathcote, James Kennedy, Benjamin Wood, and Charles Chichester were the parliamentary candidates. At the time of the election, Kennedy, one of the successful candidates, was requested by some of the electors to take the oath of qualification. Kennedy proceeded to do so, claiming that he had a landed estate, and that such lands were in the parishes of St. Andrew, Holborn, and Holy Trinity, in Middlesex and the Town of Kingston-upon-Hull. These claims were doubted by the petitioners, who did not think that Kennedy was the rightful representative of the people of Tiverton.[35] Before the House of Commons could take action on the petition, Kennedy sent a letter to the Speaker of that body informing him that he would not defend his return for the Borough of Tiverton.[36] Disregarding Kennedy's letter, the House of Commons appointed a Select Committee; and after due time, Mr. Abercromby, the chairman, reported that Kennedy was not the duly elected representative for the Borough of Tiverton.[37]

34 See Halévy, E., *The Growth of Philosophic Radicalism*, translated by Mary Morris (New York, 1928).

35 Perry, H. J. and Knapp, J. W., *op. cit.*, pp. 269-271. *J. H. C.*, LXXXVIII, 17.

36 *Ibid.*, LXXXVIII, 102.

37 *Ibid.*, LXXXVIII, 380.

On February 18, 1833, the House of Commons was petitioned by Lovell Edgworth, Barry Fox, and other freeholders of the County of Longford, to the effect that illegal practices at the time of the election had returned James Rorke and Luke White to the House of Commons. They charged that corrupt practices had prevailed at the election, and that Rorke, in spite of his assertions to the contrary, was not the possessor of a landed estate which would qualify him for a parliamentary seat.[38] After an investigation of the charges had been made by the Select Committee, Mr. Thomas Wood, the chairman, reported that White and Rorke were not the duly elected representatives for the County of Longford, and that their opponents, Anthony Lefroy and George John Forbes, were the rightful representatives.[39] On February 19, 1833, some of the qualified voters of the Borough of Mallow, in the County of Cork, complained that in the recent election, Henry Hume, the returning officer, had allowed unqualified voters to take part in the election. As a result, William Daunt had been returned to the House of Commons as a representative of the electors. The petitioners declared that they were certain that Daunt could not be their rightful representative because he failed to meet the provisions of the Qualification Act.[40] Lord John Eastnor reported for the House committee, which found that Daunt was not duly elected, and that Charles Jephson was the rightful representative for the Borough of Mallow.[41] Many of these contested election cases involved the return of liberal members to the House of Commons. These liberals were exerting every effort to further the reform program, which included abolition of property qualifications for membership in parliament. Their conservative political opponents found no difficulty in charging them with evasion of the Qualification Act. But the liberal spirit had permeated the

38 *Ibid.*, LXXXVIII, 53-54.

39 *Ibid.*, LXXXVIII, 251. Perry, H. J. and Knapp, J. W., *op. cit.*, pp. 174-201.

40 *Ibid.*, pp. 266-268. *J. H. C.*, LXXXVIII, 76-77.

41 *Ibid.*, LXXXVIII, 304-305.

House of Commons, and with the exceptions of the three cases mentioned, the petitioners were unsuccessful in unseating their political rivals.[42]

While these election petitions were being considered by the House of Commons, still other petitions were presented. There was a petition from the members of the Protestant Conservative Society of Ireland which prayed " That the Acts relating to the Qualification of Members of the House of Commons may be amended; "[43] and on April 1, 1833, the members of the Norwich Union of the Working Classes and other inhabitants of Norwich, as well as Timothy Hutt and Mark Anthony Johnson, petitioned the House of Commons to amend the representation of the people in such a manner that no property qualifications would be required of the electors or their representatives. Not only did these petitioners pray for the abolition of property qualifications for members of the House of Commons, but they also advocated the repeal of the Septennial Act, and the adoption of secret ballot.[44] On August 5, 1833, an unusual petition

42 Reformed House of Commons — January, 1833–December, 1834. Controverted Elections concerning the Qualification Act.

	DECISION
Bath	John Roebuck, liberal sitting member, duly elected.
Carlow County (Ireland)	Walter Blackney and Thomas Wallace, sitting members, duly elected.
Coventry	Edward Ellice and Henry Earle Lytton Bulwer, liberal sitting members, duly elected.
Dover	John Halcomb, sitting member, duly elected.
Lincoln	Edward George Earle Lytton Bulwer, sitting member, duly elected.
Longford (Ireland)	James Rorke, sitting member, not duly elected.
Mallow (Ireland)	William Daunt, sitting member, not duly elected. Charles Jephson (liberal) should have been returned.
Tiverton	James Kennedy, sitting member, not duly elected. In 1833, the liberals were doubtful about Kennedy, but later he supported the cause of the reformers.

43 J. H. C., LXXXVIII, 70.

44 Ibid., LXXXVIII, 243.

was submitted by the freemen of Dover, calling the attention of the House of Commons to an earlier petition which had been presented (March, 1833), questioning the landed qualification of John Halcomb.[45] According to the parliamentary records Halcomb had been ordered by the House of Commons to comply with the Standing Orders of the House, adopted on November 21, 1717. These orders, it will be recalled, provided that the qualifications of a member whose election to the Commons was contested by petition must be submitted to the House within fifteen days after the petition against that sitting member had been received. Halcomb had not followed these requirements, claiming that ill health had prevented such action; and he requested the House to give him more time. A motion " that Mr. Halcomb be permitted to deliver to the House of Commons a paper containing details of his landed qualifications " was not adopted by the House, and no further action was taken against Halcomb.[46] This apparent indifference on the part of the members of the House of Commons did not please the freeholders of Dover, who stated in their petition that either the Commons should carry out its Standing Orders, or such Orders should be declared " nugatory ".[47]

When the election petitions were out of the way, the House of Commons turned to the numerous other problems that confronted it. The reformers were not idle; Grote moved for the adoption of secret ballot; Tennyson, for shorter parliaments; and others worked for political, social, and economic reforms. But they discovered that their group was much too small to gain their desired reforms.[48] Moreover, they were not highly organized, and dissensions among themselves were frequent. Consequently, it was impossible for them to gain the support

45 *Ibid.*, LXXXVIII, 636.

46 *Ibid.*, LXXXVIII, 293. Perry, H. J. and Knapp, J. W., *op. cit.*, pp. 412-424.

47 *J. H. C.*, LXXXVIII, 636.

48 See Thomas, J. A., *The House of Commons, 1832-1901* (Cardiff, 1939), pp. 3-6.

or even the attention of the members of the House. Besides, the attention of the Commons was now claimed by the Factory Law of 1833 and the problems of slavery in the British colonies, as well as the government of India. The reformers, afraid that the populace would forget their program of parliamentary reforms, began, in their speeches and writings, to urge the people to agitate for parliamentary reforms in public meetings and in petitions to the House of Commons. Until his death in 1835, Henry Hunt, one of the reformers, never lost an opportunity to address the people and to urge them to work for annual parliaments, universal suffrage, and the ballot.[49] When a speaker at a meeting in Newcastle in 1835 advocated the adoption of the above demands, recommending that a petition be sent to the House of Commons, the people drew up such a petition, urging not only the adoption of these three demands, but also the reduction of their taxes and the abolition of the Corn Laws.[50] Until 1835, the efforts of the reformers were concentrated on the extension of the suffrage, shorter parliaments, and secret ballot. Like their predecessors, the reformers of 1835 recognized the existence of a vital popular interest in these demands, and believed that their adoption would place the government in the hands of the people. Once the lower classes controlled the government, they felt that it would be easy to bring about other reforms, including the abolition of property qualifications for membership in the House of Commons.

As the election of 1835 approached, the reformers increased their efforts to have liberal-minded representatives elected to the House of Commons. Nor were their efforts in vain, for when the House met in February, 1835, after an uneventful election which had aroused little interest in the country, the reformers observed an increase in their number and regarded it as a good omen.

49 Huish, R., *The History of the Private and Political Life of the Late Henry Hunt* (London, 1836), II, 13.

50 *Proceedings of a Public Meeting held on the Town Moor of Newcastle-upon-Tyne*, May 27, 1833 (Newcastle, 1833), pp. 27-34.

But their plans and proposals for reforms had to wait, as usual, until the Commons had taken action on election petitions. Compared with earlier elections, there were few seats contested after the election of 1835; but as was always the case, some petitions did complain about the evasion of the Qualification Act. Three of these petitions were successful in unseating certain questionable members of the House of Commons.

On March 2, 1835, James McCartney and other qualified voters of the Town and County of the Town of Drogheda complained of the election of Andrew O'Dwyer. They stated that unfair practices had been used to return O'Dwyer to the Commons, and that they were certain that he had not had a landed estate of the required amount either at the time of his election or at the time of his return to the House. When called upon to take the oath of qualification at election time, O'Dwyer had given the necessary form to a friend, who proceeded to fill in the blank with the statement that O'Dwyer's landed estate was in the County of Dublin. This form had been signed later by O'Dwyer and handed to the presiding sheriff. The petitioners asserted that O'Dwyer's claims to a landed estate were false, and that since he was not qualified according to the law, he was not the legal representative of the voters.[51] The House of Commons appointed the customary Select Committee, and some time later, the chairman reported that Andrew O'Dwyer was not duly elected to serve as a burgess.[52]

In March, 1835, the members of the House of Commons heard a similar petition from the qualified voters of the Borough of New Windsor, complaining that bribery and corrupt practices had returned Sir John Edmond de Beauvoir to the House. They charged that during the election, qualified voters had not been permitted to vote, while unqualified voters had been permitted to participate in the election. They complained

51 J. H. C., XC, 35-36. Knapp, J. W. and Ombler, E., *Cases of Controverted Elections in the twelfth Parliament of the United Kingdom* (London, 1837), pp. 201-210.

52 J. H. C., XC, 204.

that Sir John had given meat, drink, and entertainment to the electors; and added the more serious charge that Sir John had no landed estate of the annual value of £300, and therefore could not serve the people as their representative.[53] After careful investigation, a Select Committee reported that Sir John Edmond de Beauvoir was not duly elected, and that his seat in the House of Commons should be taken by his parliamentary opponent, Sir John Elley.[54]

In the same month, March, 1835, a petition of Richard Longfield was read to the House of Commons. In this petition, Longfield claimed that in the recent election for the County of Cork, Feargus O'Connor, himself, and two others had been the parliamentary candidates. Feargus O'Connor had been returned to the House, although Longfield knew that O'Connor was not the owner of a landed estate of the annual value of £600.[55] After investigating the facts of the case, Mr. Barneby reported for the Select Committee that O'Connor was not duly elected to serve in the House of Commons, and that Richard Longfield should have been returned.[56] O'Connor lost his seat, and later, when he stood as a parliamentary candidate for Nottingham, a friend came to his rescue, and conferred upon him lands bringing in an annual income of £300.[57] Other petitions in the spring session of 1835 were not destined to meet with similar success. Very often the House committees decided in favor of the sitting member, despite the complaints of the petitioners that he was without the proper qualifications. Still other petitions were not even considered by the House, because the petitioners had neglected to hand in declarations of their own landed estates.

After the House of Commons had disposed of the problem of contested elections, and while many Englishmen, including

53 *Ibid.*, XC, 56-57.

54 *Ibid.*, XC, 198. Knapp, J. W. and Ombler, E., *op. cit.*, pp. 139-199.

55 *J. H. C.*, XC, 74-75. Knapp, J. W. and Ombler, E., *op. cit.*, pp. 391-408.

56 *J. H. C.*, XC, 320.

57 Holyoake, G. J., *Bygones Worth Remembering* (London, 1905), I, 41. According to Holyoake, Mr. Allsop qualified Feargus O'Connor.

the unseated members of the Commons, were still concerned with the operation of the Qualification Act, the time seemed ripe for the introduction of a measure abolishing property qualifications for membership in the House of Commons. On July 3, 1835, the House ordered Mr. Hume and Mr. Aglionby to prepare and bring in a bill to regulate election expenses, to limit the duration of the polls, and to abolish the landed qualification for membership in parliament for England and Wales.[58] Later, when the measure had been introduced, and while it was being considered by the House, two interesting petitions were received by that body. Andrew O'Dwyer, who had been unseated by the Select Committee, petitioned the House, complaining bitterly about his fate. He closed his petition by praying

That the House will not permit this Session to pass over without the enactment of a law more liberally regulating the qualification of Members of Parliament, if they should deem a qualification to be necessary . . . [59]

In contrast with the above petition begging that the existing Qualification Act be modified, was one which sought the enactment of a law which would require every candidate for a borough or county to be in possession of his landed qualification for membership in the House for six months prior to his election.[60] This petition was obviously a plea for effective action against the wholesale evasion of the Qualification Act and the widespread practice of acquiring fictitious landed qualifications on the eve of an election.

But during the general discussion of the Election Expenses and Qualification of Members Bill, no reference was made to either of these petitions. Hume was definitely opposed to any kind of qualification for membership in the House of Commons,

58 *J. H. C.*, XC, 415. Bill to define and Regulate the Expenses of Elections, to limit the duration of the Poll, and to abolish the Qualification of Members of Parliament for England and Wales, 1835.

59 *J. H. C.*, XC, 446.

60 *Ibid.*, XC, 477.

whether pecuniary or landed. He asserted that some of the
" worst scamps in the country were men of property," [61] and
recommended that, since the law was constantly evaded, it be
removed from the statute book. If the House of Commons proposed to maintain some qualifications, he hoped the qualifications would extend to all kinds of property, and not simply to
landed property.[62] Lord John Russell agreed with him that the
operation of the Qualification Act was often injurious, but he
advised caution in abolishing it, and even in changing the law
so as to include other kinds of property.[63] Eventually, the Election Expenses and Qualification of Members Bill was divided
into two distinct bills; [64] and in August, 1835, probably because of Lord John Russell's attitude as the leader of the House,
that dealing with qualification of members was withdrawn.[65]
The withdrawal of the measure was the second defeat for the
reformers. On June 3, 1835, Grote had introduced his second
measure in favor of secret ballot; but it had found no support
in the House of Commons. In fact, it had met with the same
lack of response that was to be shown to the Qualification of
Members Bill two months later. Nor were these two failures the
only blows that the reformers were to suffer; for in 1835, their
ranks were grievously broken by the death of William Cobbett
and Henry Hunt, two staunch supporters of the rights of the
people.

Outside the House of Commons, the reformers did not relax
their efforts in favor of their program of parliamentary reforms.
While the country was discussing the Municipal Reform Act
and the activities of the Orange Societies and their leader the
Duke of Cumberland, the reformers kept alive their ideas of reform in pamphlets and speeches. In 1835, Roebuck sponsored

61 Hansard, op. cit., 30 : 619.

62 Ibid., 30 : 618-619.

63 Ibid., 30 : 619.

64 J. H. C., XC, 481.

65 Ibid., XC, 558. Bill to dispense with the Qualifications of Members
of the Commons' House of Parliament, 1835.

Pamphlets for the People; through this organ, the reformers kept in touch with the people. Friends of Roebuck contributed to the paper, which was designed to bring about shorter parliaments, universal suffrage, secret ballot, and the abolition of property qualifications of members of the House of Commons.[66] These political demands were supported by many Englishmen, but all efforts on the part of Molesworth, Grote, and their followers to gain the approval of the House of Commons, were fruitless. The year 1836 passed without any of their political demands being accepted by the government. Undaunted by failure, this group looked forward to 1837. In that year, their active work in the House was evidenced in motions, proposals, and bills for every kind of project cherished by nineteenth century progressives. Not only did they work for the adoption of their own program; but they also advocated the repeal of the Septennial Act and the Corn Laws, the abolition of primogeniture, and the adoption of educational reforms. Their efforts in the House of Commons received the enthusiastic support of the working people of Great Britain.

The spirited approval of the Reform Movement by the lower classes rose chiefly out of their dissatisfaction. Unlike the upper classes, who had accepted the 1832 Reform Act as a final settlement of the questions of suffrage and representation in the House, the working people looked upon it as merely a step in the growth of political democracy. By 1836, they were clamoring for further political reforms; but these the upper classes were unwilling to concede. As in other periods of English history, the workers founded various organizations. As early as 1831, through the efforts of Lovett and Hetherington, both working men of outstanding character, the National Union of the Working Classes had been functioning, collecting and organizing peaceful expressions of public opinion both for the protection of the working people in the free disposal of their labor, and for effective reforms in parlia-

66 Roebuck, J. A. (Ed.), *Pamphlets for the People* (London, 1835), "Progress of Democracy," p. 14.

ment.[67] In the field of parliamentary reform, this organization reiterated political demands which had been heard frequently in England during the nineteenth century. They demanded universal suffrage, ballot, annual parliaments, and election of representatives for intellectual fitness and mental worth, and not for property.[68] But clashes with the police together with the increase in the number of trade unions, caused the National Union of the Working Classes to sink into oblivion.

For a time the Grand National Consolidated Trades' Union, which was started through the interest of Robert Owen in 1834, held the attention of the working people. With a membership of one half million men and women of various trades, this organization worked for the betterment of the working classes. Robert Owen firmly believed that if the workers were organized in their various crafts and industries so as to control the means of production, they would also control the political reins of the government. But before Owen was able to put his idea of cooperatives into practice—a plan which he thought would eradicate all the evils resulting from the Industrial Revolution—a series of unsuccessful strikes brought discredit to the Grand National Consolidated Trades' Union. The use of the lockout, a forceful weapon of the employer, and the arrest and conviction of members of the union dampened the workers' spirit, and the movement collapsed in the summer of 1834.[69]

The various leaders of the trade union movement, however, never lost interest in the general effort to improve the conditions of the working people; and on June 16, 1836, William Lovett, Henry Hetherington, Francis Place, and others founded the London Working Men's Association.[70] It aimed to agitate for

67 Maccoby, S., *op. cit.*, pp. 159-160. Linton, W. J., *James Watson, A Memoir* (Manchester, 1880), p. 40.

68 *Ibid.*, p. 42.

69 Rosenblatt, F. F., *The Chartist Movement* (New York, 1916), p. 80. Woodward, E. L., *The Age of Reform, 1815-1870* (Oxford, 1938), pp. 122-126. Maccoby, S., *op. cit.*, pp. 105-111, 397.

70 Tawney, R. H., *Life and Struggles of William Lovett* (London, 1920), I, 99.

parliamentary reforms, and to disseminate social and industrial information among the English people.[71] The organization hoped to accomplish these purposes through the medium of public meetings, and by " missionaries " who were most successful in establishing societies throughout the country. The success of these organizations was due not only to the personality of the men, who sincerely believed in their aims, but also to the revival of the working classes' interest in politics, and to their growing discontent with the existing economic conditions. In the period from 1832 to 1836, England was fairly prosperous, and even the poor people were contented. But the depression, which began in 1836, and was later augmented by the adverse economic conditions in the United States in 1837, brought to the lower classes a false interpretation of the significance of the New Poor Law. Poverty stricken people could not understand that the introduction of labor-saving devices and over-production had brought on their plight. They attributed it to the operation of the New Poor Law.[72] Accordingly, in 1836-1837, membership and interest in the London Working Men's Association increased, partly because of conditions in England, and partly because the purposes of the organization were regarded by the working people as a panacea for all their ills. This was especially true of the political purposes of the organization, which were later stated in the famous petition approved on February 28, 1837, at a meeting held at the Crown and Anchor Tavern.[73]

It was only natural that the radicals in the House of Commons should take advantage of the situation of the country; and Sir William Molesworth was ready to seize the opportunity. On February 14, 1837, he moved for leave to bring in a bill to abolish the Qualification Act of Queen Anne's reign, and the amending act passed in the time of George II, which con-

71 *Ibid.*, I, 94-95. Maccoby, S., *op. cit.*, pp. 160-161.

72 Rosenblatt, F. F., *op. cit.*, pp. 47-58.

73 Tawney, R. H., *op. cit.*, I, 104.

cerned landed property qualifications for membership in the House of Commons. He added that he sought the repeal of these laws because he knew they were vicious in principle, sometimes producing pernicious consequences, and oftentimes causing great individual hardships. Sir William stated the provisions of the Acts and of the Standing Orders of the House pertaining to the Qualification Act of 1710 and pointed out that without these orders, the Qualification Act would become inoperative and easily evaded.[74] He then took up the problems confronting the members of the Select Committees who were called upon to settle the validity of the landed qualifications of a sitting member. He pointed out that these men, in many cases without legal knowledge, and oftentimes swayed by political partisanship, were called upon to settle questions which in many contested elections concerned fictitious landed qualifications. Nothing was easier to obtain than a fictitious landed qualification, as Molesworth proceeded to explain. A gentleman who needed one would apply to his broker, who would give him a rent charge. This was a mere matter of business and an accommodation, for almost every important London banker possessed landed property. If the gentleman in question possessed no money, he would apply to a friend or lawyer who would be able to find among his own friends or clients some man possessing landed property. The landowner, if willing, would become a party in the following transaction. A deed was drawn up conveying a rent charge to the person who needed the landed qualification, but this deed never left the hands of the lawyer. To make the transaction legal, two persons witnessed the exchange of money. The last step was very important, for should a petitioner question the landed qualifications of a sitting member of the House of Commons, these two witnesses would appear before the Select Committee and swear that the transaction was a bona-fide one. Did the possession of such a legal landed qualification make the member of parliament the legal owner of a landed estate? This was the vexatious problem which con-

74 Hansard, *op. cit.*, 36: 524-525.

fronted every Select Committee called upon to render a decision in a case that involved a fictitious landed qualification.[75] Sir William said it was a well known fact that one-half the members of the House of Commons, if not more, were not the legal possessors of landed estates as required by law, and had obtained their membership in the House through the use of fictitious landed qualifications.[76] He supported his argument by reading the following letter which had been written by an eminent lawyer:

If the law were effective, it would unquestionably deprive the community of the services of many of our past and present public men. Certainly many of the old luminaries would never have shone in the British Legislature. Burke, Pitt, Fox, and Sheridan, in my early days, were always notoriously fictitiously qualified. The law has been nearly inoperative as an exclusion. Some few " conscientious " men have refused to enter the House of Commons on a fraudulent qualification; perhaps a few men of considerable talent have been unable to obtain a fictitious qualification; of the latter there is known only one instance; but he would, if qualified, have represented one of the largest towns in England . . . To be brief, and being at the end of my paper, the law is a disgrace to the statute book, and ought to be burned by the common hangman.[77]

Having shown the Qualification Act to be easily evaded, Sir William advocated the repeal of property qualifications for membership in the House of Commons. With the repeal of the act, Molesworth saw a return to the ancient constitutional principles of freedom for the electors in the choice of their representatives. Molesworth believed the only qualifications needed for membership in the House of Commons were ability and willingness to perform the duties of a legislator. Property could never be a test of the intelligence and knowledge of an individual; and the possession of large landed estates might in some

75 *Ibid.*, 36: 525-526.
76 *Ibid.*, 36: 526.
77 *Ibid.*, 36: 526-528.

cases retard rather than develop the intellectual growth of the individual. Molesworth, himself the owner of large estates, opposed the old theory that men of property had stakes in the country, and that men of great property were never biased by motives springing from their own pecuniary needs. He thought that the poor man was more interested in good laws and government than was the rich; and he pointed out that bad laws were injurious to both rich and poor alike.[78] Mr. Leader seconded Molesworth's motion; and in a very long speech, he restated that the object of the Qualification Act of 1710 had been to enlarge and confirm the power of the landed group at the expense of the moneyed group, and that perhaps there had been at that time a sincere desire on the part of some of the members of parliament to uphold the popular or country party against the corrupting influence of the court. He also pointed out that Scotland was exempt from the operation of the act, and yet her representatives were outstanding men.[79] He described the Qualification Act as a legal cobweb through which small flies as well as large ones could break with perfect ease. He mentioned the fact that Ireland had lost two of her representatives in the present session because of the existing laws. He recommended the repeal of the Qualification Act because it was bad in principle, contrary to the ancient constitution, easily evaded, and because it had a bad moral effect on the constituencies.[80]

The seconding of Molesworth's motion was followed by a lengthy debate in the House of Commons. The arguments in favor of the abolition of the Qualification Act, so ably presented by Molesworth and Leader, were warmly supported by many members of the House. One member stated that it was his firm conviction that a property qualification of any description would be evaded by the representatives of the voters. But the supporters of the existing Qualification Act vehemently denounced

78 *Ibid.*, 36: 528-530.
79 *Ibid.*, 36: 536-538.
80 *Ibid.*, 36: 538.

Sir William's motion as an attempt to weaken the most respectable class in the nation—the country gentlemen of England. Again the opinion held by many Englishmen was stated: representatives of the people should have something equivalent to a stake in the country. For this reason, the repeal of the Act was opposed, because it would open the House of Commons to landless men who would be called upon to legislate for property in which they had no interest.[81]

A few of the members were willing to compromise on the question, and they suggested that property other than landed property should be used as a qualification for membership in the House of Commons.[82] In support of this argument, a member described the case of Mr. Fairley,[83] who at the time of his election had had personal property to the amount of £100,000, but not enough land for a legal qualification. After his election he purchased the required amount of land, but the Select Committee decided the purchase was made too late, and he was, therefore, disqualified.[84] The suggestion that property other than landed property should be used as a qualification did not meet Hume's approval. He remarked that a pecuniary qualification would tend to limit the choice of the electors. Like Molesworth and others, Hume recommended the complete abolition of property qualifications of members of the House of Commons.[85] During the discussion, one member raised an interesting point by showing that if the property qualifications for representatives of the House were abolished, there would be objections to property qualifications for electors. For that reason he vigorously denounced the proposed repeal as the first step toward universal suffrage.[86] Lord John Russell, though he was not certain that

81 *Ibid.*, 36: 539.

82 *Ibid.*, 36: 541-543.

83 According to parliamentary records the name was Fairlie. *J. H. C.*, LXXIV, 20-21, 127.

84 Hansard, *op. cit.*, 36: 542-543.

85 *Ibid.*, 36: 544-545.

86 *Ibid.*, 36: 545.

evil would follow from the complete abolition of the Qualification Act, favored an amendment of the existing law. He thought that men possessed of personal property, as well as those of landed property, should be allowed to serve as representatives.[87] Lord John had many supporters in the House of Commons; and Charles Buller urged Sir William Molesworth to follow Lord John's recommendation, and to change his motion accordingly.[88] In spite of the suggestion made by Buller and supported by many members of the House, the original motion for leave to bring in a bill to abolish property qualifications was put. One hundred and four members of the House voted in favor of Molesworth's motion, but one hundred and thirty-three members, including Lord John Russell and his friends, voted against the motion. Molesworth's valiant struggle to abolish property qualifications for membership in the House of Commons was lost by a mere twenty-nine votes.[89]

The reaction of the general public to Sir William Molesworth's defeat in the Commons varied. The conservative attitude of the country was ably stated by *The Times* of February 16, 1837. That paper supported the opinion that Sir William's motion was the first step toward universal suffrage; and because Sir William had not stated that as the ulterior motive behind his proposal, *The Times* accused him of insincerity. It added that Sir William's plan would certainly have admitted artisans to the House of Commons; and it severely condemned Lord John Russell for his shuffling indecisiveness regarding the motion.[90]

Molesworth's defeat in the Commons was accepted by the reformers as a challenge to increase their efforts to keep their political demands before the public. No paper was more important in carrying out this purpose than *The National Reformer*.

87 *Ibid.*, 36: 548-549.
88 *Ibid.*, 36: 549.
89 *Ibid.*, 36: 552. *J. H. C.*, XCII, 46.
90 *The Times*, February 16, 1837.

Its editor, James Bronterre O'Brien, was a talented and radical writer. O'Brien, a young Irishman in his early thirties, and a friend of Hume and other radicals, used his talented pen to expound the six points of the Chartists. In the February 11, 1837, issue of his paper, he attacked the Qualification Act, and pointed out to his readers that if property qualifications of members of the House were abolished, any man could be a member of the House of Commons.[91] After Molesworth's defeat in the Commons, O'Brien, in the February 18 issue of his paper, openly attacked the Conservative members of the House, of whom Peel was the leader. He questioned whether Peel and his followers, being themselves men of property, were qualified to legislate for the people of Great Britain. He thought that on the contrary, their property gave them direct cause for " crushing labor into the dust." Since the true purpose of a representative body was to give all interests a voice in their procedure, he questioned whether this end could be obtained when only men of property legislated for the entire nation. Such a body would protect the interests of property without a doubt, but what of the other interests of the country?[92]

While its leaders kept in touch with the people by means of speeches and literature, the London Working Men's Association made careful plans for a public meeting to be held at the Crown and Anchor Tavern on February 28, 1837. At that famous meeting, crowded but orderly, a petition was drawn up and signed by three thousand people. In it they sought universal suffrage, annual parliaments, secret ballot, equal representation, salaries for members of parliament, and the abolition of property qualifications for members of the House of Commons. This petition was later entrusted to Roebuck, a radical member of the Commons, for presentation to parliament.[93] The interest shown by many of the English people in the Crown and Anchor Tavern

91 Bronterre O'Brien's *National Reformer*, February 11, 1837.

92 *Ibid.*, February 18, 1837.

93 Tawney, R. H., *op. cit.*, I, 104-105.

meeting did not languish; in the spring of 1837, many large public meetings were held, and Working Men's Associations were organized in various parts of England.[94]

Undoubtedly this interest in and agitation for the six points induced Henry Warburton to take up the struggle which Molesworth had abandoned. Henry Warburton's part in the Reform Movement of the thirties was not as colorful as that of Lovett, Hetherington, O'Brien, and other outstanding leaders. Perhaps, because he was overshadowed by contemporaries, Warburton does not figure greatly in the writings of the period. The son of a lumber merchant, Warburton received his education at Eton and at Cambridge. Evidently he was of a studious nature, for at Cambridge his search for knowledge earned him the title " scholar and man of science." Upon the completion of his education, he entered the field of business, which he left in 1826 to follow a parliamentary career. In that year, he was returned for the Borough of Bridport, and he continued to be a representative for the next decade. While a member of the House of Commons, he was on friendly terms with Buller, Grote, Hume, Molesworth, and other leading radicals of the day. Although he gave his support to all reform measures, his particular field of interest was medicine. He sponsored many medical measures in the House of Commons, and his work earned him the praise of the medical profession. Such was the man who proposed to do something about the Qualification Act.[95]

On April 6, 1837, Mr. Warburton moved for leave to bring in a bill to alter the property qualifications for members of parliament. He would much prefer to see the property qualifications abolished altogether; but since there was little chance of such a motion's being carried, he proposed to amend the existing Qualification Act in the following manner. He proposed to allow the substitution of personal property for landed property as a qualification for members of parliament. Such a change

94 *Ibid.*, I, 113. Maccoby, S., *op. cit.*, p. 163.
95 *The Dictionary of National Biography.*

would make possible the substitution of leasehold property or any other form of property, such as money in the funds or a valuable collection of pictures, for landed property as a qualification for a seat in the House of Commons.[96] He thought the Commons would agree to his proposal, since the same principle had been acknowledged by the Reform Act of 1832, which permitted a man holding leasehold property of a certain value to vote. More recently, men other than landed property owners had been given the right to sit on juries. If changes had been made in these cases, Warburton saw no reason why the Qualification Act could not be amended. The attitude of the members of the House of Commons towards Warburton's proposal varied. One group favored no change whatsoever in the existing Qualification Act, while another group threw its support to Warburton. Roebuck and his friends denounced any future amendment of the Qualification Act for they were not in sympathy with property qualifications of any kind for members of the House of Commons.[97] Some members of the House had grave doubts concerning the practicability of Warburton's proposal. Personal property such as that described by Warburton could be borrowed and transferred from hand to hand. The problem of bona-fide qualifications and evasion would remain unsolved under such a plan.[98] These men were assured that any amendment to the Qualification Act would be vigorously enforced. Roebuck's friend, Mr. Leader, was undecided. He admitted that the proposed amendment would open the House of Commons to owners of personal property, and considered that a good thing; but he likewise supported Roebuck's contention that no qualification, except the confidence of the electors in their representatives, should be required of members of the House of Commons.[99] Following the debate, which was not

96 Hansard, op. cit., 37 : 802-805.
97 Ibid., 37 : 805-806.
98 Ibid., 37 : 806-807.
99 Ibid., 37 : 808.

very long, leave was granted to Mr. Warburton and Mr. Wallace to bring in a bill to amend the laws relating to the qualifications of members of the House of Commons.[100]

This action of the House of Commons, considered by some people as a step in the right direction, a step which might ultimately lead to the complete abolition of property qualifications for membership in the House of Commons, had no effect on the demands and plans of the London Working Men's Association. On May 31, 1837, a meeting was called to ascertain " how far Members of Parliament were prepared to make exertions for carrying those principles [the six points of the petition] into practice." [101] Hume, O'Connell, Leader, and a few other radical members of the House attended the meeting; and it was soon apparent that the parliamentary members were at odds on some of the political demands of the petition. This lack of unity on the part of the radical members caused Lovett to charge that they professed democratic opinions in order to gain the support of the people, but once in the House of Commons, they forgot to take any step to further the cause of democracy.[102] Such bickering could lead nowhere, and the meeting was adjourned. A week later, on June 7, 1837, a similar meeting was held, and several resolutions were adopted. One of them read:

We agree to support and vote for a Bill or Bills to be brought into the House of Commons, embodying the principles of universal suffrage, equal representation, free selection of representatives without reference to property, the ballot, and short parliaments of fixed duration, the limit not to exceed three years.[103]

To carry this aim into effect, another resolution was adopted requiring that a committee of twelve persons be appointed to

100 *J. H. C.*, XCII, 233.
101 Tawney, R. H., *op. cit.*, I, 114.
102 *Ibid.*, I, 114-115.
103 *Ibid.*, I, 116.

draw up a bill or bills embodying these general principles.[104] But before this able committee could acomplish anything, William IV died on June 20, 1837.

The death of the sovereign brought about the dissolution of parliament; and a general election confronted the people of Great Britain. Nor did the London Working Men's Association fail to see the potential value of a general election for them. In the *Address to Reformers on the forthcoming Elections,* the organization, in a carefully worded account, reviewed the political situation of the English people since the passage of the Reform Act of 1832, and the complete history of the London Working Men's Association. They urged the electors of the country to return to the House of Commons members who would support their principles.[105] Copies of the address were circulated throughout the country; and during the election, it was not unusual for parliamentary candidates to state their opinions on property qualifications for members of the Commons, as well as on various other questions.[106] But in spite of the untiring efforts of the radicals and their organizations, the general election of 1837 failed to return many of their outstanding leaders to the House. Roebuck, Thompson, Ewart, and Crawford lost their seats, and superficially, it seemed that the radical cause had been successfully crushed.[107] An analysis of the membership of the new House, however, would have indicated that it contained almost as many radical members as there had been in the preceding one.[108]

104 *Ibid.,* I, 117. The members of the committee were:

D. O'Connell	Col. Thompson	J. Watson
J. A. Roebuck	W. S. Crawford	R. Moore
J. T. Leader	H. Hetherington	W. Lovett
C. Hindley	J. Cleave	H. Vincent

105 *Ibid.,* I, 118-124.

106 Morley, J., *op. cit.,* p. 78.

107 Fawcett, Mrs. *op. cit.,* pp. 133-134.

108 Harris, W., *op. cit.,* p. 286. Thomas J. A., *op. cit.,* p. 7, gives the following number of members holding radical ideas and opinions. 1832-64; 1835-66; 1837-55.

Queen Victoria's first parliament met on November 15, 1837. The customary formalities occupied the first days, and then the House of Commons turned to the problem of contested elections. On November 21, 1837, Jonathan Robinson and John Cumberland petitioned the House, claiming that in the recent election, Sir Samuel Whalley had been one of the members returned for the Borough of Marylebone. The petitioners complained that qualified voters had not been permitted to cast their votes; and they concluded with the more serious charge that Sir Samuel was not properly qualified in respect to land for holding a seat in the House of Commons.[109] The parliamentary career of Sir Samuel Whalley had been an interesting one. Following his election in 1833, a petition had been presented to the House of Commons questioning his landed qualifications. His friend, Thomas Murphy, a radical utterly opposed to landed qualifications for members of the House, was a member of the Select Committee which had been called upon to decide the case. It was probably through his influence that the case was dropped, and Sir Samuel kept his seat in the House of Commons. Now in the election of 1837, Whalley was again returned by the voters of Marylebone, and once again his election was contested. This time he was not so fortunate; the Select Committee appointed by the House of Commons included several Conservative members. When Whalley admitted to the committee that he did not possess a landed estate as required by law, his seat was declared vacant.[110] *The Morning Herald* of February 22, 1838, made the following comment on Whalley's landed qualification:

Sir Samuel Whalley swore to a qualification of £300 per annum in freehold property; the petitioners were prepared with evidence beyond dispute (as we are assured), that he possessed only a freehold of £5 per annum in London, and one of £75 per annum in

109 *J. H. C.*, XCIII, 29-30.

110 Brooke, J. W., *The Democrats of Marylebone* (London, 1839), pp. 169-170. *J. H. C.*, XCIII, 295.

Birmingham, and the rest of the property on which he grounded his qualification was a leasehold in London, yielding rents to the extent of about £130 per annum, which with the property in Birmingham, would give him an income of little more than £200 per annum leaving a deficiency, without reference to legal questions, of nearly £100 upon his actual income. In addition, however, to these facts, the leasehold property is charged with a mortgage of £4000, and an annuity of £200 per annum. This property was acquired, it was stated, by the marriage of Sir Samuel with Amelia Smith, chére amie of the late Sir Jonathan Miles, proprietor of the private madhouse at Hoxton. Part of the qualification was building land at Birmingham, the extent of which is three yards eight inches wide by thirteen yards deep. The whole is now covered with a coal shed, and if applied to building purposes, would admit the erection of a single stall stable. Such is the qualification, which Sir Samuel Whalley at a meeting of his constituents, most solemnly pledged his honour, was amply sufficient to entitle him to sit in Parliament.[111]

Although Whalley was not the only member of the 1837 House of Commons against whom charges were brought for evasion of the Qualification Act, he was the only member of that session to lose his seat solely because he lacked adequate landed qualifications. In the cases of James Patrick Somers, Peter Borthwick,[112] William Wilberforce,[113] and James Gibson,[114] corruption and bribery as well as lack of proper landed qualifications, were the basis upon which their elections were declared null and void.

With preliminary matters out of the way, the House of Commons settled down to business; and on December 21, 1837, leave was granted to Warburton and Hume to bring in a bill to amend the Qualification Act.[115] Warburton was ready with just

111 Brooke, J. W., *op. cit.*, pp. 170-171.

112 *J. H. C.*, XCIII, 52-53, 374, Borough of Evesham.

113 *Ibid.*, XCIII, 68-70, 489, Borough of Kingston-upon-Hull.

114 *Ibid.*, XCIII, 93-97, 342, Borough of Belfast.

115 *Ibid.*, XCIII, 221, 222.

such a bill, for he had been working on it since the spring of 1837. In introducing the measure, he stated that his main purpose was to extend to personal property a quality hitherto reserved for landed property: that of serving as a qualification for membership in the House of Commons. On February 8, 1838, Warburton's measure was severely attacked because it provided that future representatives should be qualified in landed property, or personal estates or " effects of any nature or kind whatsoever." The wording of the bill caused Sir Edward Sugden to request a statement of Her Majesty's government regarding the measure, the purpose of which, it seemed to him, was to confer upon something which was not a qualification, the character of a qualification. He argued that a person of property gave some assurance to his constituency that he would be faithful in the discharge of his duties. If personal property were substituted for landed property, the question of true valuation would arise. Suppose a man used the furnishings of his own home for a qualification; who would evaluate the furniture? [116] Warburton did not answer Sir Edward's question, but he restated his reasons for proposing such an amendment. He pointed out that when the Great Reform Bill was being debated in the House a minister of the Crown, Lord Althorp, said:

that it was never intended that the statutes regulating the qualification, should bear a stringent construction or be rigidly adhered to; that the only object was to secure the return of Members who would be respectable in station and character; that the object was not that they should actually possess the qualification required, but that they should be of a sufficient degree of respectability.[117]

Warburton added that the present session of the House of Commons had been presented with no less than eighteen petitions claiming that returned representatives were not properly qualified.[118] A member, in a critical mood, said that he had

116 Hansard, *op. cit.*, 40: 922-923.
117 *Ibid.*, 40: 923.
118 *Ibid.*, 40: 923.

never heard Lord Althorp utter the statement mentioned by Warburton, and while the proposed amendment was an improvement, it nevertheless would be conducive to acts of fraud.[119] Colonel Sibthorp objected to the measure which, he said, would allow any man who possessed a common stallion to sit in the House of Commons. He added, moreover, that he would like to see the required qualification trebled and not decreased.[120]

Sir Robert Inglis maintained that the best qualification possible was land: freehold, copyhold, or leasehold, and the next best qualification was money in the funds.[121] Lord John Russell, in answering one of the members, said that he did not think that the government need state its attitude on the bill, since it was merely a matter of general legislation which confronted the House of Commons. Although he considered the issue of little importance, he said he would, however, give his consent to the proposed change since it was supported by public opinion. He doubted whether any great changes would result from the adoption of such a measure, he added, as he saw no difference between English members of the House, who were forced to meet the requirements of the Qualification Act, and the Scottish and university members, who were exempt from the operation of the law. Any landed qualification for a borough representative seemed to him to be adverse to the ancient principles of the constitution. Since he thought a wealthy banker, although he possessed no landed estate, might be capable of being a worthy member of the House of Commons, he recommended that Warburton's bill be adopted.[122] Sir Robert Peel agreed with those who held the existing qualifications unsatisfactory, for although land was a proper qualification, he felt it ought not to be the only qualification. He would have the qualification of a

119 *Ibid.*, 40: 924-925.
120 *Ibid.*, 40: 925.
121 *Ibid.*, 40: 925.
122 *Ibid.*, 40: 926-927.

member of the House of Commons as simple as possible, requiring only that all parliamentary members be possessed of a certain amount of real or personal property.[123] In answering his colleagues, Warburton opposed the extension of the qualification to funded property, and recommended that the county qualification be the same as that of the borough.[124] This last proposal was vehemently opposed by Sir Robert Peel.[125]

During the month of February, 1838, while the measure was before the House of Commons, petitions were sent to the legislature praying that secret ballot and universal suffrage be adopted, and that property qualifications for members of the House of Commons be dispensed with. These petitions came from Colchester, Wakefield, the Chairman of the Ipswich Working Men's Association, members of the Braintree and Bocking Working Men's Association, Abernathy, Carshalton, and from others.[126] Meanwhile, Warburton's measure continued its journey through the legislative bodies. Warburton found it impossible to carry his original proposal to reduce the qualification of a county member to £300 per annum. The measure, which received the approval of the Queen on July 27, 1838,[127] provided that a county representative was to possess a landed or personal estate of any nature whatsoever of the yearly value of £600, while the borough representative was to meet similar requirements to the amount of £300 per annum. The other provisions of the Qualification Act regarding excluded classes and oaths remained the same. One change, however, was necessary —henceforth the elected member would hand to the Clerk, while the House was in session, a paper signed by himself, containing a statement of his real or personal property.[128]

123 *Ibid.*, 40 : 927-928.

124 *Ibid.*, 40 : 929.

125 *Ibid.*, 40 : 929.

126 *J. H. C.*, XCIII, 279.

127 *Ibid.*, XCIII, 757.

128 1 & 2 Vict., c. 48.

Warburton might well have been proud of his success, for he had been able to secure the amendment of an act which had been on the statute book of the kingdom for over one hundred years; but curiously enough, his achievement received little notice at that time. The absence of comments, from friend and foe alike, might imply that the amendment was accepted by the people because a change in conditions had necessitated it, or because the amendment would ultimately lead to complete abolition of property qualifications for members of the Commons. Very likely, however, neither conclusion is the correct one; for the Qualification Act was of secondary importance in comparison with other more pressing problems of the day, which included the Canadian problem, the Irish tithes question, the agitation of the people over the Corn Laws, and the People's Charter.

The accession of Victoria to the throne of Great Britain did not have much effect on the plans and activities of the London Working Men's Association. The members regarded her as a young and inexperienced woman, whose policies would be formed and executed by conservative Whig ministers, and saw in her little hope for the fulfillment of their six political demands. Following the dissolution of William IV's parliament, Roebuck and Lovett had been designated by the organization to draw up a bill based on the provisions of the petition which had been accepted at the Crown and Anchor Tavern on February 28, 1837. Other duties called Roebuck; and Lovett, therefore, aided by Francis Place and a few others, was mainly responsible for the bill.[129] After the bill had been approved by the organization, and while Warburton's measure was being considered in parliament, Lovett's bill was published on May 8, 1838, and became known in history as the People's Charter.[130] On the question of qualification for membership in the House of Commons, the Charter stated:

129 Maccoby, S., *op. cit.*, pp. 166-169. Tawney, R. H., *op. cit.*, I, 168-169.
130 *Ibid.*, I, 176.

That no other qualification shall be required than the choice of the electors . . . [131]

The People's Charter was enthusiastically received by the working people and by the reform associations throughout the country. One of these organizations, the Birmingham Political Union, had been largely responsible for the adoption of the Reform Act of 1832. Following the passage of that act, the Birmingham Political Union had declined in power, and had been finally dissolved in 1834. Two years later, a Reform Association had been established, and in 1837, the name of Birmingham Political Union had been restored. At first that body had been more interested in the demand of universal suffrage, but in 1837, it gave its support to the political demands of the London Working Men's Association, and henceforth both organizations worked for the same principles.[132] These organizations were responsible for the great public demonstrations which were held in the summer and fall of 1838. At first the speakers of the meetings merely expounded the principles of the Charter; but gradually other leaders, such as O'Connor, Harney, Stephens, and Vincent, began to attack the government, and to advocate the use of physical force in obtaining their demands. The perturbed state of the country, evidenced in the Chartist demonstrations and the Anti-Corn Law agitation, led the government to take action; and torch-light meetings were declared illegal. Violations of the proclamation resulted in the arrest of Stephens and many others.[133]

The advent of the new year, 1839, did not put an end to the unrest in England. Chartist and Anti-Corn Law agitation continued unabated, and the anxiety of the British government increased daily. The National Petition, embodying the demands of the workers, was presented to the House of Commons on

131 *Ibid.*, II, 469.

132 Maccoby, S., *op. cit.*, pp. 169-170. Hovell, M., *The Chartist Movement* (London, 1918), pp. 99-101.

133 Rosenblatt, F. F., *op. cit.*, pp. 141-152.

July 14, 1839; [134] but the House refused to consider the prayer of over one million people. By that time Chartist had become a household word; and the organization's political demands were criticized favorably and adversely by different groups of the populace. The political demands of the Chartists were vigorously supported by the Kettering Radical Association. In considering the question of property qualifications of members of the House, that organization in its pamphlets pointed out that when a doctor or lawyer was needed, neither was chosen on the basis of the wealth he possessed. Skill and knowledge were the deciding factors. Why then was this not true of the law-makers of the country? The circle from which representatives were chosen was comparatively small, and the best men were more often than not excluded from it. For this reason, the laws of the kingdom were " slovenly " enacted, and called for frequent amendments. The program of the government was carried on in opposition to the indisputable principles of political economy, and contrary to the dictates of common sense.[135] Not only would the abolition of property qualifications of members of the Commons give the constituencies freedom of choice in electing their representatives, but the return of working men to the House would result in the passage of legislation for their benefit. Until the qualifications for membership in the House were changed, the laws of Great Britain would be against the workers of the nation.[136] So the Kettering Radical Association marshalled its arguments for reform. In contrast to this opinion, there was the perennially offered theory expressed again in *A Few Words to the Chartists,* that persons of property were more likely to protect the rights of property owners since in so doing they were also protecting their own rights. A representative who had no property was very likely to use his vote to advance his own

134 Hansard, *op. cit.,* 48: 222.

135 *Our Rights: or The Just Claims of the Working Classes,* issued by the Kettering Radical Association (London, 1839), p. 14.

136 *Ibid.,* pp. 14-15.

interests rather than those of the entire nation.[137] These pamphlets, however, had no effect on the government, which did not propose to change its policy in regard to the property qualifications for the House. In 1838, the British government had supported Warburton's measure, and had allowed personal property to be substituted for landed property as a qualification for membership in the Commons. But it was not yet ready to take the step leading to the complete abolition of the existing qualifications for membership. While it was powerless to eradicate the political demands of the Chartists from the minds of the people, it could and did remove many of their leaders; and the closing months of the Reforming Thirties saw the arrest of Frost and several other radical leaders.

137 *A Few Words to the Chartists* (London, 1839), pp. 13-14.

CHAPTER VI

THE ABOLITION OF THE QUALI-
FICATION ACTS

THE opening year of the new decade, 1840, held for the reformers very little promise of the fulfillment of their political
demands. The late thirties had witnessed not only the rejection
of the National Petition by the House of Commons, but also
the imprisonment of many of the Chartist leaders. These events,
however, had not discouraged the Chartists; and on July 25,
1840, Lovett and other imprisoned leaders were released to
continue the work which their arrest had interrupted.[1] It soon
became apparent that a lack of unity of purpose was militating
against the Chartists' achievement of the desired parliamentary
reforms. Lovett, Hetherington, Cleave, Rogers, Mitchell, and
others, had become interested in a new project, the National
Association of the United Kingdom for Promoting the Political and Social Improvement of the People.[2] The main purpose
of this organization was to promote educational facilities for
the people.[3] This new project was strongly opposed by the
other Chartists, and was denounced particularly by O'Connor
in his paper, the *Northern Star,* because it opposed his objec-
tives: the National Charter Association and a land scheme.[4]
This dissension among the Chartist leaders was not the sole
factor which weakened the likelihood of the movement's achiev-
ing parliamentary reforms for the people. Simultaneously, the
rapidly growing absorption of the workers in the Anti-Corn
Law movement diverted their interest from the question of
parliamentary reform. Anti-Corn Law agitation had revived in
Manchester in 1838, and one year later the Anti-Corn Law

1 Tawney, R. H., *op. cit.,* II, 247.

2 *Ibid.,* p. 250.

3 *Ibid.,* pp. 253-255.

4 *Ibid.,* pp. 255-256. Maccoby, S., *op. cit.,* pp. 214-216.

League had been formed. Although Villiers had worked incessantly in the House of Commons for the repeal of the Corn Laws, it was as the result of the interest and work of Richard Cobden and John Bright that the movement suddenly gained in popularity. The Anti-Corn Law movement attracted many members of the Chartist Movement; and so the latter lost to the former not only a great deal of the popular interest, but also some of its members. It is unfortunate that the two movements were not able to unite, for then the forties would very likely have seen not only the repeal of the Corn Laws, but also the adoption of some of the political demands of the Chartists.

Although dissension among the Chartists continued, the political demands of the People's Charter came to the foreground again in the general election of 1841. In that election, under the influence of the Chartist leaders and their publications, many of the parliamentary candidates pledged themselves to work for the attainment of the six points of the charter. One of these candidates was Peter McDouall, and on the question of property qualifications for membership in the House of Commons he said:

I am an advocate for the Abolition of all Property Qualifications —because I believe that natural ability is superior to artificial wealth, and the treasures of genius more valuable than the gold of the gambler. The gifts of nature were designed for the many, the up-turnings of chance for the benefit of the few. That House of Commons will do the most good which contains a greater amount of brain than bricks, and more patriotism than purses; therefore, as we choose an architect, a general, and a seaman, by testing their qualifications, let us also elect that man as representative who is best endowed for the office of a legislator.[5]

In spite of all efforts to the contrary, the election of 1841 failed to restore to the Commons two outstanding reformers, Grote and Hume. Fortunately, however, the cause of the people was still supported in the election of Roebuck and Milner Gibson.

5 McDouall, P., *Chartist and Republican Journal*, July 10, 1841, p. 114.

The reformers in the House were immediately aware of the difficulties that confronted them,[6] for the government was in the hands of Sir Robert Peel, who responded to general ideas only when those ideas had been accepted by the average person. He would not accept any idea that was endorsed by only the outstanding intellects or philanthropists.[7] But the reformers were not totally discouraged by the great odds against them; and on September 7, 1841, one of their members introduced four resolutions relating to the qualifications of members of the House of Commons. The resolutions were very similar to the Standing Orders which had been adopted by the House in 1717; but the proposed resolutions concerned personal property and reduced the period of time in which petitioners or sitting members were required to submit to the Clerk of the House their qualifications in writing.[8] Mr. Buller, friend of Durham and Molesworth, thought it unwise to consider such an important question in the absence of so many members;[9] and another member of the House not only agreed with Buller, but also made the suggestion that the subject be postponed.[10] This suggestion was adopted, but postponement was the death knell of the resolutions, for never again were they presented to the Commons.

The attention of the members of the House then turned to the more important financial problem which confronted the nation. The war with China, and a series of bad harvests, had resulted in a huge deficit which Peel now proposed to remove. His revival of the income tax, and the alterations in the tariff, although bitterly opposed by many, raised the revenue which Great Britain needed to carry on her projects. Besides the financial policies of Peel, the question of the employment of

6 Thomas, J. A., *op. cit.*, According to Thomas there were only 42 radicals in the House of Commons in 1841, p. 7.

7 Woodward, E. L., *op. cit.*, p. 105.

8 Hansard, *op. cit.*, 59: 501.

9 *Ibid.*, 59: 502.

10 *Ibid.*, 59: 502.

women and children in mines and factories occupied the attention of parliament. The appalling working conditions of women and children as described by Lord Ashley in parliament, resulted in the passage of some legislation in their behalf. These measures, though important, brought very little relief to the distressed people of the kingdom.

In 1842, the liberal organizations in England were particularly active in demanding parliamentary reforms for the people. On April 21, 1842, Mr. Sharman Crawford, radical member of parliament for Rochdale and an active Chartist, moved that the House of Commons consider the laws relating to the representatives of the people, " with a view of giving to every portion of the community a full, fair, and free representation in the Commons' House of Parliament." [11] In a long speech, Crawford discussed the six points of the People's Charter, the adoption of which he felt would bring contentment to the people. On the question of property qualifications for members of the House, he compared the English representatives with the Scottish representatives, and doubted whether the latter, without qualifications, were in any way unfit or inferior to the former. He pleaded that the laws be made consistent. Moreover, he deplored the fact that the door of the House of Commons was shut to members returned by the choice of the voters, when the door of the House of Lords was open without reserve to men selected by the Crown. Why should a poor but meritorious servant of the people be banned from the House of Commons? The Crown, in appointing officials, was not hampered by property qualifications; and neither should the people be hampered in their choice by the Qualification Acts.[12] Crawford's speech was a very long and comprehensive one, embracing all six points of the Charter; and while some members of the House gave their opinion on all six points, others voiced their support or opposition to only some of them. Of the latter, Mr. Bowring, one of the philosophical radicals, a disciple of Bentham, strongly

11 Hansard, *op. cit.*, 62: 921.

12 *Ibid.*, 62: 916.

supported the abolition of property qualifications. He expressed a high opinion of the ability of the Scottish representatives, and he further argued that wealth changed daily. A man could be poor one day, and wealthy the next. Poverty should not exclude a man from membership in the House of Commons, because other characteristics—talent, ability, knowledge, and character —should be considered for membership in that body. Yet wealth, and wealth alone, he said, was regarded as the test of a man's senatorial capabilities.[13] Crawford and Bowring were ably supported by their friends. One said that he had always supported any attempt to abolish property qualifications, and that he rejected the theory that the elimination of property qualifications would introduce into the Commons men without stakes in the country. He added that he thought the existing property qualifications for membership in the House were " very little better than a fraud." [14] The famous Irish member, Daniel O'Connell, although more interested in the demand for triennial parliaments, was quick to point out that Ireland, before 1801, had had no property qualifications for membership in the Irish parliament; he also raised the question whether the United Kingdom should have property qualifications for some members of the House and not for others.[15] Another member was very certain that with or without property qualifications, members of the House of Commons would continue to be qualified in landed or personal property.[16] Villiers, Cobden, and Roebuck spoke for the motion; but Sir Robert Peel and his followers advised delay and pointed out that other problems were more pressing. When the vote was taken, Crawford's motion was defeated by two hundred and twenty-six votes to sixty-seven.[17]

13 *Ibid.*, 62 : 931.
14 *Ibid.*, 62 : 931.
15 *Ibid.*, 62 : 942.
16 *Ibid.*, 62 : 948.
17 *Ibid.*, 62 : 982.

The defeat, however, did not quench the spirit of the reformers; and on May 2, 1842, Mr. Duncombe, an aristocrat by nature but ever on the side of the people,[18] presented to the House of Commons a petition with three million signatures, praying that the six points of the People's Charter be adopted by the legislature. The petition described at great length the social, economic, and political conditions which necessitated reforms, and advocated the disestablishment of the Anglican Church in Ireland, and the repeal of the Act of Union of 1801. On the following day, May 3, 1842, Duncombe took up the demands as stated in the petition, and read letters describing the poor economic conditions existing in the country. These conditions, the people believed, could be remedied by the adoption of the six points of the Charter.[19] Mr. Leader and Mr. Bowring were heartily in sympathy with the pleas of the petitioners. Mr. Bowring repeated his previously stated opinion on the Qualification Act, which allowed only wealthy men to be members of the House of Commons. On this question, and on all others, he implored the House to listen to the prayer of the people.[20] Thomas Babington Macaulay, parliamentary orator of note, vigorously opposed the idea of universal suffrage, but he did support the abolition of property qualifications for membership in the House. He considered it absurd that some members had to have property qualifications, while others were not affected by the operation of the acts. His argument was that the qualifications should apply to all or to none. He added that property qualifications were neither part of the constitution, nor the result of the English Revolution, and that they should be abolished. The main reason for adopting the Qualification Act in 1710, he said, had been to exclude Protestants from the throne of England.[21] Unfortunately, the petition included too many political reforms. The proposed repeal of the Act of Union

18 Linton, W. J., *op. cit.*, pp. 55-56. Maccoby, S., *op. cit.*, pp. 231-232.
19 Hansard, *op. cit.*, 63 : 21-32.
20 *Ibid.*, 63 : 37-38.
21 *Ibid.*, 63 : 45.

caused added opposition; and it was not surprising that only forty-nine members of the House of Commons supported the adoption of the petition while two hundred and eighty-seven followed Russell in opposing it.[22]

Parliament was prorogued on August 12, 1842, not to meet again until February, 1843. The defeat of the National Petition of 1842 was, of course, not agreeably received by the workers of England; and during the long recess, their suffering, which seemed to increase rather than diminish, expressed itself in the form of strikes, public meetings, and innumerable pamphlets. Wage reductions and the ineffectiveness of the measures which the government had so recently adopted caused many strikes in the summer of 1842. The Chartists, influenced by the industrial unrest at Wolverhampton, Ashton, Manchester, and other large factory towns,[23] held huge public meetings at which the six demands of the People's Charter were advocated as the cure for all the causes of discontent. The membership of the National Charter Association increased rapidly. There were over forty thousand names on its books, and its county and district branches were scattered throughout the country.[24] Chartist lecturers were active, and their pamphlets demanded government action. Mr. Spencer, one of their members, writing in 1842, advocated universal suffrage, secret ballot, and the abolition of property qualifications for members of the House of Commons. On the last issue he said:

And whereas the requiring that a Member of Parliament must possess a certain amount of property is founded on distrust, implying that the people would elect persons who are unworthy of the honour, while in fact it has frequently operated to the admission into Parliament of wealthy ignorance and gambling poverty; and whereas the basest of men are sometimes rich, and have not un-

22 *Ibid.*, 63 : 88.

23 Gammage, R. G., *History of the Chartist Movement, 1837-1854* (London, 1894), pp. 217-225. Maccoby, S., *op. cit.*, pp. 236-241.

24 Gammage, R. G., *op. cit.*, p. 213.

frequently acquired their riches by their baseness, whilst the wisest and best men are sometimes not rich; therefore it is necessary to destroy all technical qualifications, and to leave the people to select, without any restriction, the men whom they deem most competent to act in their name.[25]

But the strikes, riots, demonstrations, and pamphlets were to no avail. Gradually the strikers returned to their work, and many of the Chartists were arrested and imprisoned. But the imprisonment of some of their leaders did not prevent the Chartists from participating in a conference held in late December of the year 1842. This consisted of several hundreds of delegates who came together to consider the program of the Complete Suffrage Union and the Chartists. Although the delegates agreed on the six points of the Charter, they disagreed on the question of leadership and whether the document should be called the Bill of Rights or continue to be called the People's Charter. Lovett and his followers, of course, insisted on keeping the name, People's Charter; but many of the members of the Complete Suffrage Union would not agree; and thereafter the two movements followed their separate paths in working for parliamentary reforms.[26]

Poor economic conditions still existed in England when parliament met on February 2, 1843. The Queen's speech noted the plight of the manufacturing industries of the country, and the House of Commons spent much time in considering the distressed state of the nation. The growth in power of the Anti-Corn Law League and the unrest that existed among the workers of the nation, resulted in lengthy debates in the House on the Corn Laws. For this reason, there was very little opportunity for the radicals in the House to bring up the question of parliamentary reform. Indeed, for a time, the powerful Anti-Corn Law League, because of its able leadership and popular appeal, seemed to overshadow the Chartists, whose cause was weakened by constant clashes among their leaders. Yet the ques-

25 Spencer, T., *The People's Rights: and How to Get Them* (London, 1842), p. 14.

26 Gammage, R. G., *op. cit.*, pp. 241-245.

tion of parliamentary reform was not entirely neglected in the House. On May 18, 1843, Crawford asked leave " to bring in a bill to secure the full representation of the people, and to shorten the duration of Parliament." [27] His proposal included universal suffrage, annual parliaments, payment of the members of the House of Commons, secret ballot, and abolition of property qualifications for members of parliament. He argued that the rights of the people had been subverted by the lengthening of the duration of parliaments and by the adoption of the Qualification Acts. Mr. Crawford stated that no qualifications for membership in the House of Commons had been required in the early period of English history, and he urged the return to the old constitutional principle which had been violated by the Qualification Acts.[28] Mr. Crawford was supported by Mr. Ward, who pointed out that the absence of property qualifications for Scottish members had not worked disadvantageously. He approved of any step which would lead to the abolition of property qualifications, because under the existing laws it was impossible for working men to become members of parliament and he felt that the absence of their views, sentiments, and questions was a great loss to the Commons.[29] Peel and other members of the House did not approve of Crawford's motion, which included many political reforms; and leave to bring in the bill was refused by a vote of one hundred and one to thirty-two.[30] Crawford had again been unsuccessful in his attempt to gain parliamentary reforms for the people. The rest of the session was devoted to the educational problem.

Fortunately for the nation, the business cycle had changed, and it was in the midst of prosperity that parliament met on February 1, 1844. Indeed, prosperous times favored the people until the summer of 1845. With the return of prosperity, agitation in the country became less acute, although agitation for re-

27 Hansard, *op. cit.*, 69 : 500.
28 *Ibid.*, 69 : 506.
29 *Ibid.*, 69 : 512.
30 *Ibid.*, 69 : 529.

forms did not completely cease. On the contrary, the Anti-Corn Law League continued its activities, and the election of John Bright [31] gave them additional support in the House of Commons. The Anti-Corn Law compaign was unsuccessful in the House in 1844-1845 because other problems, especially the Bank Charter and Irish agitation, claimed the attention of the legislators. On the whole, the country was most interested in the financial policies of Sir Robert Peel. His problem of attempting to control periods of depression and boom by the expansion and contraction of credit and currency was an old one. Peel attempted to solve this problem by reforming the banking system of the kingdom. His comprehensive financial program and the comparatively quiet and prosperous state of the country afforded little opportunity for the parliamentary reformers or the Anti-Corn Law members to reintroduce their projects in the House of Commons.

But though the reformers were unsuccessful inside the House of Commons, the Chartists outside of the House never relaxed their efforts to keep alive the six political demands of the organization. In 1845, through the influence of Feargus O'Connor, the Chartist Land Cooperative Society was founded, the main purpose of which was " to show the working classes the value of land as a means of making them independent of the grinding capitalist." [32] While O'Connor's project received support from some of the Chartists, most of them continued to devote all their energy to the political demands of the organization. Meetings were held and pamphlets issued, upholding the six points as a panacea for all evils. In *An Address to the Chartists of the United Kingdom* issued by the National Association in 1845, the Chartists were urged to present a united front in working for their cause.[33] W. J. Fox, friend of the Chartist leaders and later parliamentary representative for Oldham, used

31 John Bright was elected to the House of Commons by the electors of Durham, July, 1843.

32 Hovell, M., *op. cit.*, p. 273.

33 Tawney, R. H., *op. cit.*, II, 315-318.

his literary ability in support of the movement. In a work which appeared in 1845, he clearly explained the reasons for each political demand of the Chartists. He thought the Qualification Acts had failed in England because of the power of money, and he regretted that the House of Commons was virtually closed to the average working man.

It is for him as though the parliament sat in the moon; he has about as much chance of getting there. The wrongs of his class, its peculiar desires, interests, and wishes—the opinion which it entertains on different topics of public concern—its thoughts and principles on internal or external policy—the redress of immediate and pressing grievances, and the application of principles that affect its future progress—these, and whatever else he wishes to say in the legislature, must be said by other voices than his own.[34]

He asserted that the Chartists stood for the abolition of the property qualifications because they were more interested in ability than in money. While the Qualification Acts remained on the statute book, representatives of the voters would be elected from only one class, with the result that

the industrious shall be represented by the idle, the poor by the rich, and those who live by their toil by those who have an interest in land.[35]

The Qualification Acts, he said, must be repealed, for only then would the majority of the people be represented in the legislature.[36] The untiring work of Fox and leading Chartists accomplished nothing; and the events of the summer and fall of 1845 turned the attention of the people to the great agricultural misfortune which, unforeseen and unprecedented, descended upon them.

The summer of 1845 had been rainy and chilly, and the English people realized that their crops would not be good. The

34 Fox, W. J., *Lectures Addressed chiefly to the Working Classes* (London, 1845), II, 4.
35 *Ibid.*, III, 205.
36 *Ibid.*, III, 205.

future grew even more forbidding when the potato disease began to lay waste the crops of Ireland. Famine was the inevitable result. These tragic events, however, proved extremely favorable for the work of the Anti-Corn Law League. In the summer and fall of 1845 Bright, Cobden, and other Anti-Corn Law leaders, unhampered by money difficulties, used their resources freely in an effort to reach the people. Nor were they disappointed, for everywhere they were enthusiastically received by the distressed population. But if events were favorable for the Anti-Corn Law advocates, they were most unfavorable for the Chartists and their political demands. When people are hungry, food, not political power, is uppermost in their minds. For a time, then, many of the English people forgot the six points of the People's Charter, and gave their wholehearted support to the Anti-Corn Law League. That body, with its singleness of purpose and capable leadership, reached the pinnacle of its power during this crisis. The disturbed state of the country necessitated emergency meetings of the cabinet; and on January 19, 1846, parliament met. The agricultural problem was, of course, the most pressing one, and all the time and energy of the House of Commons were directed toward its solution. Within a very short time, and in spite of the opposition of a strong protectionist group in the House, the Corn Laws were repealed. In June, 1846, however, Peel and his colleagues resigned, and Lord John Russell became the Prime Minister.

Parliament met on January 19, 1847, and the distressed state of the Irish nation was the main topic of interest in the Queen's speech. Immediately, Lord John Russell proposed a plan to relieve the Irish people. The House responded not only by adopting measures to aid their poverty-stricken neighbors, but also by passing laws to improve the educational facilities and the working conditions of the factory people of England.

Conditions in England favored the reformers in the general election of 1847. Tory forces were not highly organized and many of their constituencies were lost to their opponents. Although the election failed to return some leading Chartist sympathizers, such as Roebuck, to the House of Commons, the political platform of the Chartists was ably supported by William J. Fox, who was elected by the people of Oldham, and George Thompson, who represented Tower Hamlets.[37] The popularity of Feargus O'Connor reached its zenith, and he was returned by the electors of Nottingham as the first Chartist member of parliament. It was hoped that he would take the place of Daniel O'Connell, whose death in 1847 had left no "connecting link between Irish and English Radicalism." [38] Colonel Thompson, radical member for Bradford, and wealthy Sir Joshua Walmsley, radical member for Leicester, could also be counted upon to lend their support to the program of parliamentary reform. On the whole, the election of 1847 returned a smaller number of country gentlemen and relatives of peers, and a larger number of lawyers, " merchants, railroad contractors, and political writers and lecturers." [39]

The new parliament met on November 18, 1847, and, as usual, petitions complaining of unfair election practices were presented to the House of Commons. On December 6, 1847, James Tucker petitioned the House to the effect that John Patrick Somers, newly elected member for Sligo, was not at the time of his election, nor at the time of his return to the House, possessed of real or personal property as required by the Qualification Acts. True, Somers owned a small estate, but the property was subject to a judgment which had been obtained by his creditors. The land had been for several years in the hands of a receiver appointed by the Court of Chancery. Before Somers' election, it had been alleged by his friends that a certain Cornelius O'Brien would supply the needed qualification. Tucker believed that O'Brien had drawn up this deed but doubted whether the deed had ever been executed. For this

37 Harris, W., *op. cit.*, pp. 357-358.

38 *Ibid.*, p. 357.

39 Maccoby, S., *op. cit.*, p. 275. According to Thomas, J. A., *op. cit.*, p. 7, there were 41 radicals in the House of Commons as a result of the election of 1847.

reason, and also because Somers had failed to take the oath of qualification at the time of the election, Tucker thought that the election of Somers should be declared null and void.[40] Mr. Grainger, the Chairman of a Select Committee appointed by the House, reported for his committee that Somers had not been the duly elected representative.[41] Similar charges resulted in a declaration voiding the elections of Charles M'Tavish, returned representative for Dundalk, and Mr. Prinsep, returned representative for Harwich. Corrupt practices and lack of proper qualifications caused another committee of the House to declare that John Jervis had not been duly elected by the qualified voters of the Borough of Horsham.[42]

In the next session of Parliament, which began on February 3, 1848, momentous problems confronted the legislature. England had not recovered from her economic distress, and Ireland was on the verge of rebellion. Suddenly, on February 24, 1848, Louis Philippe was overthrown, and a republican form of government was established in France. The news " filled the Democrats with hope," [43] and gave an impetus to the Chartist cause in England. In the fall of 1847, the Chartists, taking advantage of the state of unrest in England, had held large public meetings in Birmingham, London, and other places; [44] and now in 1848, influenced by the march of democracy in Europe, the Chartist leaders addressed large meetings, urging the people to support their political program. On April 4, 1848, the long anticipated National Convention assembled in London, and after hearing many speeches in which the delegates described the poor economic conditions of the country, a decision was reached to pre-

40 *J. H. C.*, CIII, 50-52.

41 *Ibid.*, CIII, 374. Power, D. Rodwell, H. and Dew, E., *Reports of the Decisions of Committees of the House of Commons in the trial of Controverted Elections, during the fifteenth Parliament of the United Kingdom* (London, 1853), I, 119-128.

42 *J. H. C.*, CIII, 83-85, 357.

43 Gammage, R. G., *op. cit.*, p. 292.

44 *Ibid.*, p. 291.

sent the Third National Petition to the House of Commons. Elaborate plans were made not only for the presentation of the petition, but also for a huge demonstration to take place on the same day.[45] The British government, forewarned as to the events about to occur, prepared itself to meet all emergencies.[46] On the appointed day, April 10, 1848, the National Petition, embracing five points of the People's Charter—universal suffrage, equal electoral districts, annual parliaments, payment of members of the House, and abolition of property qualifications for members—was presented in the House of Commons.[47] Throughout England, great gatherings of people voiced their approval of the National Petition. Fortunately, there were no serious clashes between the people and the armed forces of the government. Three days later, on April 13, 1848, the Commons' Committee on Petitions reported that the actual number of signatures appendant to the National Petition was a little less than two million.[48]

The failure of the House of Commons to act favorably upon the National Petition and upon the petition presented by John Bright on April 10, 1848, praying for the six points of the People's Charter, did not arrest the activities of the Chartists. In an effort to unite the reformers of the country, a new organization, the People's League, was formed, the purpose of which was to work for political reforms.[49] Another organization, the membership of which included Sir William Molesworth, Joshua Walmsley, Locke King, George Thompson, W. J. Fox, and others, worked for secret ballot, household suffrage, triennial parliaments, the abolition of property qualifications for members of the House of Commons, and equal electoral districts. Its activities attracted the attention of the public, and even Bright,

45 Maccoby, S., op. cit., p. 280. Gammage, R. G., op. cit., pp. 301-309.

46 Slosson, P. W., The Decline of the Chartist Movement (New York, 1916), pp. 97-98.

47 Hovell, M., op. cit., p. 287.

48 Hansard, op. cit., 98 : 285.

49 Tawney, R. H., op. cit., II, 343-348.

in a letter, acknowledged the value of the organization when he said:

Household suffrage, with the ballot and three-year parliaments, and more equal electoral districts, and the removal of the property qualification for members, would ensure a real representation; and I believe this would be as far as the middle and wealthier classes could be prevailed upon to go.[50]

The activities of the reformers were recorded in the *Reformer's Almanac* for 1848 by Joseph Barker, a new addition to the ranks of the reformers. Not only were the outstanding events of the day described in this publication, but Barker's opinions on current events were also expressed. He vigorously supported the People's Charter and vehemently denounced the aristocratic character of the House of Commons, which he described as a body of men who

are not chosen by the common people, nor are they taken from the common people, nor do they represent the views, the wishes, or the interests of the common people. . . . The members of the House of Commons are, in general, chosen from the Aristocratic class, and they are, in effect, chosen by the Aristocratic class.   By far the majority of the House of Commons are chosen by persons directly under the influence and control of the Aristocracy . . . it is a tool in the hands of the Aristocrats. The Aristocrats elect the members: the Aristocratic order supplies the candidates: the members of the House of Commons represent Aristocratic interests, give efficiency to the Aristocratic will, protect Aristocratic corruptions from popular influence, and keep back and suppress the views and the feelings of the common people. In short, as I have said, we have no House of Commons.[51]

This general unrest in England produced repercussions in the House of Commons. Although no bill for the abolition of

50 *New Movement—Household Suffrage, Triennial Parliaments, Vote by Ballot, No Property Qualification, and equal Electoral Districts* (Manchester, 1848). Letter written by John Bright, April 18, 1848, p. 5.

51 Barker, J., *The Reformer's Almanac for 1848* (Wortley, 1848), pp. 216-217.

the Qualification Acts was introduced in 1848, the question of property qualifications for members of the House did come to the foreground on several occasions. On April 12, 1848, two days after the presentation of the National Petition, leave was granted to Mr. Moffatt and Mr. Brotherton to bring in a bill " to enforce and render more effectual the Laws relating to the Qualification of Members to sit in the House of Commons, and to provide for the Exclusion therefrom of Persons who shall be proved to be unable or unwilling to satisfy their just Debts." [52] Mr. Moffatt, member for Dartmouth, introduced the measure and added that while the members of the House were free from arrest for debt, this freedom had been abused. His bill would allow creditors to take action against debtor members of the Commons.[53] While it was acknowledged that the principle of not protecting debtors in parliament from their creditors was a very good one, there were strenuous objections to the machinery set up by the bill.[54] Opponents of the bill thought it unfair that a committee of the House should act as a court for the trial of cases of debt.[55] Although the House received petitions from the people of Wallingford praying that the bill be passed,[56] opposition forced Mr. Moffatt to withdraw his measure.[57] On another occasion, on May 29, 1848, the Speaker of the House acquainted that body with the fact that Mr. Harcourt had taken the oath of qualification but had not handed in a written statement of his qualifications. He had not done so because at the time of his election he had been the heir apparent of the Archbishop of York, and had, therefore, been exempt from the provisions of the Qualification Acts. Since his election, however, his father had died, and the Speaker was now in possession of a

52 *J. H. C.*, CIII, 437.

53 Hansard, *op. cit.*, 100: 461-462.

54 *Ibid.*, 100: 462-463.

55 *Ibid.*, 100: 462.

56 *J. H. C.*, CIII, 603.

57 *Ibid.*, CIII, 714.

written qualification which he requested the House to receive. The members willingly accepted Mr. Harcourt's qualification, and that gentleman thanked the House, explaining that for over forty years he had been a member of the House of Commons without ever having had the occasion to submit his qualifications.[58]

On June 20, 1848, Joseph Hume moved that the national representation be amended and that

the Elective Franchise shall be so extended as to include all Householders—that votes shall be taken by Ballot—that the duration of Parliaments shall not exceed three years—and that the apportionment of Members to Population shall be made more equal.[59]

In the course of the debate, Hume said the agricultural unrest of the country had been augmented by the operation of the Qualification Acts, and he added:

In Ireland matters were pretty much the same; but in Scotland a better system prevailed. There, any man who was an elector might be elected; no qualification was required. In Scotland, therefore, a working man might be returned as well as a man of land; and he wished to know what good reason there was against the return to that House of a working man, if a body of constituents thought fit to elect him, although he had not £300 a year.[60]

Hume also said that he represented a Scottish constituency and was, therefore, not required to have a qualification. He was most anxious to put England and Ireland on an equal footing with Scotland, where no property qualifications existed, and where a talented working man could become a member of the House of Commons. For this reason, he recommended that the United Kingdom follow the example of Scotland.[61] Mr. Henry Drummond, a Tory of the old school, declared that equal electoral districts, universal suffrage, and no property qualifications

58 Hansard, *op. cit.*, 99:70-71.
59 *Ibid.*, 99:879.
60 *Ibid.*, 99:894.
61 *Ibid.*, 99:901.

for the members of the House were the means of "obtaining an end which I think we should all most studiously resist,"[62] since political power must be held by men who have property and since "those who have no property must be entirely excluded from it." [63] The debate lasted for two nights, and while Cobden, Locke King, Villiers, and others supported Hume's motion, the opposition was too strong, and the motion was defeated by a vote of three hundred and fifty-one to eighty-four.[64] With the defeat of Hume's motion the House of Commons turned its attention to other problems, and the reformers of the country knew that the House was again in no mood to consider democratic measures. Failure in the House of Commons, however, was not the only reversal that the Chartists suffered, O'Connor's land scheme collapsed; Ernest Jones, McDouall, Cuffey, and other leading Chartists were imprisoned; and the year 1848 ended dismally for reformers and reform in England.[65]

While Hume and his friends in the House of Commons were exerting every effort to obtain parliamentary reforms for the people, other reformers were organizing new groups to keep alive the democratic ideas of the People's Charter. Although their efforts were not as successful as they had been in previous years, new organs, such as the National Parliamentary and Financial Reform Association, and the National Reform League, were founded to carry on the interest of democracy. Many of the outstanding reformers of the country were members of the National Parliamentary and Financial Reform Association, the platform of which embraced extension of the suffrage, secret ballot, triennial parliaments, equal electoral districts, and the abolition of property qualifications for members

62 *Ibid.*, 99:911.

63 *Ibid.*, 99:913.

64 *Ibid.*, 100:226.

65 Gammage, R. G., *op. cit.*, pp. 338-340.

of the House of Commons.[66] The platform of the National Reform League included the six political demands of the Charter as well as Bronterre O'Brien's plan for the nationalization of land. Because of its economic interests, this organization failed to become a successful rival of the National Charter Organization, which continued to be the chief organ of Chartist activities.[67]

The Reform Movement had lost prestige in 1848 but, as hope springs eternal in the human breast, the reformers renewed their efforts in 1849. Within the House of Commons, attempts were made to shorten the duration of parliaments and to obtain a secret ballot. On June 5, 1849, Hume, the veteran reformer, again introduced a plan which included extension of the suffrage, secret ballot, shorter parliaments, and the appointment of representatives in accordance with population.[68] Hume told his colleagues that " so long as he remained in that House, no Session should pass without witnessing his humble individual efforts to persuade the House to adopt further reforms." [69] His long speech was followed by an equally lengthy debate, but at no time did the question of the abolition of property qualifications enter the general discussion. When the vote was taken, only eighty-two members supported Hume, while two hundred and sixty-eight opposed his plan.[70] Nor was Mr. Moffatt more successful on the following day, June 6, 1849, when he introduced his Bill for Bankrupt and Insolvent Members. The echo of the Chartist Movement, however, was heard on July 3, 1849, when Feargus O'Connor moved that the House of Commons adopt the six principles of the People's Charter.[71] He said that the

66 Williams, W., *An Address to the Electors and Non-Electors of the United Kingdom on the Defective State of the Representative System* (London, 1849), p. 29.

67 Hovell, M., *op. cit.*, pp. 297-298.

68 Hansard, *op. cit.*, 105: 1156-1171.

69 *Ibid.*, 105: 1157.

70 *Ibid.*, 105: 1233.

71 *Ibid.*, 106: 1277.

people " would never look for anything short of the People's Charter, whole and entire." [72] Speaking on the question of property qualifications for members of parliament, O'Connor said there were fifty-three members of the present legislative body who had not been required to meet the qualifications. In this group he included the representatives of the universities, whom he considered " the most prejudiced and bigoted men in the House." [73] Since there was no reason to require qualifications from the English and Irish members, he recommended the adoption of the provision of the People's Charter which called for the abolition of the property qualifications for members of the House of Commons. Crawford, Hume, and Thompson spoke in favor of parliamentary reforms, but made no mention of the Qualification Acts. One parliamentary member urged the repeal of the Qualification Acts for, he said, it was a notorious fact that men had been members of the House of Commons with a nominal qualification while they possesed no property whatsoever.[74] Lord John Russell led the opposing group, and although two hundred and thirty-five members were present in the House of Commons, only thirteen supported O'Connor's motion.[75]

The opening year of a new decade brought no change in the fortunes of the reformers. The year 1850 was a mere repetition of 1849. In the House of Commons, Hume, faithful to the promise which he had made in 1849, requested leave to introduce a bill providing for household suffrage, secret ballot, triennial parliaments, and equal electoral districts; but his motion, as well as that of Berkeley for the adoption of secret ballot, was defeated. O'Connor was once again unsuccessful on July 11, 1850, when he proposed that the House of Commons adopt the principles embodied in the People's Charter.[76]

72 *Ibid.*, 106: 1272.
73 *Ibid.*, 106: 1274.
74 *Ibid.*, 106: 1303.
75 *Ibid.*, 106: 1304.
76 *Ibid.*, 112: 1282-1284.

Throughout the country, the reformers continued their agitation. Pamphlets and newspapers kept in touch with the people, and new organizations, such as the National Charter League [77] and The National Reform Association, were established to keep alive the spirit of reform. Sir Joshua Walmsley, member of the House, was president of the latter association, the aims of which were triennial parliaments, equal electoral districts, universal suffrage, secret ballot, and the abolition of property qualifications for membership in the House of Commons.[78] The reformers, however, realized that so many small organizations weakened their cause, and an attempt was made to unite the democratic societies. In 1850, delegates of the various organizations met, but differences of opinion, as well as conflicting personalities among the leaders, made unity impossible.[79] Unable to accomplish the formation of a single strong organization, the small societies continued to exist as such and to work through speeches and pamphlets for the democratic cause.

In 1851 the reformers in the House of Commons restated their plans for liberal reforms. Locke King, the member from East Surrey, worked for the extension of the suffrage; and Henry Berkeley, who had taken up Grote's cause in the House, made his annual resolution in favor of secret ballot. The same session witnessed another attempt to admit Jews into the House of Commons. On May 10, 1851, leave was granted to Mr. Hutt and Mr. Adderley to bring in a bill which would allow property in any part of Her Majesty's empire to be used as a qualification for membership in the House of Commons.[80] Mr. Hutt, parliamentary member for Gateshead, presented the Colonial Property Qualification Bill; and on May 30, 1851, one member opposed the second reading of that bill, because of the difficulties

77 Gammage, R. G., op. cit., p. 353.

78 Speech of George Thompson delivered to The National Reform Association on September 18, 1850. Officers and purposes of the organization were stated.

79 Gammage, R. G., op. cit., p. 356.

80 J. H. C., CVI, 214.

which would arise in determining the value of a £600 landed estate in Ceylon or the Punjab. How could the members of the House of Commons determine the truth or falsity of a member's declaration? Would they accept a certificate of some government official in that possession, or send out a committee to investigate the case? If the House of Commons demanded qualifications, it should afford the means of ascertaining the existence of them. The same member saw no reason for the proposed measure, and recommended the abolition of property qualifications. He suggested, however, that, since the promise to consider the question of parliamentary reform in the next session had been given by Lord John Russell, alterations in the laws should be considered at that time. He therefore moved that the bill be read six months thence.[81]

This motion was not carried; and on July 9, 1851, while the bill was being considered by the House, Mr. Tufnell, Whig member for Devonport, expressed the opinion that, while he thought it best to wait until Lord John Russell brought forth his plan for parliamentary reform, yet, since Mr. Hutt's bill had raised the question of property qualifications of members of the Commons, he failed to see the necessity of such qualifications. He did not believe that the aim of the Qualification Act of 1710 had been to promote the general welfare of the people, but to pave the way for the restoration of the Stuart dynasty.[82] Mr. Tufnell traced the history of the 1710 Qualification Act and criticized Warburton's Act of 1838, which permitted personal property to be substituted for real property, because he thought it would lead to an even wider evasion of the law. Not only had a declaration been substituted for the oath, but the description in that act of the personal property of a member of the House of Commons had been so vague and indefinite, that even a sharp-witted committee of the House found it extremely difficult to determine the validity of a qualification.[83] Added to this

81 Hansard, *op. cit.*, 117: 325-326.
82 *Ibid.*, 118: 393-394.
83 *Ibid.*, 118: 396.

criticism was the one that the Qualification Acts were unfair in their operation. In the current session, Mr. Prinsep, a director of the East India Company, had included in his qualification, a pension of £1000 per annum and a house. The " corpus " of the pension fund was in India and not in the United Kingdom, and this induced the committee of the House of Commons to reject the qualification which had been submitted.[84] Mr. Tufnell pointed out that had Mr. Prinsep's attorney been vague and indefinite in describing the qualification of his client, the House Committee would have found it impossible to determine the exact qualification. He condemned the existing laws which made property alone a test of qualification for a seat in the House of Commons. The laws, he pointed out, were evaded, and the law-makers should certainly not be law-breakers.[85] For all these reasons, Mr. Tufnell called upon his colleagues to support him in his attempt to return to the old constitutional principle whereby the electors of the community had free choice in their election, and he moved:

That it be an Instruction to the Committee, to provide for the abolition of any Property Qualification for the Election of Members to serve in Parliament.[86]

The motion was duly seconded,[87] and the members were anxious to hear Lord John Russell's opinion on the subject. But Lord John pointed out that a great inconsistency existed between Hutt's bill and Tufnell's motion. Russell admitted that Tufnell's arguments against the Qualification Acts were good ones; for, he thought, the Qualification Act which had been adopted in the time of Queen Anne was an inadvisable one. While Warburton's Act had been justified by changing conditions, nevertheless parliamentary members still found it com-

84 *Ibid.*, 118: 396.

85 *Ibid.*, 118: 397-398.

86 *Ibid.*, 118: 399. *J. H. C.*, CVI, 347.

87 Hansard, *op. cit.*, 118: 399.

paratively easy to evade the existing laws. Without actually acquiring the necessary landed or personal property, prospective members of the House of Commons found ways of obtaining fictitious qualifications. Now and then some member of the House lost his seat because he lacked the necessary qualification, but usually there were fifty or more sitting members of the House who were not properly qualified. Scottish representatives, without qualifications, were not inferior to the other members of the House of Commons. In short, Lord John was in sympathy with Tufnell's idea, but could not endorse the procedure adopted by that gentleman in presenting his motion. He thought that either a measure for the abolition of property qualifications of members of the House of Commons should be introduced, or a comprehensive bill for the improvement of the whole system of representation should be presented. Lord John concluded with the general statement of his belief that even though property qualifications of members of the Commons were abolished, only men of means would be returned to the House anyway. The time involved and the great expense of residing in London would make it impossible for poor men to aspire to parliamentary seats.[88]

Mr. Newdegate, member for Warwickshire, condemned the tactics of the reformers in the House of Commons, who made attempts to deprive Lord John Russell of the privilege of introducing a general reform bill in 1852. He realized that changes should be made in the existing laws if they were defective, but he doubted whether the House was prepared at that time to consider such changes.[89] Another member, while agreeing with Lord John on many points, questioned Lord John's opinion that even with the removal of property qualifications of members of the House, only men of means would be returned to the legislature. He was quite sure that there were political adventurers in the country who, if there were no Qualification Acts,

88 *Ibid.*, 118: 399-402.
89 *Ibid.*, 118: 402-403.

would be returned by the voters of some of the constituencies; and it would be a great national injury to have such men in the House of Commons. Lord John had said that members found no difficulty in securing fictitious qualifications; but that at least indicated that these men had connections or credit, and were deemed worthy of being given sufficient support to enable them to enter the House.[90] Mr. Vernon Smith, representative for Northampton, supported his friend, Mr. Tufnell; but Tufnell thought he could best serve the cause of reform by leaving the question in the hands of Lord John Russell.[91] Hutt, following the stand taken by Tufnell, would not proceed with the presentation of his bill, and the measure was withdrawn.[92]

Interest in political matters revived in England in the winter of 1851. Events in France in December of that year proved that the march of democracy had been checked. In that month, Louis Napoleon staged his famous *coup d'état,* overthrowing the French constitution which he had promised faithfully to maintain, and quickly disposed of his enemies. Contrary to the cabinet's recommendation that strict neutrality be observed on the question, Lord Palmerston, the British Foreign Secretary, expressed his approval of Napoleon's action to the French Ambassador. Palmerston's conduct of British foreign affairs had been a source of anxiety to the cabinet and court; his approval of events in France caused Prime Minister Russell to take action, and Palmerston was dismissed from office. Lord Palmerston, however, had been a power in the kingdom, and there was widespread interest in the outcome of his dismissal. The people, moreover, eagerly awaited the approach of the new session of parliament, which they hoped would result in the adoption of parliamentary reforms. Nor were they disappointed in the Queen's speech, which intimated that changes would be made in the system of representation. On February 9, 1852, Lord

90 *Ibid.,* 118: 403-404.

91 *Ibid.,* 118: 405.

92 *Ibid.,* 118: 406. *J. H. C.,* CVI, 348. Bill to make property in any Colony or Possession of Her Majesty, a Qualification for a Seat in Parliament, 1851.

John Russell moved to bring in a " Bill to extend the Right of Voting for Members of Parliament, and to amend the laws relating to the representation of the People." [93] Lord John proposed to enfranchise some large towns, to lower the borough and county qualifications for the franchise, and to abolish property qualifications for members of the House of Commons. On the last item, he said:

. . . no good end was attained in retaining the present property qualification of Members of Parliament, seeing that it was so capable of being evaded; that I thought it had been introduced contrary to the general principles of representation, and that for my part I should willingly see it abandoned. Sir, maintaining that opinion still, I avail myself of this opportunity of repealing all those acts, beginning with the Act of Anne, by which those various property qualifications were imposed.[94]

The bill was not favorably received either by the country or by the House of Commons. In the House, Hume desired a greater extension of the suffrage, and Berkeley and his followers were dissatisfied because of the omission of secret ballot. The reformers of the country were displeased because the bill had failed to meet their expectations, and some of the people believed that the existing qualifications for franchise were already far too low. When he realized that his measure would receive support from neither the country nor the House, Lord John Russell moved for its withdrawal. Throughout the month of February, 1852, he failed to receive the necessary support from the members of the House of Commons; and on February 23, 1852, the resignation of his cabinet was announced, and the Earl of Derby succeeded him as Prime Minister.[95]

With the appointment of the Earl of Derby, himself a Tory, and a Tory cabinet, there was little likelihood of any advance in the line of parliamentary reform. But in spite of the attitude

93 Hansard, *op. cit.*, 119: 252.

94 *Ibid.*, 119: 265.

95 Harris, W., *op. cit.*, p. 390.

of the government, the reformers in the House of Commons continued to introduce their plans for parliamentary reforms. On March 17, 1852, Mr. Tufnell moved for leave to bring in a bill to abolish property qualifications for members of the House of Commons.[96] Spencer Walpole, the historian, saw no reason to oppose the introduction of such a measure, for the abolition of property qualifications had been one of the provisions of the bill which Lord John Russell had introduced. He pointed out that there had been no great opposition to that clause of the bill.[97] Opposition to the proposal, however, was voiced by Colonel Sibthorp, who asserted that the existing laws were constitutionally necessary.[98] But in spite of objections, the members of the House gave permission to Mr. Tufnell, Sir William Molesworth, and Mr. Ewart to bring in a " Bill to abolish Property Qualifications for Members of Parliament." [99] Mr. Tufnell presented the bill, but the apathy displayed by the House resulted in the withdrawal of the measure.[100] In the same month, March, 1852, Hume brought forth his annual motion for electoral reform and secret ballot; and Berkeley again raised the question of secret ballot. But the session brought no success to Tufnell, Hume, Berkeley, or Locke King, who had also worked for the extension of the franchise. Other questions continued to hold the attention of the Commons, and parliament was finally prorogued and dissolved on July 1, 1852.

The election of 1852 was a very quiet one, for no question of great significance faced the country. In many cases parliamentary candidates promised their constituencies that they would exert every effort to advance the cause of democracy. One such candidate was Sir William Molesworth, who promised the

96 Hansard, *op. cit.*, 119: 1222.

97 *Ibid.*, 119: 1222.

98 *Ibid.*, 119: 1223.

99 *J. H. C.*, CVII, 99.

100 *Ibid.*, CVII, 210. Bill to abolish Property Qualifications for Members of Parliament, 1852.

voters of Southwark that among other things he would work for the extension of the suffrage, the redistribution of seats in the House of Commons, secret ballot, the abolition of property qualifications for members of the House of Commons, national education, and income tax.[101] The outcome of the election was very disappointing, for there was little change in the relative strength of the political parties in the House. Slight gains had been made by the Conservative government at the expense of the Peelites, but the position of the reformers remained unchanged.[102] Their exact position in the House is difficult to determine, for available statistics on the subject are not adequate. The number of radicals in the House had steadily declined since 1832,[103] not only because some of them had failed to be reelected to the House, but also because by 1852 many of them had been absorbed by the other political parties. Since the election of 1852 caused no great change in the strength of any political party in the House of Commons,[104] the adoption of parliamentary reforms in the new session seemed extremely unlikely.

Following the preliminary business of organization, the House of Commons considered election petitions which complained of bribery, corruption, and evasion of the Qualification Acts. On November 12, 1852, the qualified voters of Tavistock petitioned the House to the effect that Samuel Carter, the liberal representative for their borough, was not qualified in real or personal property to be a member of the House of Commons. At the time of the election, Carter had been requested to state his qualification, and he had presented a written statement as-

101 Fawcett, Mrs., *op. cit.*, p. 303.

102 Harris, W., *op. cit.*, pp. 394-395.

103 According to Thomas, J. A., *op. cit.*, p. 7, only 18 radicals were returned to the House of Commons in 1852.

104 Harris, W., *op. cit.*, p. 397. According to the Earl of Derby, the composition of the House of Commons included 310 adherents of the government, 260 mixed Whigs and Liberals, members of the Peel Party, and Irish Roman Catholics. Maccoby, S., *op. cit.*, pp. 435-436.

suring the electors that his qualification had been deposited in the Crown Office and could be examined by any interested person. Later, in an effort to remove suspicion that still persisted, he made the following statement:

I, Samuel Carter, do solemnly and sincerely declare that I am, to the best of my knowledge and belief, duly qualified to be elected as a Member of the House of Commons, according to the true intent and meaning of the Act passed in the second year of the reign of Queen Victoria . . . and that my qualification to be so elected doth arise out of leasehold houses and tenements, annuities and shares in Joint Stock Companies, monies, goods and chattels, as hereunder set forth, leasehold houses, tenements, tan yard and premises in the parish of Tavistock . . . [105]

But in spite of the above, the petitioners carried their complaint to the House of Commons; and on February 21, 1853, Lord Robert Grosvenor reported for the Select Committee, which had spent much time in questioning people and examining the assets of Carter, that

Samuel Carter, Esquire, not being qualified according to the Provisions of the Act of the 1 and 2 Vic. c. 48, intituled, "An Act to amend the Law relating to the Qualification of Members to serve in Parliament," is not duly elected a Burgess to serve in this present Parliament for the Borough of Tavistock.[106]

For a time it seemed likely that the same fate would befall Charles Duffy, extreme liberal representative for New Ross. His friend, William O'Hara, admitted to a House committee that he had supplied the necessary property qualification to enable his good friend Duffy to obtain a parliamentary seat. Despite this admission of the violation of the Qualification Act, Duffy was permitted to remain a member of the House of Com-

105 *J. H. C.*, CVIII, 13.

106 *Ibid.*, CVIII, 263. *Parliamentary Papers*, Reports from Committees, Elections 1852-1853, XIX, Tavistock Election.

mons.[107] Like Duffy, William Keogh, liberal representative for Athlone, and Richard Guinness, conservative representative for Barnstaple, were successful in retaining their seats in the House of Commons.

The 1852 winter session of parliament was not outstanding. The question of the budget aroused considerable opposition, and Lord Derby resigned in December, 1852. Lord Aberdeen assumed the leadership of the government, with a cabinet consisting of seven Peelites, five Whigs, and one Radical.[108] The radical member of Lord Aberdeen's cabinet was Sir William Molesworth, whose office was that of First Commissioner of Works. While Molesworth never lost interest in the question of parliamentary reform, and could be expected to give his support to any reform measure introduced into the House, yet at this time he seemed more interested in the field of colonial affairs.

Following the Christmas recess, parliament resumed its session on February 10, 1853. Financial and educational reforms were adopted, and careful consideration was given to a government bill for India. Although Berkeley introduced his motion for secret ballot, and Locke King moved for leave to bring in a bill to extend the suffrage, on the whole the reformers in the House of Commons were not very active. King's motion was withdrawn because the government promised to introduce a Reform Bill in the session of 1854. But more important than legislative successes and failures was the matter of foreign affairs. For a long time the people and the government had been following the growth of friction between Russia and the Ottoman Empire. In 1853, the long expected war finally broke out; and the contest was not to end until Great Britain, France, and Sardinia had been drawn into the struggle.

107 Power, D. Rodwell, H. and Dew, E., *Reports of the Decisions of Committees of the House of Commons in the trial of Controverted Elections, during the sixteenth Parliament of the United Kingdom* (London, 1857), II, 188-200. Samuel Carter—liberal. Dod, C. R., *The Parliamentary Companion for 1852*, p. 148. Charles Duffy—liberal. *Ibid.*, 1853, p. 169. William Keogh—liberal. *Ibid.*, 1852, p. 209. Richard Guinness—conservative. *Ibid.*, 1856, p. 196.

108 Harris, W., *op. cit.*, p. 398.

The session of 1854 convened on January 30th. The Queen's speech called for changes in the shipping laws and in the legal administration of the poor laws. It further recommended civil service and parliamentary reforms for the people of the kingdom. True to his promise, Lord John Russell introduced his long awaited Reform Bill two weeks later, on February 13, 1854. His carefully worked out measure was an extension of the Reform Act of 1832.[109] Like his proposal of 1852, the bill was not favorably received by either the people of England or the House of Commons. Liberal-minded people had expected Russell's measure to be an all-inclusive one dealing with the entire question of parliamentary reform. Within the House of Commons the measure was severely attacked because it did not include secret ballot, and Mr. Tufnell voiced his disapproval because Russell had omitted the question of property qualifications for members of the House. Tufnell asserted that he would take the earliest opportunity for introducing a measure for the abolition of the Qualification Acts.[110] His stand was supported by Murrough, who expressed great disappointment at Russell's failure to include the abolition of property qualifications. He said:

This law has ever been systematically evaded, but . . . to its systematic evasion this House, at the most brilliant periods of its history, has been indebted for its most illustrious ornaments.[111]

Murrough named Addison, Sheridan, Sheil, and Curran as some of the " illustrious ornaments " of the Commons who had not had bona-fide property qualifications when they first entered the House.[112] Other members of the House continued their attack on Russell's bill. The opposition in the House and the lack of enthusiasm in the country forced Lord John to withdraw his measure.

109 Maccoby, S., *English Radicalism, 1853-1886* (London, 1938), pp. 27-28. Hansard, *op. cit.*, 130: 491-524.

110 *Ibid.*, 130: 520.

111 *Ibid.*, 130: 527.

112 *Ibid.*, 130: 528.

The failure of Russell's Reform Bill to include all their demands caused the reformers in the House to take further action. On February 18, 1854, leave was granted to Mr. Tufnell, Mr. Ewart, and Sir Benjamin Hall to bring in a " Bill to Abolish Property Qualifications for Members of Parliament." [113] The bill was introduced by Sir Benjamin Hall, Chief Commissioner of Works. Sir Benjamin had already shown keen interest in municipal problems by improving the parks of London. The bill was read a first time and ordered to be read a second time on March 8, 1854.[114] On several occasions the second reading of the measure was postponed, and finally in May the bill was withdrawn.[115] Sir Benjamin was not the only one who was unsuccessful in his attempt to bring about reforms for the people. Locke King found it impossible to abolish the law of primogeniture, and Berkeley's annual motion for the adoption of secret ballot met with its customary defeat. The lack of legislation proved that domestic affairs, including the problems of parliamentary reforms, no longer held the attention of the populace. After March 27, 1854, one question only was uppermost in the minds of the people: the conduct and the fortunes of the British forces in the Crimean War.

When parliament met on January 23, 1855, public opinion had been so aroused over the miscarriage of the Crimean War by the British government that it forced Lord John Russell, leader of the House, and later the Aberdeen Ministry, to resign. Lord Palmerston, who had often held ministerial office in the past, now became Prime Minister. At the time, the selection of Palmerston, whose chief interest lay in foreign affairs, was considered an excellent one, but time eventually proved that he was a stumbling block in the path of political change. Palmerston was not a reactionary, but his ultra-conservatism resulted in stagnation in domestic policy.

113 *J. H. C.*, CIX, 81.

114 *Ibid.*, CIX, 86.

115 *Ibid.*, CIX, 225.

The war with Russia continued to be the most absorbing topic of interest, and no progress was made in the field of parliamentary reform. Indeed, the Reform Movement suffered a great loss in the death of that veteran reformer, Joseph Hume, who died on February 20, 1855, at the age of seventy-eight. Throughout his life he had been the champion of parliamentary reform, never permitting a single opportunity to pass without exerting every effort to advance the cause of the people. Speaking of his fellow-reformer, Joshua Walmsley said:

In him the Reform party lost its oldest leader, and the country the man whose keen, firm sense of justice and indomitable resolution had raised a standard of integrity, and established principles of order and economy, that made a mark that can never be effaced on the public administration of affairs.[116]

No longer was his voice to be heard in the Commons; but his colleagues, dedicated to the cause of parliamentary reform, carried on his unfinished work. On March 3, 1855, Mr. Murrough, like Molesworth and Tufnell before him, requested permission to introduce a bill for the abolition of property qualifications for members of the House.[117] The granting of such permission was opposed by Mr. Macartney, who thought not only that there were too many members absent from the House, but also that the government, and not a private member of the Commons, should propose such a measure.[118] Murrough received some support; but Mr. Henley, member for Oxfordshire, voiced the opinion that the abolition of property qualifications of members of the House was only one aspect of the whole question of parliamentary reform. Such a question should be left in the hands of the government, which had already made the promise that careful consideration would be given to it after the termination of the war.[119]

116 Walmsley, H. M., *The Life of Sir Joshua Walmsley* (London, 1879), p. 309.

117 Hansard, *op. cit.*, 137 : 76.

118 *Ibid.*, 137 : 76.

119 *Ibid.*, 137 : 76.

Colonel Sibthorp, a life-long opponent of democracy, denounced Murrough's proposal, asserting that propertied members were the only ones who would protect the property of other people. He would have liked, he added, to see the property qualifications of the House members ten times greater than they were; thus making for a respectable legislative body. He added that for over twenty-six years he had been a member of the House, and that he was sorry to say that every session saw the House of Commons sinking in respectability. In his opinion, some of the members of the House belonged to the "tagrag and bobtail of society." Propertied members would assure a respectable House of Commons, and would bring satisfaction to the people, who would then know that their true interests were being safeguarded.[120] Lord Palmerston, representing the government, took the stand that if any changes were proposed in the representative system of the country, such changes should not be considered at that time but postponed to some future date. In short, he was opposed to Murrough's motion.[121] Very likely, the attitude taken by Lord Palmerston induced other members to oppose Murrough's proposal; yet when the vote was taken, it was very close.   Twenty-seven members supported Murrough, and twenty-eight opposed him.[122] The same session witnessed the defeat of Berkeley's motion in favor of secret ballot. The defeat of these proposals, the attitude of the government as expressed by Lord Palmerston, and the public's absorbing interest in the war, made the success of any parliamentary reform measure quite impossible.

If it is true that the old motto, *silent leges inter arma,* was applicable during the Crimean War, then it is equally true that following the war a sort of languor enveloped the parliament and the people.[123] In the spring of 1856, two problems held the attention of the nation. The negotiation of the Treaty of Paris

120 *Ibid.,* 137 : 76-77
121 *Ibid.,* 137 : 77.
122 *Ibid.,* 137 : 78. *J. H. C.,* CX, 103.
123 McCarthy, J., *A History of Our Own Times* (London, 1880), III, 1.

was eagerly followed by the public; and for a time the national educational policies of Lord John Russell held the limelight. The reformers in the House of Commons were not very active, although they made some attempts to abolish the church rates and to obtain secret ballot. As the year drew to a close, however, the relations between China and Great Britain became strained, and before long the two countries were at war.

For the first time in several years, no mention of property qualifications for membership in the House of Commons was heard during the parliamentary session of 1856. Interestingly enough, the mismanagement of the Crimean War by the British government induced Lovett, who had been largely responsible for the People's Charter, to consider the composition of the House of Commons, and to draw up a petition on that subject. His old friend Roebuck presented the petition to the House; in it Lovett stated that he was one of many Englishmen who had come to the conclusion that the Commons was exclusively and most unjustly elected by a select and trivial number of voters. Not only was the electorate restricted, but the qualifications required for membership in the House resulted in a legislative body whose members were the representatives of parties and factions, with interests opposed to the general welfare and prosperity of the country.[124] In the past years, incompetent and selfish administrations had resulted in a needless sacrifice of human life, and in unnecessary expenditures of the resources of the nation. Accordingly, means must be taken to prepare and qualify proper representatives of the voters.[125] Lovett recommended the abolition of the property qualifications for the members of the House and proposed the substitution of intellectual and moral qualifications.[126] These qualifications, he thought, should be established by law, and a Public Court of Examiners should be appointed to enforce the law. This court

124 Tawney, R. H., *op. cit.*, II, "A Higher Intellectual and Moral Standard for Members of Parliament," pp. 376-377.

125 *Ibid.*, II, 377.

126 *Ibid.*, II, 377.

would examine all men who desired to enter the House of Commons, and all successful candidates would receive diplomas to that effect. Only those who survived the scrutiny of the court would be permitted to serve as representatives. A qualified representative who had served for seven years would have his name placed on a list of " Persons Competent to Share in the Government of their Country," and Her Majesty would be asked to make all appointments from this list.[127] Lovett believed that this system would improve the character of the House and promote the welfare of the nation; but such was not the attitude of the House of Commons. His proposals were not adopted, and his petition aroused little interest within or without the Commons.

When parliament met on February 3, 1857, hostilities with China had already commenced; and once again foreign affairs overshadowed affairs domestic. The reformers in the House, however, were not contented to be as inactive as they had been in 1856, and during the month of February they brought forth their favorite projects. Clay worked for the abolition of church rates; Locke King, for the extension of the county suffrage; and on February 24th, Sir Joshua Walmsley moved for a committee to consider the subject of representation and to report upon means of extending to the unenfranchised their share of political power.[128] The reformers were unsuccessful in their efforts, and they realized that they lacked the support of the government, which regarded the entire question of parliamentary reform with indifference, and did not even encourage the hope that the question of political reform might be considered at some future date. But parliamentary reforms were forgotten when Richard Cobden moved a resolution on the Chinese question which stated:

. . . That this House considers that the Papers which have been laid upon the Table fail to establish satisfactory grounds for the

127 *Ibid.*, II, 378-379.

128 Hansard, *op. cit.*, 144: 1249-1255, 1266.

violent measures resorted to at Canton, in the late affair of the Arrow:

That a Select Committee be appointed to inquire into the state of our commercial relations with China.[129]

Cobden's resolution, which was regarded as a vote of censure on the government, was carried; and on March 5th, Lord Palmerston announced that he would take the issue to the country. Accordingly, on March 5, 1857, parliament was prorogued and dissolved.

The question confronting the electors in the election of 1857 was whether or not they had confidence in Lord Palmerston. Parliamentary reform was not a prominent feature of the electoral contest in any district, although a few of the parliamentary candidates promised their constituents that they would exert every effort to advance the cause of democracy.[130] The election was a great triumph for Palmerston; and the return of his supporters to power proved that his foreign policy, talent, and personality had won the approval of the electorate. The total rout and dissolution of the so-called " Manchester party " came as a complete surprise to the public. The defeat of Cobden, Bright, Milner Gibson, W. J. Fox, Sir Joshua Walmsley, and others proved that the voters had not approved of their views on the great question of national policy.[131]

The new parliament met on April 30, 1857. The Queen's speech recommended to the legislators the question of law reform. Nothing was said about parliamentary reform; and in the course of a later debate in the House of Commons, Lord Palmerston made the announcement that in the near future the government intended to bring forth a program of that nature. The program of the government was not explained by Lord

129 *Ibid.*, 144: 1421.

130 *The Edinburgh Review*, 1857, CVI, 257.

131 *Ibid.*, 1857, CV, 571. Harris, W., *op. cit.*, p. 425. Composition of the House after the election of 1857. Liberals, 366, Conservatives, 287. According to Thomas, J. A., *op. cit.*, p. 7, only 19 radicals were returned to the House of Commons. Maccoby, S., *op. cit.*, p. 63.

Palmerston, but the announcement of this future program had the desired effect: it resulted in the postponement of many measures of parliamentary reform. Berkeley's motion in favor of secret ballot, and Locke King's attempt to extend the county franchise met with defeat in the House of Commons.   Only one ray of hope was evident; Locke King was given permission to introduce a measure for the abolition of property qualifications of members of the House.

Peter Locke King, who took up the struggle abandoned by Molesworth, Warburton, Tufnell, and Murrough, was a man in his middle forties. Born in 1811, and educated at Harrow and Trinity College, Cambridge, he had become friendly with the reformers of his day. In 1847, King was returned for East Surrey, and he continued to be a member of the House of Commons until 1874. During that period he gave his support to all liberal measures proposed in the House. For many years he worked for alterations in the law of primogeniture, and he was responsible for many important acts of legislation pertaining to real property. In 1856 he succeeded in bringing about the repeal of one hundred and twenty laws, many of them minor in character, which had been dormant on the statute book for many years, but which nevertheless could have been executed at any time. He worked for the abolition of church rates, the adoption of secret ballot, and on eight occasions he introduced into the Commons the question of county franchise.[132] It was Peter Locke King who, on May 12, 1857, moved for leave to bring in a bill to abolish the property qualifications for members of the Commons.[133]

King told his colleagues that the time was ripe for the introduction of such a measure, because the recent election had caused the members of the House of Commons (and many of them at considerable trouble and expense) to hand in statements of their qualifications. He attacked the Qualification Acts

132 *The Dictionary of National Biography. The Times*, November 14, 1885, p. 9.

133 Hansard, *op. cit.*, 145 : 221.

because of the anomalies by which they were characterized. County representatives were obliged to have property qualifications of £600 per annum, while borough representatives were compelled to have property qualifications of £300 per annum. There were, of course, many exceptions to the law, such as Scottish members and eldest sons of peers; and he did not see that the propertied members were in any way superior to the landless members.

The origin of the Qualification Act went back to 1710, a period when it was thought desirable to keep out the trading class; but in 1857 the trading class, having been able to meet the personal property requirement, was already represented. If members of the House of Commons were elected by universal suffrage, there might be some argument in favor of the existing laws; but the adoption of universal suffrage did not seem imminent. King, therefore, recommended the abolition of the Qualification Acts.[134] He was answered by Lord Palmerston, who, speaking for the government, said that he thought that it had been understood that all questions pertaining to the representation of the people in parliament and to the organization of the House of Commons, were to be postponed till the next session. He would not oppose the introduction of such a measure, but he would suggest that King permit it to lie on the table for consideration between this and the next session of parliament.[135] The question was put to a vote, and leave was granted to Mr. Locke King, Mr. Henry Langton, and Mr. Cobbett to introduce a " Bill to abolish Property Qualifications for Members of Parliament." [136]

Locke King presented his bill, and on June 10, 1857, he urged the second reading of the measure. He said there had been objections to his bill because some members of the House thought the whole question of parliamentary reform should be

134 *Ibid.*, 145 : 221-222.

135 *Ibid.*, 145 : 222-223.

136 *J. H. C.*, CXII, 140.

postponed until the next session of parliament. He opposed this idea because he felt that his measure concerned the elected and not the electors. No one could call his bill an innovation, he said, for he proposed merely to restore constitutional conditions as they had been before the adoption of the Qualification Act of 1710. It was well known that the present laws were evaded; qualifications for membership in the House were bought and sold, and many men when taking their seats in the House, were not the possessors of bona-fide qualifications. He moved that the bill be read a second time, for he was quite sure that his measure would prove beneficial to the people of the kingdom.[137] Sir George Grey, a member of Palmerston's cabinet and a person of sound judgment, stated that he would not discuss the merits of the bill; but since the government intended to introduce a Reform Bill in 1858, he would move that the bill be read a second time six months thence.[138] But this proposal aroused opposition from one of the members, who said that there was no assurance that the question of property qualifications of members of parliament would be a part of the proposed Reform Bill. To this another member replied that no more than a pledge could be expected from the government. The latter member agreed with Mr. King that the property qualifications should be abolished, but like members in the previous session, he proposed to leave the entire question of parliamentary reform in the hands of the government. Nothing along that line could be accomplished in this session, he felt, and he hoped that King would withdraw his bill.[139] Mr. Duncombe came to the rescue and asserted that, as representatives of the voters, they had the right to discuss the question of parliamentary reforms needed in the country, and that he would recommend the withdrawal of King's measure only when some member of the government assured him that the abolition of property qualifications would be a part of the Reform Bill.[140]

137 Hansard, *op. cit.*, 145: 1539-1540.
138 *Ibid.*, 145: 1540-1541.
139 *Ibid.*, 145: 1541.
140 *Ibid.*, 145: 1541-1542.

The position assumed by Duncombe was supported by Samuel Greer, a member of the reform group in the House of Commons. As a representative for the City of Londonderry, Greer had shown his interest in the Reform Movement by supporting all motions for the adoption of secret ballot, and he worked indefatigably to improve the system of land tenure in Ireland. On the question before the House, Greer stated that the reason underlying the adoption of the Qualification Act of 1710 had been to insure a House of Commons comprised of members possessed of a high degree of intelligence and honesty. He did not think, however, that people became more honest or more clear-headed as they increased in worldly goods; nor that a man's property was an adequate test of his moral or intellectual qualities. Like Lovett, who had originally advanced the theory, Greer thought that moral and intellectual tests were needed for members of the House. To carry out his idea, he offered the suggestion that the Educational Committee of the Privy Council should consider the question, and formulate plans to carry out the idea.[141] Lord Palmerston was very brief on the subject. He hoped that the members of the House would follow the recommendation of Sir George Grey, and that Locke King would not press the House to a division upon the present occasion.[142] King did not agree with the noble Lord, and when the question was put to a vote, Grey's motion that the bill be read a second time six months later, was passed.[143] Palmerston, Sir George, and their supporters had won the day; but Locke King was not discouraged. Before he could resume the struggle the following year, however, his case had been greatly aided by the outcome of the Beverley Election Case.

On May 20, 1857, the House of Commons received a petition from William Wells, an unsuccessful parliamentary candidate, claiming that Edward Auchmuty Glover, one of the returned

141 *Ibid.*, 145 : 1543-1544.
142 *Ibid.*, 145 : 1544-1545.
143 *Ibid.*, 145 : 1545. *J. H. C.*, CXII, 206.

representatives for the Borough of Beverley, was not properly qualified in real or personal property to be a member of the House of Commons.[144] In 1852 Glover had been a parliamentary candidate for the same borough, and at that time it was said that in 1849 he had taken the benefit of the Insolvent Debtors Act.[145] Glover had been unsuccessful in 1852; but when he became a candidate in 1857, the rumors concerning his qualifications were again circulated, and handbills were printed and distributed. To silence the rumors Glover made the following statement concerning his qualifications:

I, Edward Auchmuty Glover, do solemnly and sincerely declare that I am, to the best of my knowledge and belief, duly qualified to be elected a Member of the House of Commons, according to the true intent and meaning of the Act passed in the second year of Queen Victoria, intituled, "An Act to amend the Laws relating to the qualification of Members to serve in Parliament," and that my qualification to be so elected doth arise out of lands, estate and premises, as hereinunder set forth, that is to say: from an estate in the lands of Curaghclonbro, in the parish of Drumcullegr, county of Cork, Ireland, held for thirty-one years, renewable for ever at a peppercorn fine, to the best of my belief; also a lease for twenty-one years of the house and estates of " The Oaks ", situate in the parish of Ospringe, in the county of Kent, of the value of three hundred pounds per year; also a rent charge or annuity of three hundred and twenty-five pounds a year charged upon the house, lands, and estates of Brewer's farm, Great Brewer's-hill, Little Brewer's hill, and all the subdenominations to them belonging, situate in the Island of Harty, county of Kent, and bearing date the seventh day of August, one thousand eight hundred and fifty-four. Not expecting such a discreditable proceeding as the demand for my qualification, I have not my title deeds here, and therefore I cannot be particular as to the date or denomination; but I make the above declaration conscientiously believing the same to be true.[146]

144 *Ibid.*, CXII, 160.

145 *Parliamentary Papers*; Reports from Committees, Elections, 1857. Minutes of Evidence taken before the Select Committee on the Beverley Borough Election Petition, pp. 16, 51.

146 *Ibid.*, p. 5.

Later Glover assured his election committee that he was properly qualified, and that committee reported to the people:

To the Electors of Beverley.

In reference to the infamous charges set forth in an anonymous placard this morning, respecting Mr. E. A. Glover, he has appeared before his committee and a great number of electors this afternoon, and has fully cleared himself of the charges contained therein to the satisfaction of all present.[147]

Glover was successful in the election, but his opponents carried their case to the House of Commons. On August 3, 1857, the Select Committee appointed by the House to hear the case, reported that Edward Auchmuty Glover was not properly qualified in real or personal property, and therefore was not the duly elected representative for the Borough of Beverley.[148] Not only did the committee declare Glover's election null and void, but it also moved

That the said Edward Auchmuty Glover, Esquire, made and signed Declarations in the form prescribed by the 1 and 2 Vic. c. 48, ss 3 and 6, and that it is the unanimous opinion of the Committee that the Evidence taken before them should be laid before the Attorney General, with a view to further Proceedings being taken with reference to such Declarations.[149]

This unexpected action of the Select Committee was received by Glover and many men with great astonishment. True, Glover was not the first member of the House to lose his seat because he lacked the proper qualifications; but it was the first time in the history of the Qualification Acts that the Attorney General was called upon to take action against an ousted member. Glover immediately petitioned the Commons to revise the recommenda-

147 *Ibid.*, p. 73.

148 *J. H. C.*, CXII, 369. Wolferstan, F. S. P. and Dew, E., *Reports of the Decisions of Committees of the House of Commons in the trial of Controverted Elections, during the seventeenth Parliament of the United Kingdom* (London, 1859), pp. 214-224.

149 *J. H. C.*, CXII, 369.

tion of the Select Committee, but the House refused to consider the petition.[150] In due time the Glover Case was tried in an English court, and Glover was found guilty of making a false declaration before the House of Commons, to the effect that he was possessed of £300 per annum when in reality he possessed no real or personal property whatsoever of the required amount. Unlike other members of the Commons, Glover, at the time of his election and entrance into the House of Commons, had not even take the precaution to obtain a fictitious qualification. The jury decided against Glover, and he was sentenced to Newgate prison.[151]

The Glover Case focused the attention of the people on the operation of the Qualification Acts. They fully realized that Glover, not an ordinary criminal in the eyes of the law, had been condemned for making a false declaration, while many of his colleagues, by virtue of equally false declarations, were occupying seats in the Commons. Such an anomalous state of affairs could not be permitted to continue; and the reformers in and outside of the Commons, as well as such organizations as the London Reform Association, were determined to remove the obnoxious laws from the statute book of the nation.

The Queen's speech on December 8, 1857, promised parliamentary reforms, but the events in the opening months of 1858 overshadowed the question of reform. The Indian problem and the Orsini Affair, which latter brought about the downfall of Palmerston's administration and the formation of a new ministry by the Earl of Derby, held the attention of the public. When it seemed unlikely that the government would be responsible for any program of parliamentary reform, the reformers, including Locke King, resumed the struggle which they had abandoned in 1857. On April 22, 1858, while the Glover Case was still fresh in the minds of the people, King moved for leave to bring in a bill for the abolition of property qualifications for

150 *Ibid.*, CXII, 408.

151 White, W., *The Inner Life of the House of Commons* (London, 1898), I, 56.

membership in the House of Commons. He strongly urged the House to grant his request, for it seemed improbable that the government would sponsor a Reform Bill, and recent events in the court had made it advisable that some action be taken regarding the evasion of the Qualification Acts.[152] King's request was granted, and the bill was presented to the House.[153] On May 6, 1858, King, the sponsor of the measure, traced the history of the Qualification Acts. He pointed out that evasions were common, and that after every general election fifty or sixty new members were admitted to the Commons without being properly qualified according to the true meaning of the law.[154] He proceeded to attack the argument used by many, that the law excluded from the House Chartists and other men of extreme political views; and he said it was better to have such men express their opinions within the Commons. Legislation which encouraged parliamentary members to swear falsely and restricted the electors of the country in their choice of representatives should be abolished, he declared as he moved the second reading of the bill.[155]

Mr. Bentinck, Tory member for Norfolk, while not opposed to the second reading of the measure, made a few comments on the Qualification Acts. The object of the original law, he thought, had been to prevent the entrance into the House of persons with means insufficient to allow the devotion of all their time to parliamentary business. Any alteration in the existing laws would introduce into the House men of this very nature; and not only would the character of the Commons be changed, but the public interests would also be affected. If King's measure became a law, Bentinck predicted that there would be a move to abolish the salaries of all public officials. Only in that way would the people have officials whose wealth and position

152 Hansard, op. cit., 149: 1543-1544.

153 Ibid., 149: 1544. J. H. C., CXIII, 129, 130

154 Hansard, op. cit., 150: 222-223.

155 Ibid., 150: 223.

would free them from temptation.[156] However, King was supported by many of his colleagues. One thought that the members of the House should recommend to the mercy of the Crown that unfortunate gentleman, Mr. Edward Glover, who had been sentenced to prison for having taken his seat in the House without a proper qualification.[157] This suggestion was warmly supported by Major Edwards, Glover's successor for the Borough of Beverley, who thought the punishment inflicted upon the late representative of Beverley too severe a retribution " for what might have been an error in judgment." [158] Mr. Walpole started his speech by examining critically the arguments which had been advanced in favor of the Qualification Acts. One such argument was that parliamentary members possessing real or personal property were independent and not open to temptation. But this argument was invalid, he pointed out, because it was a well known fact that the laws were notoriously evaded, and besides, there were many exemptions to those laws. If the laws were to be maintained, he said, exemptions should be abolished and the laws should be made applicable to Scotland. Another argument advanced by the supporters of the Qualification Acts was that they prevented adventurous candidates from putting bona-fide candidates to unnecessary expense at elections. Mr. Walpole doubted whether political adventurers could add to the already high expense of election. For these reasons, he thought that the Qualification Acts should not be maintained in their present state; and believing that the electors and parliamentary candidates should not be restricted in any way, he supported the opponents of the Qualification Acts.[159] King's motion was carried and his measure was read a second time amid some cheering in the House of Commons.[160]

156 *Ibid.*, 150: 224.

157 *Ibid.*, 150: 225.

158 *Ibid.*, 150: 226.

159 *Ibid.*, 150: 226-227.

160 *Ibid.*, 150: 227. *The Times*, May 7, 1858, p. 8.

Seven days later, on May 13, 1858, the question of going into committee on King's measure arose. Opposition quickly developed, and Mr. Bentinck moved that the debate be adjourned because of the lateness of the hour.[161] Another member came to Bentinck's support because he did not think that ample discussion had been given to the second reading of the measure.[162] King's anger was aroused, and he declared that a full consideration had been given to the second reading of the bill, and that if further discussion were desired, it might take place then.[163] But King realized that opposition in the House was strong. One of the members declared that although Her Majesty's Government had abandoned conservative principles, many of the members of the House would not follow the policy of the government, but would continue their opposition to King's measure and to all other liberal reforms.[164] When Disraeli, the Chancellor of the Exchequer, and supporter of King's measure, stated that he would support Bentinck's motion because more time was needed for the discussion, King decided that under the circumstances he would not press his bill, but would postpone it instead to some later day.[165]

The month of May passed, and it was not until June 2, 1858, that the question of going into committee again arose. On that day, Bentinck said that he should have voiced his opposition to King's measure at an earlier date, and that he would have done so, had he not expected opposition which had never developed. But now he would voice his objections to that measure, he said, because he believed that a property qualification was " an essential ingredient in the constitution of that House ", and that the abolition of property qualifications for members of the House was a part of a general Reform Bill, and as such should not be

161 Hansard, *op. cit.*, 150: 576.

162 *Ibid.*, 150: 577.

163 *Ibid.*, 150: 577.

164 *Ibid.*, 150: 577.

165 *Ibid.*, 150: 578.

treated as an isolated question of parliamentary reform.[166] Even though the Acts were evaded, if the object behind them was as good as many men thought, the existing laws should be amended and not repealed, he felt. The repeal of the Acts would enable bankrupts, spendthrifts, and paupers to enter the House of Commons. These men would not be able to devote all their time to the business of the nation, and some of them would fall prey to temptation. The admittance of such members, moreover, would make it impossible to maintain the privilege of freedom from arrest for debt, since the House of Commons would then be little more than a refuge for bankrupts and other disreputable characters.[167] Bentinck closed his long speech by making the following amendment:

This house will, upon this day six months, resolve itself into the said Committee.[168]

Action on Bentinck's amendment was delayed while the House members continued their discussion. Mr. Ker Seymer, member for Dorsetshire, asserted that the existing laws were not effective in keeping out of the House men not possessed of property of the required amount. His experience on Election Committees had proved that fictitious qualifications were easily obtainable, and that in some cases, members of the House who were well qualified in property had lost their seats because of some legal point relating to their qualifications. He hoped that the property qualifications of the members of the House of Commons would be abolished, for he would be extremely sorry to see another general election take place under the existing laws.[169] Property found an able supporter in the person of conservative Mr. Henry Drummond, who believed that if property were divorced from political power, it would be impossible to preserve the framework of society. He assured his colleagues

166 *Ibid.*, 150: 1422.

167 *Ibid.*, 150: 1422-1423.

168 *Ibid.*, 150: 1425. *J. H. C.*, CXIII, 203.

169 Hansard, *op. cit.*, 150: 1425-1426.

that the admittance of some of the reformers into the Commons would throw the burden of taxation upon the rich, and the wealthy class would be reduced to the uniform state of pauperism. Not content with discussing the membership of the House of Commons, Drummond asserted that only men of property should be members of the House of Lords.[170] His statements were strenuously opposed by Sir George Lewis, author and statesman, who did not think that property qualifications afforded any safeguard for the social, intellectual, or educational standards of the members who were returned to the House of Commons. The real safeguard, he held, was in the hands of the voters.[171] Drummond's position was supported, however, by Mr. Knightley, who pointed out the inconsistencies of Spencer Walpole and his supporters. These men, he said, approved of the abolition of property qualifications for members of the House and yet rejected the principle of universal suffrage. Surely there was a close connection between the property qualifications of the voters and those of the members of the Commons. Property qualifications for members of the legislature insured an independent and incorruptible House of Commons. He did not doubt the honesty of poor men; but if a man were in want or in debt, the temptation which membership in the House would throw in his way, might be too great for him.[172] The discussion continued, but when Bentinck's proposed amendment was put to a vote, it was lost; and the House of Commons went into committee to consider King's measure.[173]

Immediately Bentinck rose and asked the reason for the change in the attitude of many members toward the question of the property qualifications for members of the House of Commons. Formerly, he pointed out, many members had opposed the abolition of the Qualification Acts; but now, several of them, including the government, seemed to favor King's meas-

170 *Ibid.*, 150: 1426-1427.
171 *Ibid.*, 150: 1427.
172 *Ibid.*, 150: 1429-1430.
173 *Ibid.*, 150: 1431.

ure.[174] Spencer Walpole took up the challenge and attempted to show that he had not been inconsistent in expressing his attitude toward the question. He restated his argument against the Qualification Acts, which in some cases prevented men of scruples like Southey from entering the House of Commons, and in other cases resulted in nothing more than mere sham.[175] Colonel North was not convinced. He saw great danger to the country if penniless men were to become members of the House of Commons. He called the attention of the House to a recent case in which a member of that body had declared in court that he did not know where to find £40.[176] Was such a person fit to serve the voters of England? [177] Lord John Russell, throwing his support to the opponents of the acts, attacked the argument that property qualifications were essential to the constitution. He declared that the Qualification Act of 1710 was an invasion, an usurpation, and a contradiction of the ancient constitution. He pointed out that men of ability had been obliged to resort to evasion of the laws which many desired to retain as essential to the constitution of the House.[178] The debate continued, but King's measure was finally reported without amendment.[179]

The next day, June 3, 1858, King moved the third reading of his bill.[180] On that occasion Bentinck said that although he had opposed the measure, since it was supported by so large a majority in the House, he felt that further opposition to it was useless. He would have liked to hear Lord Palmerston's opin-

174 *Ibid.*, 150: 1431-1432.

175 *Ibid.*, 150: 1432-1435.

176 The member was probably John Townsend, who had been declared a bankrupt. The House of Commons passed the following motion: That John Townsend, having been found a Bankrupt, has since been, and still is, by Law, incapable of sitting and voting in the House. Mr. Townsend to withdraw until creditors have been paid. *J. H. C.*, CXIII, p. 229.

177 Hansard, *op. cit.*, 150: 1436.

178 *Ibid.*, 150: 1436-1437.

179 According to *The Times*, the measure was received with cheers in the House of Commons. *The Times*, June 3, 1858, p. 6.

180 Hansard, *op. cit.*, 150: 1506.

ion on the measure, but this was impossible since that gentleman had already left for the evening.[181] After a very brief discussion, Locke King's measure to abolish the property qualifications of the members of the House was read a third time and passed by the House of Commons.[182]

The bill was sent to the House of Lords, and on June 10, 1858, the second reading of the measure was moved by Earl Fortescue. He maintained that the measure was justified, since the requirement of property qualifications limited the freedom of choice and was an infringement of the rights of the people. If there were to be property qualifications for the members of the House, he added, there should also be property qualifications for membership in the House of Lords. Many peers who sat and voted in the Upper House, had incomes smaller than the requirements of the borough representatives. Eldest sons of such peers, and even of bankrupt peers, were eligible for membership in the House. The nobleman related the story of an Irish member of the House who needed a qualification. With a map of one of the largest counties of Ireland before him, the representative marked out an estate in a mountainous section of the country, and then proceeded to fill out his qualification. With such a qualification, the member sat through two parliaments.[183] Earl Fortescue mentioned the case of Edward Glover, and said that King's measure would abolish what had been justly called a delusion and a sham.[184] This peer was supported by a colleague who asserted that the abolition of the Qualification Acts would relieve the members of the House of Commons from the painful and unsatisfactory duty of serving on Election Committees to determine the qualifications of their members.[185] The Duke of Newcastle also supported the repeal of the Qualifi-

181 *Ibid.*, 150: 1506.
182 *Ibid.*, 150: 1507. *J. H. C.*, CXIII, 208.
183 Hansard, *op. cit.*, 150: 1830.
184 *Ibid.*, 150: 1832.
185 *Ibid.*, 150: 1837-1838.

cation Acts. Such action, he thought, need not open the door of the House of Commons to bankrupts and swindlers; it would however, offer opportunity to artisans and poor men, who, after all, should be represented in the law-making body.[186] The supporters of the Qualification Acts bravely attacked the arguments of their opponents. Earl Grey, whose father had been responsible for the Reform Act of 1832, cautioned the members of the House of Lords that there were in England numerous reform organizations which wanted to effect a complete change in the representative system of the country. He said that they were demanding a secret ballot, universal suffrage, and many other political reforms; he added that the abolition of property qualifications for members of the House of Commons was but one step in the fulfillment of their demands. He firmly believed that the majority of the people were opposed to these demands, and pointed out that democracy as it had developed in France and in the United States was not wholly satisfactory.[187] The Duke of Rutland also opposed the repeal of the Qualification Acts; but the Earl of Derby doubted that the repeal would make any real or substantial change in the nature of the membership in the House of Commons.[188] The debate continued, and when the motion was finally put to the House of Lords, it was adopted and King's bill was read a second time.[189]

A few days later, on June 11, 1858, when the question of going into committee was before the House of Lords, Earl Grey, supporter of the Qualification Acts, moved:

That it be an instruction to the Committee to amend the Bill by introducing Clauses rendering the Members of both Houses of Parliament liable to Arrest for Debt under the Judgment of a Court of competent Jurisdiction, and by altering the Title of the Bill accordingly.[190]

186 *Ibid.*, 150: 1842-1845.
187 *Ibid.*, 150: 1832-1837.
188 *Ibid.*, 150: 1839-1842.
189 *Ibid.*, 150: 1848.
190 *Ibid.*, 150: 1916. *J. H. L.*, XC, 237.

The proposed amendment aroused great opposition, not only because it had been introduced without notice, but also because it was considered a rider to King's bill. Earl Grey met the criticism of his opponents with the contention that there was a connection between the bill and his amendment. The bill, according to Earl Grey, proposed to abolish a security, even though imperfect, and something should be substituted to insure the independence of members of parliament. The amendment was sound in principle, he added, and should be adopted.[191] The House of Lords refused to accept the opinion of Earl Grey, and the bill was reported without amendment.[192]

Events moved swiftly after that, and on June 15, 1858, the motion that the Bill to abolish Property Qualifications of Members of the House of Commons be read a third time, was before the House of Lords. Lord Ravensworth remarked that while he would not oppose the bill, he wished to call attention to the results that would surely follow the passage of such a measure. The reformers in the country would not stop with this, but would continue their agitation for all remaining points of the Charter. If the property qualifications for House members were abolished, the reformers would question the right of insisting upon property qualifications for the electors. If, moreover, the upper classes accepted this measure, there would be an attempt to abolish qualifications for other public officers. With the abolition of property qualifications for the members of the Commons, poor men would be returned to the House; and it was only logical to suppose that they would then begin to work for salaries for the members of the Commons. He warned their lordships that they must take a stand against further attempts at legislation in this direction.[193] The Earl of Clancarty not only agreed with Lord Ravensworth that the march of democracy must be arrested, but further recommended that another bill abolishing freedom of arrest from debt should follow if the present measure

191 Hansard, *op. cit.*, 150: 1918.

192 *Ibid.*, 150: 1919. *J. H. L.*, XC, 237.

193 Hansard, *op. cit.*, 150: 2089-2091.

were accepted.[194] The Earl of Wicklow and Lord Denman also opposed King's measure. The former ridiculed the argument that evasion warranted the abolition of the Qualification Acts. There were very few laws that had not been evaded, he said. In spite of the evasions, the Qualification Acts gave some security to the people, by preventing property-less men from becoming members of the House of Commons. If their lordships adopted the bill, they would be injuring the people.[195] Lord Denman believed that the proposed bill was unconstitutional, and he moved that it be read six months later.[196] This motion was strenuously opposed, and upon the appeal of his friends, Denman withdrew it. After a third reading, King's measure was passed by the House of Lords.[197] Lord Denman and his followers registered their protest to this action in the following statement:

1. Because the passing of this Bill without the retaining any Qualification whatsoever (of Land or Houses, or the substituting that of Money or Property in the Funds, or Stock of the East India Company, or Railway Shares) is a far more sweeping Measure than is needed to correct the Anomalies of the Property Qualification Law.

2. Because such Change as may suddenly be effected by the Act now in progress would only be necessary if the Evasion of the late Law had been always carried on with Impunity, and had been practised by very many former and present Members of the House of Commons; whereas the Law has but lately been vindicated, and the great Majority of the former and present Members of the House of Commons had at the Time of their Elections and still have legal Qualifications.

3. Because the qualification of Property in Land or Houses having been requisite for Members of Boroughs as well as Counties, it would have been better to render the Ownership of a Money or Funded Property, or of British or Indian Stock or Railway

194 *Ibid.*, 150: 2091-2093.

195 *Ibid.*, 150: 2093-2095.

196 *Ibid.*, 150: 2095. *J. H. L.*, XC, 251.

197 Hansard, *op. cit.*, 150: 2096. *J. H. L.*, XC, 251.

Shares, a Qualification of Burgesses to sit for Boroughs, and a Qualification of an Estate, Lease, Tenancy, or Reversion to Land or to a Title, a Qualification for Knights of the Shire, than to reduce the Qualification both of Burgesses and Knights below that of the Electors who may return them.

4. Because the Possession of a moderate Sum beyond Incumbrances, such as is required in the Case of Persons to be intrusted with the Collection or Distribution of Money, is necessary as a Safeguard in those who have to legislate extensively as to the Rights, Property, Liberties, and Lives of the Electors and People of Great Britain and Ireland, and her Majesty's Colonial Possessions, as well as with regard to the Affairs of the East India Company.

5. Because in the event of any moderate Qualification being soon hereafter found to be advisable by the Legislators and Electors and People of Great Britain and Ireland, it might be supposed that the Writer of this Protest could not advocate such a Measure without Inconsistency, if he had agreed to the passing of the present Measure without expressing his Opinion of its possible Disadvantages.[198]

This protest, however, could not check the sequence of events; the repeal of the Acts had been too long demanded, and the Glover Case had made it impossible for any Ministry, Liberal or Conservative, to maintain the laws. On June 28, 1858, King's measure received the approval of Queen Victoria, and the Qualification Acts disappeared from the statute book of the nation.[199] Thus were consummated the untiring efforts of several generations of men, in their march toward their ideal of democracy. But as is often the way in such cases, the actual repeal of the Acts caused little excitement in the country. Commenting on the repeal, Charles Greville, political diarist, seems to have captured the spirit of the general public when he wrote:

Amongst the concessions of last week was the passing of Locke King's Bill for abolishing a property qualification, which was done

198 *J. H. L.*, XC, 251.

199 *J. H. C.*, CXIII, 259. 21 and 22 Vict., c. 26. Hansard, *op. cit.*, 151 : 272.

with hardly any opposition. There can be no doubt that the practice was a mere sham, and that a property qualification was very often a fiction or a fraud, and such being the case, that it was useless to keep up the distinction . . . [200]

Though a moral victory for the reformers, the repeal of the Qualifications Acts brought no immediate change to the people. The reformers had argued that it was only the Acts which prevented the working people from representation; but actually, the average working man was in no position to become a member of the House, with or without the Qualification Acts. The general election of 1859 made little change in the character of the Commons. According to *The Annual Register,* the results of the election of 1859 were as follows:

Members reelected for the same places 511
Members reelected by other constituencies 13
New members, formerly in parliament 40
New members, not before in parliament .... 91 [201]

Of the total number of representatives returned to the Commons, only ninety-one were new members; and possibly some of these owed their election to the repeal of the Qualification Acts. But on the whole, despite the dire warnings of some of the leaders of the country, the years immediately following the abolition of property qualifications were very much like those that preceded the repeal. Until the introduction of other reforms, especially the payment of salaries to parliamentary members, the majority of the representatives of the voters continued to be men of real or personal property.

200 Strachey, L. and Fulford, R. (Ed.), *The Greville Memoirs, 1814-1860* (London, 1938), VII, 374.

201 *The Annual Register,* 1859, p. 508.

CONCLUSION

THE history of the 1710 Qualification Act is closely woven into the economic and political fabric of British history. Born at a time when great economic changes caused bitter rivalry between the Whigs and the Tories, the Qualification Act remained on the statute book of the kingdom for nearly one hundred and fifty years. In 1710, its Tory sponsors considered the Act an absolute necessity; yet the repeal of the Acts in 1858 caused little apprehension on the part of the people, and was accompanied by no great political upheaval. Despite the dire warnings of the conservative leaders that the Acts safeguarded the constitution, the abolition of the Acts was hailed by liberal men and reformers as another progressive step in the growth of political democracy in Great Britain.

The role played by the Qualification Acts in the complicated setting of British politics in the eighteenth and nineteenth centuries will always remain debatable. Its supporters, the landed gentry, who believed in the " stake in the country " theory, were certain that without the 1710 Act, landless men would have dominated the House of Commons. But historical research refutes this argument, for throughout this period the landed men were the political overlords of the nation, the independent landless men almost a political nonentity. The landed interest found its chief stronghold of support in the county; and it was not unusual for English counties to be represented by successive members of old parliamentary families. Occasionally, wealthy political adventurers, in violation of the Qualification Act, made vain attempts to invade the counties and oppose the country gentlemen; but outsiders were regarded as foreigners and received little support from the voters of any county. A parliamentary candidate of no landed estate and no territorial connections in the county had little chance of becoming a knight of the shire. Long established custom could not be changed or influenced by th: Qualification Act of 1710.

Looking back to 1710, however, the landed men feared that the moneyed classes, already gaining entrance into the Commons by means of boroughs, might in time gain political control of the counties. To check once and for all the growing power of these moneyed men was the main purpose of the Qualification Act of 1710. But how successful were the landed men in carrying out their aim? Political leaders, contemporary writers, pamphlets, and speeches in the Commons give evidence that the Acts were notoriously evaded by House members, who swore to the ownership of landed estates which they never possessed. In 1783, one writer asserted that one third of the House members were fictitiously qualified.[1] In the opening decade of the nineteenth century, a political pamphleteer claimed that one hundred of the members of the Commons were not the true owners of landed estates.[2] Many years later, in 1837, Sir William Molesworth, in pleading for the abolition of the Acts, told his House colleagues that about one half, if not more, of the Commons were not properly qualified in landed estates.[3]

How was it possible that so many members, including Pitt, Burke, Fox, Sheridan, and others, were fictitiously qualified? Careful investigation would prove that obliging relatives and friends, especially borough patrons, had enabled them to take their seats in the Commons. Borough patrons were the territorial magnates of the nation. At one time Wendover was the sole property of Earl Verney;[4] Tiverton, the property of Lord Harrowly;[5] Weymouth and Melcombe-Regis, the property of Bubb Dodington;[6] and Gatton, the property of Sir George

1 Hist. MSS. Comm., *Rutland MSS.*, Letter of D. Pulteney to the Duke of Rutland, May 14, 1783, p. 95.

2 Cobbett's *Parliamentary Register*, Letter to *The Political Register*, October 19, 1806. Found in November 1, 1806 issue.

3 Hansard, *op. cit.*, 36: 526.

4 Oldfield, T., *op. cit.*, I, 34.

5 *Ibid.*, p. 137.

6 *Ibid.*, p. 189.

Colebrooke.[7] If a patron had complete control over his borough, he could easily persuade his voters to return his relatives or nominees to the House. Seldom did the parliamentary candidates appear on election days, and no questions were raised concerning their landed estates. In many cases borough patrons, fully prepared to meet such emergencies as contested elections, placed landed property at the disposal of their candidates. In actuality, the great landowners of the kingdom and advocates of the " stake in the country " theory, were the evaders of the Qualification Act of 1710.

Borough patrons were not, however, the only ones responsible for the widespread evasion of the 1710 Qualification Act. Important political leaders, including Walpole, Henry Pelham, and the Duke of Newcastle, found the Act no barrier in maintaining their political supremacy. These officers used government money freely to purchase parliamentary seats and votes for their supporters. During his administration as First Lord of the Treasury, the Duke of Newcastle was able to control the elections in Hastings, Harwich, Rye, Queensborough, Sandwich, and Winchelsea.[8] George III interfered in elections in favor of his candidates. Government candidates, like the favorites of the borough patrons, rarely appeared on election days, and nobody was concerned about their landed qualifications. These members entered the House of Commons with fictitious qualifications or none at all.

Moneyed men, whose intellectual shrewdness had enabled them to amass huge fortunes, were quick to realize that this political situation worked to their advantage. Ambitious politically-minded men of this class never found the Qualification Act a bar to the realization of their aspirations. In many instances, part of their newly acquired wealth was invested in land; and as landowners, the former merchants, bankers, and stock-brokers found access to the parliamentary chamber. By the acquisition of land and by intermarriage, these moneyed men

7 *Ibid.*, II, 138.

8 Porritt, E. and A., *op. cit.*, I, 340.

were gradually absorbed by the old landed gentry. But some of this group, refusing to become landowners, still cherished the hope of membership in the House of Commons. These men used their wealth to purchase votes, parliamentary seats, and fictitious landed qualifications. To them it seemed a better business proposition to obtain temporary fictitious landed qualifications than to purchase the land outright; for landed investments were not as lucrative as other investments. These moneyed men relied upon government officials, borough patrons, bankers, and lawyers to obtain seats in parliament.

The latter group of independent moneyed men found entrance into the House of Commons an enlightening experience and a costly proposition. They were considered political upstarts by the landed gentry, and viewed suspiciously by the rightful candidates of any constituency. Large sums of money had to be spent to gain parliamentary seats, and often petitions of unsuccessful political opponents meant additional expense. The Qualification Act operated to their disadvantage; for it was easy for the defeated opponent to claim evasion of that Act, and hand-in-hand with that charge often went charges of bribery and corruption. In many cases, it was less difficult for House committees to probe the latter charge than to prove the former one. If found guilty of bribery and corruption, the moneyed man lost his seat in the Commons. House committees, in weighing the charges of evasion of the Qualification Act, considered the political ideas of the defeated parliamentary candidate and the returned House member. The moneyed man was less likely to retain his seat in the House if his political ideas differed from those of his opponent and the party in power. In that case, evasion of the Act would be used as a cloak for ridding the House of a non-supporter of the government. Well aware of the numerous difficulties which confronted them in gaining parliamentary seats, the moneyed men apparently resorted to careful planning, for few of their number lost their parliamentary seats during the long period in which the Qualification Act was in operation.

From 1710 to 1858, the supporters of the "stake in the country" theory worked indefatigably against this moneyed group of political adventurers. Contemporary pamphlets and speeches in the Commons condemned their growing political power. Within the House every effort was made to amend the original Qualification Act. The purpose of the 1760 amendment was to abolish the use of temporary fictitious landed qualifications. After that year, a member of the House had to give a schedule of his landed qualification to the Clerk of that body, and subscribe to an oath. The supporters of the Qualification Act firmly believed that this amendment would return properly qualified members to the legislative body. But this was wishful thinking on the part of the landed men, and fictitious landed qualifications continued to be used down to 1858.

The events of the eighteenth and nineteenth centuries, moreover, continued to favor the moneyed men of the nation. The French and Indian War, the American Revolution, the French Revolution, and the Napoleonic Period increased the importance of the men of liquid wealth, who refused to be excluded from the portals of the Commons. The factory system of production and the improved means of transportation brought China, Japan, India, and Africa closer to Great Britain. Wealth flowed to the mother country, and the growing capitalist class strengthened the ranks of the moneyed men. In addition to the capitalist class arose another group, the working men of the nation. Neither could be expected to follow willingly the ideas and doctrines of the landed men. The political supremacy of the landed men was challenged, but to wrest their power from the landed gentry was a herculean task. Progress was slow, and there were many setbacks. The late twenties and the thirties of the nineteenth century were most encouraging and the agitation of the forties and fifties produced the desired results. The march of democracy could not be arrested, and in 1858 property qualifications for members of parliament were abolished. Evolution, not revolution, was the method used by the British people to gain their democracy.

BIBLIOGRAPHY

I. General Bibliographies.

II. Contemporary Material.

    A. Parliamentary.

    B. Pamphlets, Periodicals, Other Writings.

    C. Letters, Diaries, Memoirs.

    D. Other Primary Sources.

III. Secondary Works.

I. BIBLIOGRAPHIES

No attempt will be made to give a complete bibliography for this work, which covers the long period, 1690-1858. The bibliographies found in the volumes of *The Oxford History of England*, ed. by G. N. Clark, and *The Political History of England*. ed. by W. Hunt and R. L. Poole, proved most valuable in the preparation of this book.

Davies, Godfrey, *Bibliography of British History, Stuart Period, 1603-1714.* 459 pp. Oxford, The Clarendon Press, 1928.

The Dictionary of National Biography.

Great Britain, Parliament, House of Commons, Catalogue of Parliamentary Reports, and a Breviate of their Contents : arranged under Heads according to the Subjects. 1696-1834. 220 pp. London, 1836.

——, General Index to the Accounts and Papers, Reports of Commissioners, Estimates, etc. 1801-1852. 1080 pp. London, 1853.

Grose, Clyde L., *A Select Bibliography of British History, 1660-1760.* 507 pp. Chicago, The University of Chicago Press, 1939.

Gross, Charles, *A Bibliography of British Municipal History including Gilds and Parliamentary Representation.* 461 pp. New York, Longmans, 1897.

Morgan, William T., *A Bibliography of British History, 1700-1715, with special reference to the Reign of Queen Anne.* 3 v. Bloomington, Ind., Indiana University Press, 1934-1939.

Poole's Index to Periodical Literature, 1802-1881. 2 v. Revised Edition. New York, Smith, 1938.

——, *Supplements, 1882-1906.* 5 v. Boston, Houghton, 1887-1908.

II. CONTEMPORARY MATERIAL

A. PARLIAMENTARY

Cobbett's Parliamentary History of England, from the Norman Conquest in 1066, to the Year 1803. 36 v. London, 1806-1820.

——, *Parliamentary Debates, 1803-1820.* 41 v. London, 1804-1820. In 1813 T. C. Hansard took over the publication of Cobbett's Debates.

A Collection of Parliamentary Debates in England from the Year 1668 to the present Time. 20 v. Dublin, J. Torbuck, 1739-1742.

Debates of the House of Commons, 1768-1771. 2 v. Arranged by Sir Henry Cavendish. London, Longmans, 1841-1843.

Great Britain. Parliament. Bills.

A Bill to Explain and Amend the several Acts for securing the Freedom of Parliament, by farther extending the Qualifications for Members to sit in the House of Commons, and for rendering the same more effectual, 1780.

A Bill to define and Regulate the Expenses of Elections, to limit the duration of the Poll, and to abolish the Qualifications of Members of Parliament for England and Wales, 1835.

A Bill to make property in any Colony or Possession of Her Majesty, a Qualification for a Seat in Parliament, 1851.

A Bill to abolish Property Qualifications for Members of Parliament, 1852.

Great Britain. Parliament. Laws and Statutes.

An Act for securing the Freedom of Parliaments, by the farther qualifying the Members to sit in the House of Commons, 1710 (9 Anne, c. 5).

An Act to enforce and render more Effectual the Laws relating to the Qualification of Members to sit in the House of Commons, 1760 (33 George II, c. 20).

An Act for further regulating the Qualification of Members to serve in the United Parliament of Great Britain and Ireland, 1819 (59 George III, c. 37).

An Act to amend the Laws relating to the Qualification of Members to serve in Parliament, 1837-1838 (1 & 2 Vict., c. 48).

An Act to abolish Property Qualifications of Members of Parliament, 1858 (21 & 22 Vict., c. 26).

Great Britain. The Statutes of the United Kingdom of Great Britain and Ireland, 1225-1865. 105 v. V. 1-46 have the title *The Statutes at Large, from Magna Charta to 46 George III.* Arranged by Danby Pickering, 1806.

Great Britain. Journals of the House of Commons.

XI	.... 1695/1696	LXXXII	 1826
XIV	.... 1702/1703	LXXXVIII	 1832–1833
XVI	.... 1710/1711	XC	 1835
XVIII	 1713–1715	XCII	 1837
XIX	 1721	CIII	 1847
XXI	 1730	CVI	 1851
XXII	 1735	CVII	 1852
XXIII	 1739	CVIII	 1852
XXVIII	 1760	CIX	 1854
LVI	 1800	CX	 1855
LVIII	 1802	CXII	 1857
LXXIV	 1818	CXIII	 1858
LXXV	 1820		

———, *Journals of the House of Lords,* XIX (1710-1711), XC (1858).

——, *Paliamentary Papers.* Reports from Committees, Elections. 1852-1853, Tavistock Election. 1857, Beverley Election.

Hansard's Parliamentary Debates, 1820-1830. New Series, 25 v. London, 1821-1831,

——, *Parliamentary Debates, 1830-1858.* 3rd Series. 152 v. for the period 1830-1858. London, 1831-1859.

The History and Proceedings of the House of Commons from the Restoration to the present Time. 14 v. London, R. Chandler, 1742-1744.

The History and Proceedings of the House of Lords from the Restoration in 1660 to the present Time. 8v. London, E. Timberland, 1742-1743.

The Parliamentary Register; or the History of the Debates and Proceedings of the House of Lords and Commons, 1775-1804. Work started by J. Almon and continued by J. Debrett. 80 v. London, 1775-1804.

B. PAMPHLETS, PERIODICALS, OTHER WRITINGS

Acherley, Roger, *Free Parliaments.* 322 pp. London, D. Browne, 1731.

An Address to Richard Brinsley Sheridan Esq., on the Public and Private Proceedings during the late Election for Westminster. 63 pp. London, J. Stockdale, 1807.

Two Addresses to the Freeholders of Westmorland. 74 pp. Kendal, Airey and Bellingham, 1818.

The Annual Register.

Authentic Copy of a Petition praying for a Reform in Parliament, presented to the House of Commons on Monday, May 6, 1793. 20 pp. London, J. Debrett, 1793.

Authentic Report on the Debate in the House of Commons on the 6th and 7th of May, 1793, on Mr. Grey's Motion for a Reform in Parliament. 150 pp. London, J. Debrett, 1793.

Barker, Joseph, *The Reformer's Almanac for 1848.* Monthly Pamphlet. Wortley, J. Barker, 1848.

Boyer, Abel, *An Essay towards the History of the Last Ministry and Parliament.* 72 pp. London, J. Baker, 1710.

——, *The History of the Reign of Queen Anne, digested into Annals, 1703-1712.* 10 v. London, A Roper, 1703-1713.

——, *The Political State of Great Britain, 1711-1737.* 54 v. London, J. Baker, 1712-1740.

Briscoe, John, *A Discourse on the late Funds, of the Million Act, Lottery Act, and Bank of England.* 187 pp. London, A. Bell, 1696.

The British Essayists. Ed. by Alexander Chalmers. 45 v. London, J. Johnson, 1802-1803.

Brooke, James W., *The Democrats of Marylebone.* 192 pp. London, W. J. Cleaver, 1839.

Burnet, Gilbert, *History of His Own Time.* 2 v. London, T. Ward, 1724-1734.

——, *A Supplement to Burnet's History of My Own Time* by Helen C. Foxcroft. 565 pp. Oxford, Clarendon Press, 1902.

Carpenter, William, *Monthly Political Magazine, September, 1831–July, 1832.*

——, *Political Letters and Pamphlets,* London, W. Carpenter, 1830-1831.

Cartwright, John, *Take Your Choice.* 97 pp. London, J. Almon, 1776.
——, *The Legislative Rights of the Commonalty Vindicated; or Take Your Choice.* 2nd Edition. 249 pp. London, J. Almon, 1777.
——, *The People's Barrier Against Undue Influence and Corruption.* 141 pp. London, J. Almon, 1780.
Carysfort, John J., *Thoughts on the Constitution, with a View to the Proposed Reform in the Representation of the People, and Duration of Parliament.* 53 pp. London, J. Debrett, 1783.
Clifford, Henry, *Observations on some Doctrines advanced during the Late Elections.* 103 pp. London, J. Budd, 1807.
Cobbett, William, *Political Register, 1802-1813.* 25 v.
——, *Weekly Political Register.* Published in New York, 1816.
Cockburn, William, *An Essay upon the Propitious and Glorious Reign of our Gracious Sovereign Anne, Queen of Great Britain, France, and Ireland.* 141 pp. London, 1710.
A Compleat History of the late Septennial Parliament. 78 pp. London, J. Peele, 1722.
The Craftsman. July 29, 1727; August 5, 1727; May 24, 1729; January 10, 1729/1730.
Davenant, Charles, *Sir Thomas Double at Court and in High Preferments.* 112 pp. London, J. Morphew, 1710.
de Cize, Emanuel, *Histoire du Whigisme et du Torisme.* 392 pp. Amsterdam, J. F. Bernard, 1717.
Defoe, Daniel, *A Plan of the English Commerce.* 368 pp. London, Rivington, 1749.
——, *A Tour through England and Wales.* 2 v. New York, Dutton [1928].
——, *Defoe's Review.* Reproduced from the Original Editions. Introd. and Bibl. Notes by Arthur Wellesley Secord. 22 v. New York, Columbia University Press, 1938.
——, *A Word against a New Election.* 23 pp. 1710.
The English Chartist Circular: Number 29.
The Examiner. Nos. 14, 15, 17, 35, 45.
The False Steps of the Ministry after the Revolution. 34 pp. London, J. Roberts, 1714.
A Few Words to the Chartists. 16 pp. London, T. Cadell, 1839.
Fox, William J., *Lectures Addressed chiefly to the Working Classes.* 4 v. London, C. Fox, 1845-1849.
The Freedom of England, in Contra-Distinction to Pitticism. 144 pp. Stamford, J. Drakard, 1818.
The Freethinker, September 19, 1718.
A Full Report of the Proceedings of the Meeting Convened by the Hampden Club at the Freemasons' Tavern, Lincoln's Inn Fields, June 15, 1816. Printed by J. M'Creery. 52 pp. London, W. Hone, 1816.
A General View of our Present Discontents. 28 pp. London, A. Baldwin, 1710.
The Gentlemen's Magazine.
September, 1740; June, 1747; August, 1747; February, 1761; May, 1784; June, 1839.

Hare, Francis, *The Management of the War*. 39 pp. London, A. Baldwin, 1710.
——, *The Negotiations for a Treaty of Peace from the breaking off of the Conferences at the Hague to the End of Those at Gertruydenberg*. 72 pp. London, A. Baldwin, 1711.
——, *The Negotiations for a Treaty of Peace in 1709*. 49 pp. London, A. Baldwin, 1711.
Harley, Richard, *Faults on Both Sides*. 56 pp. London, 1710.
Hutcheson, Archibald, *A Collection of Advertisements, Letters and Papers, and some other Facts, relating to the last Elections at Westminster and Hastings*. 55 pp. London, T. Payne, 1722.
An Inquiry Concerning the Author of the Letters of Junius. 114 pp. London, T. Bensley, 1814.
Knox, Vicesimus, *The Spirit of Despotism*. 94 pp. London, W. Hone, 1821.
A Letter to the Right Honourable William Pitt upon the Nature of Parliamentary Representation. 77 pp. London, J. Stockdale, 1784.
The London Magazine.
February, 1740; January, 1761; March, 1761.
Luttrell, Narcissus, *A Brief Historical Relation of State Affairs from September 1678 to April 1714*. 6 v. Oxford Press, 1857.
MacPherson, James, *Original Papers containing the Secret History of Great Britain, from the Restoration to the Accession of the House of Hanover*. 2 v. London, Strahan and Cadell, 1775.
McDouall, P., *Chartist and Republican Journal, April 1841–October 1841*.
The Medley.
February 5, 1711; February 26, 1711; April 23, 1711.
Memoirs of Queen Anne: being a Compleat Supplement to the History of Her Reign, wherein the Transactions of the Four Last Years are fully related. 317 pp. London, A. Millar, 1729.
National Reformer
February 11, 1837; February 18, 1837.
National Reform Tracts, Speech of George Thompson delivered to The National Reform Association on September 18, 1850. 12 pp. London, B. D. Cousins, 1850.
New Movement—Household Suffrage, Triennial Parliaments, Vote by Ballot, No Property Qualification, and Equal Electoral Districts. 11 pp. Manchester, A. Heywood, 1848.
Our Rights: or the Just Claims of the Working Classes. Issued by the Kettering Radical Association. 29 pp. London, J. Toller, 1839.
Owen, R., *An Antidote against Modern Slanders and Calumnies*. 24 pp. London, 1713.
Parties and Factions in England at the Accession of William IV. 55 pp. 2nd Edition. London, Longmans, no date.
Petyt, George, *Lex Parliamentaria*. 434 pp. London, 1734.
Pittis, William, *The History of the Present Parliament and Convocation*. 368 pp. London, J. Baker, 1711.
The Post Boy—October 26, 1710.

Proceedings of a Public Meeting held on the Town Moor of Newcastle-upon-Tyne, May 27, 1833. 36 pp. Newcastle, E. MacKenzie, 1833.

Proceedings of the Society of Friends of the People. 69 pp. London, 1793.

Ralph, James, *Of the Use and Abuse of Parliaments.* 2 v. London, 1744.

Roebuck, John A. (Ed.), *Pamphlets for the People.* London, C. Ely, 1835.

A Short State of War and Peace. 24 pp. London, J. Morphew, 1715.

Sidney, Algernon, *Discourses on Government.* Printed for Richard Lee. 3 v. New York, Deare and Andrews, 1805.

Somers, John, *A Collection of Scarce and Valuable Tracts on the most interesting and entertaining Subjects* . . . Arranged by Walter Scott. 13 v. London, T. Cadell, 1809-1815.

Spencer, Thomas, *The People's Rights: and How to get Them.* 20 pp. London, T. Green, 1842.

Speeches of the Right Honourable William Pitt and Right Honourable Charles J. Fox on Mr. Grey's Motion for a Reform in Parliament, May 7, 1793. 70 pp. London, J. Debrett, 1793.

Stuart, Daniel, *Peace and Reform, against War and Corruption.* 160 pp. London, 1794.

The Thoughts of an Honest Whig upon the Present Proceedings of that Party. 16 pp. London, 1710.

The Times
February 16, 1837; May 7, 1858; June 3, 1858; November 14, 1885.

Toland, John, *The Art of Governing by Partys.* 180 pp. London, B. Lintott, 1701.

Torrens, Robert, *A Letter to the Independent Freemen of the City of Rochester.* 33 pp. London, 1819.

Towers, Joseph A., *Vindication of the Political Principles of Mr. Locke.* 113 pp. London, 1782.

[Trapp, Joseph], *The Character and Principles of the present Set of Whigs.* 26 pp. London, 1711.

Trenchard, John and Gordon, Thomas (Ed.), *A Collection of Tracts.* 2 v. London, Cogan, 1751.

Tucker, Josiah, *A Treatise Concerning Civil Government.* 428 pp. London, 1781.

Wagstaffe, William, *The State and Condition of our Taxes Considered.* 43 pp. London, 1714.

——, *Miscellaneous Works of William Wagstaffe.* 414 pp. London, J. Bowyer, 1726.

Warrington, Earl, *The Works of the Right Honourable Henry, late L. Delamer, and Earl of Warrington.* Printed for John Lawrence and John Dunton. 684 pp. London, 1694.

The Whig Examiner—September 14, 1710.

Williams, William, *An Address to the Electors and Non-Electors of the United Kingdom on the Defective State of the Representative System.* 31 pp. London, E. Wilson, 1849.

Wilson, Effingham, *Workings of the Borough System.* 12 pp. London, B. Steil, circa 1830.

Wyvill, Christopher, *A Letter to the Right Honourable William Pitt.* 35 pp. London, 1793.

Yate, Walter H., *A Candid and Admonitory Address to the Independent Electors of the United Kingdom.* 32 pp. London, M. Jones. Published in 1812, and also in 1825.

Young, Arthur, *The Example of France—A Warning to Britain.* 256 pp. London, W. Richardson, 1794.

C. LETTERS, DIARIES, AND MEMOIRS

Bamford, Samuel, *Passages in the Life of a Radical.* 2 v. London, Simpkin, Marshall, 1844.

Bolingbroke, Henry St. John, Viscount—*Memoirs of Lord Bolingbroke.* Ed. by George Cooke. 2 v. London, R. Bentley, 1836.

——, *A Collection of Political Tracts.* 388 pp. London, R. Francklin, 1748.

——, *The Works of the late Right Honourable Henry St. John, Lord Viscount Bolingbroke.* Edited by David Mallet. 5 v. London, 1777.

——, *Letters and Correspondence, Public and Private, of the Right Honourable Henry St. John, Lord Viscount Bolingbroke.* Ed. by Gilbert Parke. 4 v. London, G. G. and J. Robinson, 1798.

Broughton, Lord, *Recollections of a Long Life.* Edited by Lady Dorchester. 6 v. New York, Scribner, 1909-1911.

Calamy, Edmund, *An Historical Account of My Own Life, with some Reflections on the Times I have lived in, 1671-1731.* Ed. by John Rutt. 2 v. London, Henry Colburn, 1829.

Chesterfield, Earl, *The Letters of Philip Dormer Stanhope, Earl of Chesterfield.* Ed. by John Bradshaw. 3 v. London, S. Sonnenschein, 1892.

——, *Miscellaneous Works of the late Philip Dormer Stanhope, Earl of Chesterfield.* Ed. by Matthew Maty. 3 v. Dublin, W. Watson, 1777.

The Clarke Papers—Selections from the Papers of William Clarke. Ed. by Charles H. Firth for the Camden Society. 442 pp. Westminster, 1891.

Colchester, Lord, *The Diary and Correspondence of Charles Abbot, Lord Colchester.* Ed. by Lord Charles Colchester. 3 v. London, J. Murray, 1861.

Coxe, William (Ed.), *Memoirs of the Life and Administration of John, Duke of Marlborough.* 6 v. London, Longmans, 1820.

——, *Memoirs of the Administration of the Right Honourable Henry Pelham.* 2 v. London, Longmans, 1829.

——, *Memoirs of the Life and Administration of Sir Robert Walpole, Earl of Orford.* 3 v. London, Cadell, 1800.

Dickins, Lilian and Stanton, Mary, *An Eighteenth-Century Correspondence.* 466 pp. London, J. Murray, 1910.

Elliot, Hugh S. (Ed.), *The Letters of John S. Mill.* 2 v. London, Longmans, 1910.

The Greville Memoirs, 1814-1860. Arranged by L. Strachey and R. Fulford. 8 v. London, Macmillan, 1938.

Hervey, John, Lord, *Memoirs of the Reign of George II, from his Accession to the Death of Queen Caroline.* Ed. by John Crocker. 2 v. London, J. Murray, 1855.

Holyoake, George J., *Bygones Worth Remembering.* 2 v. London, T. F. Unwin, 1905.

Holland, Lady, *A Memoir of the late Sidney Smith.* 2 v. London, Longmans, 1855.

Newton, Lady Evelyn (Ed.), *Lyme Letters, 1660-1760.* 322 pp. London, Wm. Heinemann, 1925.

Laprade, William T., *Parliamentary Papers of John Robinson, 1774-1784.* 198 pp. London, Offices of the Royal Historical Society, 1922.

Linton, William J., *James Watson, A Memoir.* 93 pp. Manchester, A. Heywood, 1880.

Nicholls, John, *Recollections and Reflections, Personal and Political, as connected with the Public Affairs during the Reign of George III.* 2 v. London, Longmans, 1822.

Oldmixon, John, *Memoirs of the Press.* 64 pp. London, T. Cox, 1742.

Paley, Edmund (Ed.), *The Works of William Paley.* 6 v. London, Rivington, 1830.

Prothero, Rowland E. (Ed.), *Private Letters of Edward Gibbon.* 2 v. London, J. Murray, 1897.

Raleigh, Walter (Ed.), *The Complete Works of George Savile, First Marquess of Halifax.* 256 pp. Oxford, Clarendon Press, 1912.

Redding, Cyrus, *Personal Reminiscences of Eminent Men.* 3 v. London, Saunders, Otley and Co., 1867.

Sharp, Thomas (Ed.), *The Life of John Sharp, Lord Archbishop of York.* 2 v. London, Livington, 1825.

Torcy, Marquis, *Memoirs of the Marquis of Torcy.* Ed. by P. Vaillant, 2 v. London, 1757.

Townshend, William C., *Memoirs of the House of Commons from the Convention Parliament of 1688-1689 to the Passing of the Reform Bill of 1832.* 2 v. London, H. Colburn, 1844.

Vernon, James, *Letters Illustrative of the Reign of William III, from 1696-1708.* Ed. by George James. 3 v. London, H. Colburn, 1841.

Waldegrave, James Earl, *Memoirs, 1754-1758.* 176 pp. London, J. Murray, 1821.

Walpole, Horace, 4th Earl of Orford, *Memoirs of the Last Ten Years of the Reign of George II.* 2 v. London, John Murray, 1822.

——, *Memoirs of the Reign of King George the Third.* Ed. by G. F. Russell Barker. 4 v. London, Lawrence and Bullen, 1894.

——, *Letters complete with Bibliography.* Ed. by Mrs. Paget Toynbee. 16 v. Oxford, Clarendon Press, 1903-1905.

Walpole, Spencer, *Essays, Political and Biographical.* Ed. by Francis Holland. 317 pp. New York, Dutton, 1908.

Wentworth Papers, 1705-1739. Ed. by James Cartwright. 568 pp. London, Wyman, 1883.

Wraxall, Nathaniel, *Historical Memoirs of My Own Times, 1772-1784.* 494 pp. Phila. 1837.

D. OTHER PRIMARY SOURCES

Great Britain. Historical Manuscripts Commission.
    10th Report: Weston MSS.
    11th Report: Townshend MSS.
    12th Report: Rutland MSS.
    14th Report: House of Lords MSS—1693-1697.
    14th Report: Onslow MSS.
    14th Report: Kenyon MSS.
    15th Report: Carlisle MSS.
    15th Report: Egmont MSS.
    15th Report: Earl of Mar and Kellie MSS.
    15th Report: Portland MSS.

II. SECONDARY WORKS

Adolphus, John, *The History of England, from the Accession of King George the Third, to the Conclusion of Peace, 1783.* 3 v. London, T. Cadell, 1802.

Allyn, Emily, *Lords versus Commons; a Century of Conflict and Compromise, 1830-1930.* 266 pp. Penna, 1927.

Ashton, John, *When William IV was King.* 355 pp. London, Chapman and Hall, 1896.

Beatson, Robert, *A Chronological Register of both Houses of the British Parliament from the Union in 1708 to the Third Parliament of the United Kingdom of Great Britain and Ireland in 1807.* 3 v. London, Longmans, 1807.

Brodrick, George C. and J. K. Fotheringham, *The History of England from Addington's Administration to the Close of William IV's Reign, 1801-1837.* Half-Title—*The Political History of England.* Ed. by Hunt and Poole. 486 pp. London, Longmans, 1906.

Brown, Louise F., *The First Earl of Shaftesbury*, 350 pp. New York, Appleton, 1933.

Brown, Philip A., *The French Revolution in English History.* 232 pp. London, Lockwood and Son, 1918.

Burton, John H., *A History of the Reign of Queen Anne.* 3 v. London, Blackwoods, 1880.

Cambridge Modern History.

Cartwright, Frances D., *The Life and Correspondence of Major Cartwright.* 2 v. London, H. Colburn, 1826.

Christie, Octavius F., *The Transition from Aristocracy, 1832-1867.* 288 pp. London, Seeley, Service Co., 1927.

Christie, William D., *A Life of Anthony Ashley Cooper, First Earl of Shaftesbury, 1621-1683.* 2 v. London, Macmillan, 1871.

Churchill, Winston S., *Marlborough, His Life and Times.* 4 v. London, G. G. Harrap and Co., 1933-1938.

Clapham, John H., *An Economic History of Modern Britain.* 3 v. Cambridge, University Press, 1930-1938.

Clark, George N., *Later Stuarts, 1660-1714.* 461 pp. Half-title—*The Oxford History of England.* Ed. by G. N. Clark. Oxford, Clarendon Press, 1934.

Cockburn, A. J. and Rowe, W. C., *Cases of Controverted Elections determined in the Eleventh Parliament of the United Kingdom.* 583 pp. London, Saunders and Binning, 1833.

Cooke, George W., *The History of Party, from the Rise of the Whig and Tory Factions, in the Reign of Charles II to the Passing of the Reform Bill: 1660-1832.* 3 v. London, J. Macrone, 1836-1837.

Corbett, U. and Daniell, E. R., *Reports of Cases of Controverted Elections, in the Sixth Parliament of the United Kingdom.* 288 pp. London, J. and W. T. Clarke, 1821.

Cunningham, George G., *The English Nation: or A History of England in the Lives of Englishmen.* 5 v. Edinburgh, Fullerton, 1863-1868.

Cunningham, William, *The Growth of English Industry and Commerce in Modern Times.* 2 v. Cambridge, The University Press, 1890-1892.

Daly, John B., *The Dawn of Radicalism.* 252 pp. London, Sonnenschein, 1892.

——, *Radical Pioneers of the Eighteenth Century.* 252 pp. London, Sonnenschein, 1886.

Davis, H. W. C., *The Age of Grey and Peel.* 347 pp. Oxford, Clarendon Press, 1929.

Day, Samuel H., *Parliamentary Elections and Petitions.* 746 pp. London, Stevens and Son, 1900.

Dickenson, Goldworthy L., *The Development of Parliament during the Nineteenth Century.* 183 pp. London, Longmans, 1895.

Digest of all Election Reports from the Earliest to the Present Time. Printed for C. F. F. Wordsworth. 191 pp. London, A. Maxwell, 1834.

Dod, Charles R., *The Parliamentary Companion,* London, Whittaker & Company.

The Edinburgh Review—1812, 1857.

Emden, Cecil, *The People and the Constitution.* 336 pp. Oxford, Clarendon Press, 1933.

The English Historical Review—Article, " The Duke of Newcastle and the Election of 1734 " by Basil Williams, July, 1897, pp. 448-488.

Falconer, T. and Fitzherbert, E. H., *Cases of Controverted Elections, determined in Committees of the House of Commons, in the Second Parliament of the Reign of Queen Victoria,* 718 pp. London, Saunders and Benning, 1839.

Fawcett, Millicent G., *Life of the Right Honourable Sir William Molesworth.* 352 pp. London, Macmillan, 1901.

Feiling, Keith G., *A History of the Tory Party, 1604-1714.* 525 pp. Oxford, Clarendon Press, 1924.

——, *The Second Tory Party, 1714-1832.* 451 pp. London, Macmillan, 1938.

Fremantle, Alan F., *England in the Nineteenth Century.* 2 v. London, Allen, 1929-1930.

Gammage, Robert G., *History of the Chartist Movement, 1837-1854.* 438 pp. Newcastle-on-Tyne, Browne, 1894.

Gibbons, Philip A., *Ideas of Political Representation in Parliament, 1660-1832.* 56 pp. Oxford, B. H. Blackwell, 1914.

Gregō, Joseph, *A History of Parliamentary Elections and Electioneering in the Old Days*. 403 pp. London, Chatto Windus, 1886.

Grote, George, *The Minor Works of George Grote*. Ed. by Alexander Bain. 364 pp. London, J. Murray, 1873.

Halévy, Elie, *The Growth of Philosophic Radicalism*. Translated by Mary Morris. 554 pp. New York, Macmillan, 1928.

——, *A History of the English People in 1815*. Translated by E. I. Watkin and D. A. Barker. 3 v. New York, Harcourt, 1924-1928.

Hallam, Henry, *Constitutional History of England from the Accession of Henry VII to the Death of George II*. 3 v. London, J. Murray, 1876.

Hammond, John and Barbara, *The Age of the Chartists, 1832-1854*. 386 pp. London, Longmans, 1930.

Harris, William, *The History of the Radical Party in Parliament*. 510 pp. London, Kegan Paul, 1885.

Hassall, Arthur A., *Life of Viscount Bolingbroke*. 237 pp. London, Macmillan, 1889.

Harrop, Robert, *Bolingbroke, a Political Study*. 357 pp. Kegan Paul, 1884.

Hatsell, John, *Precedents of Proceedings in the House of Commons: with Observations*. 4 v. London, Hansard, 1818.

Heaton, H., *Economic History of Europe*. 775 pp. New York, Harper, 1936.

Hill, Richard L., *Toryism and the People, 1832-1846*. 278 pp. London, Constable and Co., 1929.

Hovell, Mark, *The Chartist Movement*. 327 pp. London, Longmans, 1918.

Huish, Robert, *The History of the Private and Political Life of the late Henry Hunt*. 2 v. London, J. Saunders, 1836.

Hunt, William, *The History of England from the Accession of George III to the Close of Pitt's First Administration, 1760-1801*. 495 pp. Half-title —*The Political History of England*. Ed. by Hunt and Poole. London, Longmans, 1905.

Jenks, Edward, *Parliamentary England*. 462 pp. London, Unwin, 1903.

Jephson, Henry, *The Platform: its Rise and Progress*. 2v. London, Macmillan, 1892.

Kebbel, Thomas E., *A History of Toryism; from the Accession of Mr. Pitt to Power in 1783 to the Death of Lord Beaconsfield in 1881*. 408 pp. London, W. H. Allen, 1886.

Kent, Clement B., *The Early History of the Tories from the Accession of Charles the Second to the Death of William III, 1660-1702*. 481 pp. London, Smith, Elder and Co., 1908.

——, *The English Radicals*. 451 pp. London, Longmans, 1899.

Knapp, J. and Ombler, E., *Cases of Controverted Elections in the Twelfth Parliament of the United Kingdom*. 497 pp. London, Sweet, 1837.

Laprade, William T., *Public Opinion and Politics in Eighteenth Century England to the Fall of Walpole*. 463 pp. New York, Macmillan, 1936.

Leadam, Isaac S., *The History of England from the Accession of Anne to the Death of George II, 1702-1760*. 557 pp. Half-title — *The Political History of England*. Ed. by Hunt and Poole. London, Longmans, 1909.

Leader, Robert E. (Ed.), *Life and Letters of J. A. Roebuck.* 392 pp. London, E. Arnold, 1897.

Lecky, William E. H., *A History of England in the Eighteenth Century.* 8 v. London, Longmans, 1878-1890.

Lodge, R., *The History of England from the Restoration to the Death of William III, 1660-1702.* 517 pp. Half-title — *The Political History of England.* Ed. by Hunt and Poole, London, Longmans, 1910.

Lolme, Jean L., *The Constitution of England.* 378 pp. Dublin, P. Byrne and J. Moore, 1793.

Lord, Walter, *Development of Political Parties during the Reign of Queen Anne.* Transactions of the Royal Historical Society. New Series XIV, pp. 69-121. London, 1900.

Low, Sidney and Sanders, L. C., *The History of England during the Reign of Victoria.* 532 pp. Half-title—*The Political History of England.* Ed. by William Hunt and Reginald Poole. London, Longmans, 1907.

Luders, Alexander, *Reports of the Proceedings in Committees of the House of Commons, upon Controverted Elections, heard and determined during the Parliament called in 1784.* 3 v. London, E. and R. Brooke, 1785-1790.

McCarthy, Justin, *A History of the Four Georges.* 2 v. New York, Harper, 1885-1890.

——, *A History of our Own Times.* 7 v. London, Chatto, 1880-1909.

——, *The Reign of Queen Anne.* 2 v. New York, Harper, 1902.

Macaulay, Thomas B., *History of England from the Accession of James II.* 5 v. New York, Harper, 1899.

Maccoby, Simon, *English Radicalism, 1832-1852.* 462 pp. London, G. Allen, 1935.

——, *English Radicalism, 1853-1886.* 432 pp. London, G. Allen, 1938.

Mackinnon, James, *The Union of England and Scotland.* 524 pp. London, Longmans, 1896.

Mahon, Philip Stanhope, Viscount, *History of England from the Peace of Utrecht to the Peace of Paris.* 2 v. Phila., Appleton, 1849.

——, *History of England comprising the Reign of Queen Anne, 1701-1713.* 584 pp. London, J. Murray, 1870.

Maitland, Frederic W., *The Constitutional History of England.* 548 pp. Cambridge, University Press, 1926.

Manning, James A., *The Lives of the Speakers of the House of Commons.* 496 pp. London, E. Churton, 1851.

Marriott, John A., *English Political Institutions.* 348 pp. Oxford, Clarendon Press, 1938.

——, *England since Waterloo.* 546 pp. New York, Putnam, 1913.

Martineau, Harriet, *A History of the Thirty Years' Peace, 1815-1846.* 4 v. London, G. Bell, 1877-1878.

Massey, William, *A History of England during the Reign of George the Third.* 4 v. London, J. W. Parker, 1855-1863.

May, Thomas E., *Constitutional History of England since the Accession of George the Third.* 3 v. London, Longmans, 1912.

Merewether, Henry, and Archibald Stephens, *The History of the Boroughs and Municipal Corporations of the United Kingdom, from the earliest to the present Time.* 3 v. London, Stevens, 1835.

Melville, Lewis, *The Life and Letters of William Cobbett in England and America.* 2 v. New York, J. Lane, 1913.

Morgan, William T., *English Political Parties and Leaders in the Reign of Queen Anne, 1702-1710.* 428 pp. New Haven, Yale Press, 1920.

——, "An Eighteenth Century Election in England." *Political Science Quarterly,* XXXVII, 585-604, 1922.

——, "The Ministerial Revolution of 1710 in England." *Political Science Quarterly,* XXVI, 184-210, 1921.

Morley, John, *The Life of Richard Cobden.* 640 pp. Boston, Roberts, 1881.

Namier, Lewis, *England in the Age of the American Revolution.* 518 pp. London, Macmillan, 1930.

——, *The Structure of Politics at the Accession of George III.* 2 v. London, Macmillan, 1929.

Nulle, Stebelton, *Thomas Pelham-Holles, Duke of Newcastle.* 204 pp. Phila., University of Penna. Press, 1931.

Oldfield, Thomas H., *An Entire and Complete History, political and personal, of the Boroughs of Great Britain, together with the Cinque Ports.* 2 v. London, B. Crosby, 1794.

——, *The Representative History of Great Britain and Ireland being a History of the House of Commons and of the Counties, Cities, and Boroughs, of the United Kingdom, from the earliest Period.* 6 v. London, Baldwin, 1816.

Oliver, Frederick, *The Endless Adventure.* 3 v. London, Macmillan, 1930-1935.

Oldmixon, John, *The History of England during the Reigns of King William and Queen Mary, Queen Anne, King George I.* 808 pp. London, T. Cox, 1735.

Paul, Herbert, *A History of Modern England.* 5 v. New York, Macmillan, 1904-1906.

Penman, John S., *The Irresistible Movement of Democracy.* 729 pp. New York, Macmillan, 1923.

Perry, H. and Knapp, J. W., *Cases of Controverted Elections in the Eleventh Parliament of the United Kingdom.* 620 pp. London, J. and W. T. Clarke, 1833.

Phillimore, John G., *History of England during the Reign of George the Third.* 2 v. London, Virtue, 1863.

Pike, Luke O., *Constitutional History of the House of Lords from Original Sources.* 405 pp. London, Macmillan, 1894.

Pollard, Albert F., *Political Pamphlets, selected and arranged.* 345 pp. London, Paul, 1897.

Pope, Alexander, *The Works of Alexander Pope.* Ed. by William Bowles. 10 v. London, J. Johnson, 1806.

Porritt, Edward and Annie, *The Unreformed House of Commons.* 2 v. Cambridge, University Press, 1909.

Power, D. Rodwell, H. and Dew, E., *Reports of the Decisions of Committees of the House of Commons in the Trial of Controverted Elections during the Fifteenth Parliament of the United Kingdom.* 2 v. London, Stevens, 1853-1857.

Redlich, Josef, *The Procedure of the House of Commons,* 3 v. London, A. Constable, 1908.

Rider, William T., *A New History of England.* 50 v. London, S. Crowder, 1762-1769.

Roberts, Michael, *The Whig Party, 1807-1812.* 453 pp. London, Macmillan, 1939.

Robertson, Joseph M., *Bolingbroke and Walpole.* 266 pp. London, Uwin, 1919.

Roebuck, John A., *History of the Whig Ministry of 1830 to the Passing of the Reform Bill.* 2 v. London, J. W. Parker, 1852.

Rogers, James E. T., *The First Nine Years of the Bank of England.* 183 pp. New York, Macmillan, 1887.

——, *A Complete Collection of the Protests of the Lords with Historical Introduction.* 3 v. Oxford, Clarendon Press, 1875.

——, *The Industrial and Commercial History of England.* 473 pp. New York, Putnam, 1892.

Rosenblatt, Frank F., *The Chartist Movement in its Social and Economic Aspects.* 249 pp. New York, Columbia University Press, 1916.

Rothstein, Thomas, *From Chartism to Laborism.* 365 pp. London, Lawrence, 1929.

Scudi, Abbie T., *The Sacheverell Affair.* 170 pp. New York, Columbia University Press, 1939.

Seymour, Charles, *Electoral Reform in England and Wales.* 564 pp. New Haven, Yale University Press, 1915.

——, *How the World Votes.* 2 v. Springfield, C. A. Nichols, 1918.

Sichel, Walter S., *Bolingbroke and his Times.* 2 v. London, J. Nisbet, 1901-1902.

Skottowe, Britiffe, *A Short History of Parliament.* 339 pp. London, Sonnenschein, 1892.

Slater, Gilbert, *The Growth of Modern England.* 642 pp. London, Constable, 1939.

Slosson, Preston W., *The Decline of the Chartist Movement.* 216 pp. New York, Columbia University Press, 1916.

Smellie, Kingsley B., *A Hundred Years of English Government.* 468 pp. London, Duckworth, 1937.

Smith, F. E. (Ed.), *Toryism.* 200 pp. New York, Harper, 1903.

Smith, George B., *History of the English Parliament.* 2 v. London, Ward, Lock, 1892.

Smith, Goldwin, *The United Kingdom.* 2 v. London, Macmillan, 1899-1901.

Smith, Henry S., *The Register of Parliamentary Contested Elections.* 260 pp. London, L. Simpkin and Marshall, 1842.

Smollett, Tobias G., *History of England from the Revolution of 1688 to the Death of George II.* 6 v. London, A. Wilson, 1811-1812.

Somerville, Thomas, *The History of Great Britain during the Reign of Queen Anne.* 674 pp. London, A. Strahan, 1798.

Stebbing, William, *Some Verdicts of History Reviewed.* 416 pp. London, J. Murray, 1887.

Stevens, David H., *Party Politics and English Journalism, 1702-1742.* 156 pp. Menasha, Wisconsin, Banta, 1916.

Sydney, William, *England and the English in the Eighteenth Century.* 2 v. New York, Macmillan, 1891.

Swift, Jonathan, *The Prose Works of Jonathan Swift.* Arranged by Temple Scott. 12 v. London, G. Bell, 1897-1908.

Tawney, Richard H., *Life and Struggles of William Lovett.* 2 v. London, G. Bell, 1920.

Taylor, G. W. Stirling, *Robert Walpole and his Age.* 343 pp. London, Cape, 1931.

Thomas, John A., *The House of Commons, 1832-1901.* 176 pp. Cardiff, University of Wales Press, 1939.

Tindal, Nicholas, *The Continuation of Mr. Rapin's History of England from the Revolution to the Accession of George II.* 28 v. London, Knapton, 1744-1747.

Todd, Alpheus, *On Parliamentary Government in England,* 2 v. London, Longmans, 1867-1869.

Torrens, William M., *History of Cabinets from the Union of Scotland to the Acquisition of Canada and Bengal.* 2 v. London, W. H. Allen, 1894.

Trevelyan, George M., *British History in the Nineteenth Century and after (1782-1919),* 512 pp. London, Longmans, 1937.

——, *England under the Stuarts.* 566 pp. Half-title—*A History of England.* Ed. by C. W. C. Oman. New York, Putnam, 1930.

——, *England under Queen Anne.* 3 v. London, Longmans, 1930-1934.

——, *The Two Party System in English Political History.* 27 pp. Oxford, Clarendon Press, 1926.

Troward, Richard, *A Collection of the Statutes now in force relative to Elections down to the present Time.* 304 pp. London, D. Stuart, 1790.

Turberville, Arthur S., *English Men and Manners in the Eighteenth Century.* 540 pp. Oxford, Clarendon Press, 1929.

——, *The House of Lords in the XVIIIth Century.* 556 pp. Oxford, Clarendon Press, 1927.

Veitch, George S., *The Genesis of Parliamentary Reform.* 397 pp. London, Constable, 1913.

Wallas, Graham, *The Life of Francis Place, 1771-1854.* 415 pp. London, Longmans, 1898.

Walmsley, Hugh M., *The Life of Sir Joshua Walmsley.* 352 pp. London, Chapman and Hall, 1879.

Walpole, Spencer, *A History of England from the Conclusion of the Great War in 1815.* 6 v. New York, Longmans, 1890-1900.

——, *The History of Twenty-five Years.* 4 v. New York, Longmans, 1904-1908.

238   BIBLIOGRAPHY

West, Julius, *A History of the Chartist Movement.* 316 pp. London, Constable, 1920.
White, William, *The Inner Life of the House of Commons.* 2 v. London, T. Fisher Unwin, 1898.
Whitworth, Charles, *The Succession of Parliaments being exact Lists of the Members chosen at each General Election from the Restoration to the Last General Election, 1761.* 316 pp. London, R. Davis, 1764.
Williams, Basil, *The Whig Supremacy, 1714-1760.* 464 pp. Half-title—*The Oxford History of England.* Ed. by G. N. Clark. Oxford, Clarendon Press, 1939.
Williams, David, *John Frost.* 355 pp. Cardiff, University of Wales Press, 1939.
Winstanley, Denys A., *Lord Chatham and the Whig Opposition.* 460 pp. Cambridge, The University Press, 1912.
——, *Personal and Party Government.* 322 pp. Cambridge, The University Press, 1910.
Wolferstan, F. S. P. and Dew, E., *Reports of the Decisions of Committees of the House of Commons in the Trial of Controverted Elections, during the Seventeenth Parliament of the United Kingdom.* 252 pp. London, Stevens, 1859.
Woodhouse, A. S. P., *Puritanism and Liberty, being the Army Debates (1647-9).* 506 pp. London, Dent, 1938.
Woodward, Ernest L., *The Age of Reform, 1815-1870.* 656 pp. Half-title— *The Oxford History of England.* Ed. by G. N. Clark. Oxford, Clarendon Press, 1939.
Wright, Thomas, *England under the House of Hanover.* 2 v. Second Edition. London, R. Bentley, 1848.
Wyon, Frederick W., *The History of Great Britain during the Reign of Queen Anne.* 2 v. London, Chapman, 1876.

INDEX